Forever French

Colin W. Nettelbeck

The French emigration to the United States during the Second World War was a phenomenon of notable cultural and political significance. While a crushed and occupied France could project little of its former grandeur, the emigration involved many of pre-war France's most influential and creative people in all fields from music, painting, writing and philosophy, to politics, atomic physics and mathematics. The French community in the United States was divided by political opinion and beset by the abrasive efforts of the Gaullists to impose their leader's supremacy, even against explicit opposition from the US administration. Nevertheless, not only did the presence and activity of so many exiled artists and writers contribute to the rise of New York as cultural capital of the West, members of the emigrant community also succeeded in maintaining an image of an independent and democratic France as an indispensable partner in the reconstruction of Europe, and hence played a significant role in the shaping of post-war France.

Colin Nettelbeck is Associate Professor in the Department of Romance Languages at Monash University.

Berg French Studies
General Editor: John E. Flower

John E. Flower and Bernard C. Swift (eds), *François Mauriac: Visions and Reappraisals*

Michael Tilby (ed.), *Beyond the Nouveau Roman: Essays on the Contemporary French Novel*

Richard Griffiths, *The Use of Abuse: The Polemics of the Dreyfus Affair and its Aftermath*

Alec G. Hargreaves, *Voices from the North African Immigrant Community in France: Immigration and Identity in Beur Fiction*

–Forthcoming–

Malcolm Cook, *Fictional France: Social Reality in the French Novel, 1775–1800*

Nicholas Hewitt, *Intellectuals and the New Right in Postwar France*

David Looseley, *Culture and Politics in Contemporary France*

Alan Morris, *Collaboration and Resistance Reviewed: Writers and the 'Mode retro' in Post-Gaullist France*

Alan Clark, *Paris Peasant: François Mitterrand and the Modernisation of France*

Forever French

Exile in the United States
1939-1945

Colin W. Nettelbeck

BERG

New York / Oxford

Distributed exclusively in the US and Canada by
St Martin's Press, New York

First published in 1991 by
Berg Publishers Limited
Editorial offices:
165 Taber Avenue, Providence, RI 02906, USA
150 Cowley Road, Oxford, OX4 1JJ, UK

Library of Congress Cataloging-in-Publication Data
Nettelbeck, Colin W.
    Forever French: exile in the United States 1939-1945
                Colin W. Nettelbeck.
    p.   cm. -- (Berg French Studies)
    Includes bibliographical references and index.
    ISBN 0-85496-632-3
    1. World War, 1939-1945 -- Refugees. 2. Refugees, Political -- United
States--History--20th century.   3.   Refugees, Political -- France-
-History --20th century.   4. World War, 1939-1945 -- Underground
movements -- France. I. Title. II. Series.
    D809, U5N4B   1992
    940, 63' 159 -- dc20   91-33214
                                                                CIP

    British Library Cataloguing in Publication Data
    Nettelbeck, Colin W.
        Forever French: exile in the United
        States 1939-1945
        (Berg French Studies)
        I. Title   II. Series
        325.440973

        ISBN 0–85496–632–3

Printed in Great Britain by
Billing & Sons Ltd, Worcester

Contents

Acknowledgements

I want to thank Carol Nettelbeck, my research assistant and companion in spy-file and microfilm-reader neck-crane; Monash University and the Australian Research Council for grants that made the research possible; and all those people who generously offered their help and advice: especially Alain Bosquet, Mrs Howard Samuels, Sarah Rapkine and Raoul Aglion.

Introduction

The French experience of the Second World War is an area of study that has been richly covered in every way – from historical, fictional and memorial perspectives, and in every medium. It is, not unexpectedly, an area constantly subject to change. With each new release of previously classified material from government archives, each emergence of new witnesses or old skeletons, there is a surge of modification in thinking, a move to redefine the motivation and importance of events and people.

And yet change is not rapid. Old ideologies squat like concrete bunkers on the high ground of history, scarring the landscape and marring our vision of it, long after their relevance has disappeared. They hamper the development of historiographical concepts adequate to serene understanding, and of newer, more effective epistemologies. We know how long, for example, it has taken (is taking) for serious accounts of the balance of collaborationist and resistance attitudes in Occupied France to gain wide acceptance. And surely many questions will always remain unsettled – particularly those that concern individual responsibility in a context where group pressures were so powerfully evident.

None the less, change has occurred, both in the way the history of the period is perceived, and in the way it is taught. From novelists like Tournier, Modiano, Duras and others, from film-makers like the Ophuls of *Le Chagrin et la pitié* or *Hôtel Terminus*, form historians, both foreign (Hoffmann, Paxton) and native (Ory, Rioux, Azéma, Duroselle, Rousso), there has been a steady flow of material contributing not only to overcome many of the barriers to knowledge and understanding, but to establish the right, once and for all, to free exploration of previously forbidden terrain.

Given the wealth of information readily available on most aspects of the French war experience, it is surprising that so little attention should have been given to the phenomenon of French refugees in the United States of America during that period. Although from an historical viewpoint, the surprise diminishes with the realisation that there has been virtually no *recognition* of such a phenomenon. To be sure, those familiar with certain major French cultural events of this century, and with their significant figures, will not be unaware that the war years in America often played a crucial role.

Those interested in surrealism will know, for instance, of the activities of Breton, Ernst, Tanguy, Duchamp, Masson, Dali, and so on, in wartime New York, and the part that they, as well as painters like Léger and Ozenfant, had in the explosion of artistic creation in that city. Scientists will perhaps have read Bertrand Goldschmidt's story of his work on atomic physics, and its relationship to the development of the French A-bomb. Anthropologists and structuralists, among others, will have encountered Claude Lévi-Strauss's *Tristes tropiques* or his later memoirs, and understood how critical to his itinerary was his stay in America. Film fans may have read Jean Renoir's autobiography, or Dalio's, or Jean-Pierre Aumont's. Specialists of authors like Jules Romains or Antoine de Saint-Exupéry or Saint-John Perse, have, of course, pondered on the significance of the fact that the last volumes of *Les Hommes de bonne volonté*, and the first editions of *Vol de Nuit*, *Le Petit Prince*, *Poèmes à l'Etrangère* and *Anabase* appeared on American soil. And anyone interested in how contemporary Europe has come into being must surely have reflected on Jean Monnet's links with the United States, particularly during the war years.

But to what degree does this assortment of individual adventures – the actual numbers of French refugees in the United States amounted to a little over 30,000 in all – constitute an identifiable, describable, collective phenomenon? To what extent was there a *French community* in exile, and what forms did it take? The answers to these questions, which stimulated the original research on which this book is based, are not obvious.

Two works exist which provide some guidance. The first, written by Guy Fritsch-Estrangin, who was the Havas News Service director in New York before joining the Giraud Military Mission in Washington, was published in Paris in 1969 – an early example of post-gaullist historical revisionism – under the title *New York entre de Gaulle et Pétain: les Français aux Etats-Unis de 1940 à 1946*. An anecdotal, gossipy book, composed by a professional journalist who had clearly hung on to his notes and clippings, it does posit the existence of a representative and significant community: 'a little *patrie* in exile, a France in miniature with its flaws and qualities, its weaknesses and its grandeur'.[1]

---

1. p. 13. Unless otherwise noted, all quotations from French sources have been translated by the author.

Fritsch-Estrangin, clearly not a gaullist, and even rather hostile towards de Gaulle, covers a large field. He delineates, albeit superficially, the institutional structures of this France-in-exile, and gives considerable detail about the people and the events which marked its existence. Always impressionistic, sometimes stridently partisan, it is very much the work of an impassioned and involved witness, rather than that of an historian, but it is seminal.

The same can be said of the other book, Raoul Aglion's *De Gaulle et Roosevelt: La France libre aux Etats-Unis* (1984) (whose English version, considerably revised and trimmed, appeared in New York in 1988 as *Roosevelt and de Gaulle*). Aglion was a gaullist, although not as 'unconditional' as some, and he ran the New York office of de Gaulle's American Delegation. Like Fritsch-Estrangin, Aglion projects an image of the exile as an entity rather than a collection of disparate experiences. He examines much of the same ground, but with greater depth, and in a broader perspective, relying more on diplomatic and intelligence service documents rather than just on journalistic ones. Fritsch-Estrangin, as his title reveals, was more interested in intra-French questions; Aglion, while he does chronicle the progress of gaullism and the obstacles it encountered within the French community, is more concerned to cast light on French–US relations during that troubled time.

Both these works are indispensable starting-points in the establishment of a new area of study in the French experience of the Second World War, but they leave many important questions unanswered – and sometimes even unasked – not only about the facts of the exile but about its wider ramifications. For the French, the Second World War was a crucible of profound changes in national self-perception and self-projection. It was the time of a sharp and major identity crisis in which many previous certainties about France's place and mission in the world were shattered. Questions of collaborationism and resistance were critical precisely because they led straight to the heart of whether France could continue to exist at all, at least as a Western democracy.

The underlying context of that situation was not new. During the whole interwar period, while the French population at large continued to be nursed along in the illusion that France had lost none of her Great Power status, the leaders, both civil and military, knew how fragile the foundations of that power were. In fact, with archaic industrial and economic structures, a shaky political regime, a weak birth rate and often geriatric leadership, France was desperately far from self-reliance. In fact, since the time of the 1919 Versailles negotiations, the importance of America as a necessary factor in any defence against German aggression was axiomatic in the French assessment of political realities.

The stubborn isolationism of the United States simply paralysed any serious peace initiatives, and was an ever-present background feature in the febrile and hopeless French diplomatic manoeuvrings of the 1930s. Saint-Exupéry knew it, when the guns on the French fighter plane he was testing froze in the high altitudes where they would be needed.[2] Jean Monnet knew it, as he frantically worked to secure American aid and increase its volume.[3] Daladier knew it at Munich, as Blum had known it at the beginning of the Spanish Civil War.

After France fell, some fled to the United States simply to escape, perhaps even reassured by isolationist policies which seemed to guarantee the 'New World' as a haven of peace. Often they were wealthy – those whom the society novelist Maurice Dekobra styled '*les émigrés de luxe*'.[4] They were able to transfer their sumptuous lifestyles from one continent to another, and live out their exile in the comfort of their normal, superficial, daily concerns, suffering no greater disorientation than a change of scenery from Maxim's or Fouquet's to the Café Pierre.

For many others, however, refuge was a way of rejecting the defeat and continuing the struggle. Coming from a wide range of different backgrounds – rich and poor, intellectual, industrial or working-class, Protestant, Catholic and Jewish – they did not share a single ideology. They did not share the same understanding of the causes of France's plight, or similar views about planning the future. Indeed, their stormy and vitriolic squabbles would become legendary, both for their own, more sanguine observers and for their American hosts, who were obliged to watch, in as much bewilderment as annoyance, the savage battles of the French among themselves.

What they did share was the faith that France's disarray would only be temporary, and the determination to make sure that that was the case. And the first task to this end was to increase American involvement in the war. In this they were not, of course, alone. The British were working in the same direction, not only through diplomatic channels, but through often ruthless covert operations. But notwithstanding Roosevelt's courageous and masterfully

---

2. See Antoine de Saint-Exupéry, *Ecrits de guerre 1939–1944* (Paris, 1982), pp. 67–87.
3. Jean Monnet, *Mémoires* (Paris, 1976), pp. 115ff.
4. This was the title of one of his novels, published in New York in 1941.

managed commitment to the British cause, isolationist sentiment ran very deep in America, and there were limits to the degree that Congress and the people could be hoodwinked. If Pearl Harbor had not happened, it would have been necessary to invent it.

In relation to France and the French, however good the general will was in the United States before the war – and although a generally positive, if somewhat romanticised image of France was maintained throughout the whole period – there is no doubt that French prestige had been severely damaged by the defeat and the Armistice. At the end of 1941, just after the United States had been forced into a generalised combat role, a Gallup poll showed that if almost half of America (49 per cent) believed that links should be maintained with the Vichy government, 58 per cent believed that Vichy favoured the Axis forces. Only 27 per cent believed that France would emerge as a Great Power, with as many (28 per cent) convinced that France would no longer be America's ally. Significantly, 63 per cent of the respondents were unable, at that time, to identify who de Gaulle was.[5] It was thus evident that the French refugees had to pursue their goals of defending France's wounded honour and of securing her future, in a climate that was often far from congenial. Their presence was met with a sometimes paradoxical mixture. On the one hand, there was a basically positive prejudice, and on the other, a suspicion born of disappointed admiration and a wakening sense in America of its new mission as global peace-keeper and policeman of democracy.

The exiles did not arrive into a vacuum. Sometimes their way had been prepared by American relief organisations that had begun their activities six or seven years earlier, with their initial focus on saving scientists and scholars or other victims of the repressions of Hitler's Germany. There was also, already established, a considerable number of specifically French networks – French veterans associations, Chambers of Commerce, the Havas news service, and groups gathered around teaching or cultural institutions like the New York Lycée and Institut, and the various Alliances Françaises. University circuits too, opened by a steady flow of visitors during the 1920s and 1930s, would prove a valuable resource. Finally, there were well-placed individuals who had settled in America before the war, or had been trapped there at the beginning of hostilities during extended stays, and whose position and experience would facilitate the life and war efforts of the refugees. Charles Boyer would play this role in Hollywood, for the motley band of

5. Figures quoted in *Pour la Victoire*, 28 February 1942, p. 5.

French actors and directors who headed for southern California looking for work. On the East Coast, the philosopher-theologian Jacques Maritain, very familiar with America, and the journalist Raoul Roussy de Sales, who had been in the United States since 1929, would serve as guides and mentors to large numbers of refugees as they gradually built themselves into a community.

It was among the permanent or long-term expatriates that moves to organise French resistance and recovery were first initiated, following de Gaulle's appeal on 18 June 1940. As early as 29 June, Dr Albert Simard, who was president of the French Veterans of the Great War, and also of the Associated French Societies of New York, called a public meeting to launch a support movement. Shortly thereafter, Eugène Houdry, an industrial engineer who had come to the United States in the 1920s, and made a considerable fortune through oil 'cracking' techniques and in pioneering plastics in Philadelphia, emerged as the president of the movement, resoundingly named 'France Forever'.

A ceremonial charter-signing was held at the Independence Hall in Philadelphia on 28 September 1940, with 300 high-profile founding members from industry and banking, most of them American. Dynamic, principled and disciplined, Houdry rapidly developed his movement into a nation-wide organisation boasting over forty chapters or committees, and 10,000–12,000 members. The vast majority of these too were Americans, and it is perhaps not a semantic accident that the English name of the association projected a much more affirmative image than the rather plaintive French equivalent – '*La France Quand Même*' – which moreover never quite took on, and quickly disappeared. It was France Forever that in due course would become the target for takeover, to be transformed into part of the official gaullist political machine.[6]

In the meantime, like Robinson Crusoe on his island, the exiled French set about trying to recreate *in situ* the civilisation they had been torn away from by the catastrophic shipwreck of June 1940. They created all sorts of social structures – artistic, cultural, educational and political. They held art exhibitions, gave concerts, wrote and produced plays, established newspapers, reviews and a book publishing industry. They founded a university and a variety of political groups. Where they found local Fridays who could be of

6. *France Forever Yearbook*, 1942. Cf. Guy Fritsch-Estrangin, *New York entre de Gaulle et Pétain* (Paris, 1969), pp. 59ff, and Raoul Aglion, *De Gaulle et Roosevelt* (Paris, 1984), pp. 117ff.

use to them, they enthusiastically enlisted their aid and knowledge of local conditions.

But they maintained their independence. Unlike many other European counterparts, they had no sense that their institutions would be permanent, because they had no intention of settling. Few of them sought to become US citizens, even if, as was too often the case, they had been officially stripped of their citizenship for unauthorised exit from France or some other poisoned Vichy motive. Even Louis Rapkine, a Russian-born ex-Canadian who had been naturalised French as late as 1939 (and hence fell under Vichy's July 1940 denaturalisation legislation), and who worked extensively with the Rockefeller Foundation in rescue operations for scientists, was not tempted to become an American: 'Would you have more respect for me if I changed my nationality the way I change my clothes?' he quipped to a State Department official, who wanted to know why he had not applied for US citizenship.[7]

To a very large extent, when France was eventually liberated, the exiles returned to the home which – although many of them had expected their absence to be longer – they had never really despaired of seeing again.

Notwithstanding the archetypically French fashion in which the community of exiles asserted its autonomy, it also engaged vigorously, as soon as the opportunity presented itself, in the American war effort, persuaded that this was indeed a common cause. Some of them, like the young poet Alain Bosquet, joined the US Army and played combat roles in US uniform. Others, like the journalist Pierre Lazareff, worked actively in propaganda at the Office of War Information. Others served in Colonel Donovan's Office of Strategic Services, forerunner to the CIA. The OSS archives demonstrate that almost all of the significant French in exile were very cooperative with US intelligence agents, and some were called on to offer advice directly to the President or his Secretaries. Former French Foreign Affairs head Alexis Léger (Saint-John Perse) was regularly consulted, as was the former prime minister (or *Président du conseil*, as it was under the Third Republic), Camille Chautemps. They did so with the conscientious and untroubled conviction that they were working with allies.

There is evidence, too, of Frenchmen spying on each other, and of trying to influence US opinion and policy to gain advantage for their own political views. It would be misleading to underestimate

---

7. Quoted by Leon Edel in 'Unwritten Lives: Memoir of Louis Rapkine', in B. and V. Karp (eds), *Louis Rapkine* (North Bennington, Vt, 1988), p. 33.

the depth of conflict within the French community. But after all, what was at stake was the future of France, and the passionate nature of the debates was proof that many understood how critical the issues were.

What kind of France would emerge from the war? There were some who were prepared to put their faith in de Gaulle, and to work blindly for his cause. This was the position of Henri Torrès, the First World War infantry sergeant, who claimed to have been decorated by Pétain's own hand, and who had become celebrated in the 1920s and 1930s as a brilliant lawyer. He was linked socially with an astonishing variety of people, from criminals, bookmakers and police, to press barons, politicians and famous writers. The transcripts of his speeches, given in Canada or New York, reveal the energy, generosity of spirit and eloquence for which he was admired, as he attacked Vichy with vehemence and rejected anything but complete loyalty to de Gaulle. There could be, he declared, 'no middle term, no compromise'.[8] Eventually, his love of polemics, as much as his uncompromising zeal, would get him into trouble with US libel laws, but he never wavered in his support for gaullism.

His enthusiasm was not shared by the majority of exiles. Few were overtly supportive of Vichy, though among those who were could be found people as distinguished and as highly regarded as André Maurois. Maurois wrote prolific pleas for Pétain, towards whom he felt strong personal gratitude and loyalty. He also defended the legitimacy of the Vichy government, and believed that the only way of achieving French unity was through its generalised acceptance.[9] But if Maurois and his wife Simone were widely and warmly entertained by his American hosts, his ideas were not: and while he maintained cordial personal relations with fellow writers such as Saint-Exupéry and Jules Romains, neither shared his views about Pétain and Vichy.

A more common position was that expressed by Raoul Roussy de Sales, who having rejected a pressing request from Eugène Houdry to join France Forever as its propaganda chief, noted sourly in his diary: 'That de Gaulle is fighting with the English is good. To bet everything on de Gaulle is stupid.'[10]

8. Quoted from his 1941 Radio-Canada speeches 'Vichy cède' and 'La France résiste', published by Hommage des Français libres au Canada, 1941. Cf. also his various books of memoirs, listed in the bibliography.
9. André Maurois, *Tragédie en France* (New York, 1940), passim. Also 'The Case for France', *Life*, 6 January 1941, pp. 63ff.
10. Raoul Roussy de Sales, *L' Amérique entre en guerre* (Paris, 1948), p. 120.

Many admired de Gaulle as a military figure who was helping through his 'fighting French' to revive the honour of their shamed and beaten nation. As soon as the possibility of a political dimension was evoked, however, reservations and objections sprang up from every quarter. Jacques Maritain would eventually support de Gaulle, but worried about whether he had an adequate commitment to democracy. Alexis Léger was convinced that the General wanted to install himself as a dictator. Henri de Kérillis, the great cagoulard tracker of the last years of the Third Republic parliament, could not accept that de Gaulle surrounded himself with people like the ex-Cagoule André Dewavrin (Colonel 'Passy', de Gaulle's Second Bureau chief). Saint-Exupéry, repelled by the political side of gaullism, considered de Gaulle's struggle against Pétain as fratricidal and needlessly divisive: he accorded no right to de Gaulle to 'represent' France, or to determine the future of the 40 million suffering French who were trapped under Nazi rule.

The task confronting de Gaulle's representatives was thus a daunting one, and it was made more so by US government diffidence towards the movement, and by Roosevelt's personal antipathy towards the General. Through its single-minded dedication and energy it eventually prevailed, eliminating its enemies, silencing its critics and imposing itself, apparently against all odds, as the only orthodoxy, and as the legitimate provisional government of liberated France. However, in the process of the struggle it was itself modified, and the French exiles in America had their part to play in those changes, just as they did in the shifts in US policy.

The little group of refugees was the point of encounter of two major historical forces that were in many ways working together, but often too were carrying different and even conflicting views of the future. There was a kind of schizophrenia. As exiles, many felt responsible to the land that welcomed them. But as French, they felt responsible for maintaining the values and honour of their own heritage. Their hesitations, their suffering, their internecine feuds, their courageous institution-building, reflect the nature of what now, in retrospect, can be seen as a major historical shift. After the changes, neither France nor America would be the same as they had been before the war, and it would inevitably modify their relations.

How actively did the French community in exile participate in the shaping of change? How much did it really contribute to the ways in which the most significant developments occurred? What was its role in the emergence of the new France, and in the realm of Franco-American relations? These are some of the questions on which this book seeks to cast light. It is not an exhaustive study. It is a narrative overview. But it does seek to bring into the mainstream of cultural and historical inquiry a neglected and important reality.

In the process, numerous individual stories are illuminated, some of them marked by the uncomplicated freedoms of youthful adventure, others more sober and even tragic. For many, the American exile was their real start in life, or the springboard to new lives in the post-war world. For others, it marked the end of their career and even the closing of an era.

Like the other institutions created by the French in America during that period, France Forever, born at a time when the future of France seemed desperately and permanently compromised by its recent past, dissolved after the Liberation and was reabsorbed into the margins of American cultural life. The community of refugees broke up, leaving little trace, as its individual members straggled into the 'liberty ships' or onto the planes that would take them back home. What had held them together was the way in which they had managed to maintain their identity, even when they could no longer be sure what it was.

To be French in the United States of 1939–45 was something short of a commitment to universal humanity, but of deeper import than a set of political beliefs or a national image. It meant affirming, often in an environment suffused with hostility and suspicion, values that could no longer be projected from France itself – values of freedom, of the rights of individuals to be different, of loyalty to friends and of international cooperation. It was not, at least initially, through flags and emblems that these values were kept alive. It was in the hearts and minds of people.

– 1 –

The Exodus

Images of the French population fleeing from the German advance in June 1940 are now familiar. From the north towards Paris, from Paris to the south, the clogged roads, the cars and carts, the trucks and tractors, vehicles of all sorts piled with luggage and furniture, whatever could be picked up and carried, a drift of tens of thousands of men and women uprooted from their homes by terror, crowded onto every available artery, blocking orderly troop movements, helping turn retreat into rout, and at the mercy of the advance guardian angels of the *Blitzkrieg*, the *stukkas*. They are images of dislocation, of lives being wrenched away from the times and place that gave them meaning and continuity. They are images too of powerlessness, of people cast onto a moving surface without horizon, where survival from the malevolent stream of bullets from the sky was a question more of chance than of judgement.

For those whose goal was the United States, the stereotype of powerlessness seems less appropriate, for many were wealthy or important public figures. The wealthy could command right of passage in a situation where places were hard to obtain. The famous, whether they were lawyers, artists, politicians, scientists or journalists, had people willing, and sometimes keen, to help them. There were others too, neither rich nor famous, whose initiative and resourcefulness were strong enough for them to overcome the very considerable difficulties facing the would-be émigré.

Fritsch-Estrangin[1] claims that a large majority of those who managed to cross the Atlantic during the big refugee movement – which lasted from the summer of 1940 to the spring of 1941 – were Jewish. While there were certainly many Jews – and among them a lot who would play a significant role in the exile – precise numbers are impossible to verify. The threat of persecution against Jews in France had become a reality by early October 1940, with the

---

1. Guy Fritsch-Estrangin, *New York entre de Gaulle et Pétain: les Français aux Etats-Unis de 40 à 46* (Paris, 1969), p. 12.

enactment of the first Vichy anti-Semitic laws, and there was a pressing need for Jews to escape, especially those who held public office or who were in other ways prominent. But Jews were not the only group whose safety and freedom were at risk. There were journalists like Geneviève Tabouis, Emile Buré or André Géraud (Pertinax), who had taken positions that singled them out for arrest by the Nazis. There were scientists like Jean Perrin, whose knowledge of atomic physics made him vulnerable to being forced to work for the enemy.

Some of those who escaped in the days following Pétain's announcement of 17 June of his intention to seek an armistice were able to make their way to England, and to cross the Atlantic from there. André Maurois did this. He met de Gaulle in London, who offered him a post, which he declined. Just before leaving for Canada, from whence he would make his way to New York, he made a radio broadcast to French Canada in support of Vichy. De Gaulle never forgave him.

Geneviève Tabouis, whose persistent and sweeping attacks on Hitler had earned her the Führer's personal enmity, recounts a very dramatic story. Urged by friends in high places to flee from Bordeaux, where she had followed the government, she burned four suitcases of her archives in the hotel furnace before being whisked away by the *Berkeley*, a British torpedo boat, along with her colleagues Buré and Pertinax, and Alexis Léger. Some miles out to sea, they were transferred to a cargo vessel for a week-long journey to Milford Haven.[2] Her departure was accompanied by anguished indecision – she was leaving her husband and family behind, and her own health was poor. She is a moving example of the fact that the conscious choice of exile did not make it any less painful. It was indeed all the more so because of her close personal identification with the collapse of her country. And it was a pain that her escape would not efface, just repress, though it would be made less unbearable by the driving sense of duty and mission that eventually turned Tabouis into one of the heroines of the exile. In London, like Maurois, she turned down an offer to work for de Gaulle, though she accepted an unspecified intelligence mission from Churchill. De Gaulle never forgave her either.

Getting out of France was a problem. Once the Vichy administration had established itself, it was necessary to obtain an exit permit before one could leave the country. And, even remembering

---

2. Geneviève Tabouis, *Ils l'ont appelée Cassandre* (New York, 1942), pp. 11–12. Also *Les Princes de la paix* (Paris, 1980), pp. 10ff.

that France and the United States had maintained diplomatic relations, these were in fact less than 'normal'. France, like other European countries, was subject to the quotas of the Immigration Act – quotas that from 1933 were systematically underfilled by a hypercautious administration.[3] Ordinary entry visas to the United States were extremely hard to get, requiring proof of employment or sufficient cash, and affidavits from suitably responsible US citizens guaranteeing that the visitor would place no financial burden on the American people.

Fulfilment of the conditions was not easy. The distinguished medieval scholar Gustave Cohen, who was helped to a visiting professorship at Yale by a former student teaching at Harvard and by Henri Peyre, points out in his *Lettres aux Américains* (Montreal, 1942, p. 142) that while the French government allowed emigrants to take out only the equivalent of $100, the trip alone would cost between $500 and $1200.

In view of such difficulties, subterfuge was common. Michel Bloit,[4] the sixteen-year-old son of the owner-manager of La Porcelaine de Paris, had gone south before the débâcle with his parents and sister, and at the time of the Armistice they were in Limoges. The Bloits were an old French-Jewish family (originally Bloch), established in Alsace since the time of Henri IV, and perhaps the long family experience had given them the foresight to plan ahead and prepare their escape to the United States in the event of a German victory. Fifty per cent of their prewar business had been in America, and their associates there were willing to sponsor them. None the less, it took time. In Limoges, Michel's father Robert set up a porcelain decoration workshop, which could serve as the basis for an official commercial mission to New York – to explore the possibility of exporting French porcelain to America. The ruse was facilitated by the president of the local Chamber of Commerce, a friend, and was sanctioned by Vichy officials eager to establish a foothold in the US market.

The Bloits travelled on a French cargo ship (the *Winnipeg*) which had berths for thirty passengers, and their route took them from Marseilles to Oran to Casablanca, and from there to Fort-de-France in Martinique, where they had to spend some months completing formalities for entry to the United States. The Mediterranean was

---

3. Jean Michel Palmier, *Weimar en exil* (Paris, 1988), vol. II, pp. 159ff. Cf. Roger Daniels, 'American Refugee Policy in Historical Perspective', in J. Jackman and C. Borden (eds), *The Muses Flee Hitler* (Washington, 1983), pp. 66–70.
4. Michel Bloit was interviewed by the author in June 1987.

not a safe sea for French shipping because of the British blockade. Claude Lévi-Strauss, in *Tristes Tropiques* (Paris, 1955, pp. 11–14), recounts how his ship, the *Capitaine-Paul-Lemerle*, laden with over 300 passengers, most of them in steerage (including André Breton, Victor Serge and Anna Seghers), dodged in and out of little ports all the way to the mouth of the Mediterranean and down the coast of Africa, in order to avoid encounters with the Royal Navy. And after the British destruction of the French fleet at Mers el-Kébir on 3 July 1940, the French sea captains were permanently on edge. Even if they escaped the British, moreover, their safety was not guaranteed. Henri Torrès, for example, had been in Casablanca, and had boarded a ship for South America. He was arrested and jailed by the Spanish in the Canary Islands. His eventual release was as arbitrary as his arrest.[5]

For the majority of émigrés, the escape route was via Spain to Lisbon. It was from Lisbon that most of the sea traffic from Europe to the western hemisphere left, and it was in Lisbon that those who could afford the $550 could vie for one of the twenty-five or so comfortable chairs and beds on board the newly established 30-hour Pan-American Clipper air service from the mouth of the Tagus to New York. The Swiss writer Denis de Rougemont, who was taking up the offer of a lecture tour in America, noted in his diary the difficulties of his journey across the hot southern summer:

> The 'road to Lisbon' will remain one of the most typical symbols of the year of grace 1940. 'Year of *rationed* grace', as one of my witty English friends remarked. For how many people isn't a ticket on the *Clipper* or a little American steamer the last coupon on the ration card of the happiness they all believe they deserve? But the *Clipper* and the steamers only leave now from a single European port. And to reach it only one way remains: the one which . . . passes through the South of France, filters with great difficulty into Spain, where it almost gets lost a score of times, and finally reaches Lisbon thanks, it seems, only to a strange quirk, or an ironic neglect, of the police gods of Europe. How easy it would be to close off, at any point anywhere, this slender artery through which our old world is being little by little emptied of its elite at the same time as of its parasites.[6]

As conditions of exit from France and transit across Spain were progressively tightened, escape would become harder and more

5. Henri Torrès, *Souvenir, souvenir que me veux-tu?* (Paris, 1964) pp. 190–1.
6. Denis de Rougemont, *Journal d'une époque* (Paris, 1968), p. 437.

dangerous. Those who had to resort to clandestine crossings of the Pyrenees and cope with a Spain still bullet-pocked from the Civil War, full of misery and patrolled by omnipresent police and militia, would have been astonished by the comfort and ease with which Jules Romains and his wife Lise were able to motor down, stopping to admire the cathedral at Burgos, and suffering little inconvenience other than an attack of bed-bugs in Madrid.[7]

The sparkling white buildings of Lisbon and nearby Estoril became the residence (more or less short-term, depending on the length of time needed to complete travel arrangements and secure passage) for thousands of refugees. According to a report by James Reston in the *New York Times*, (15 December 1940) the numbers reached a peak of 11,000, 90 per cent of them Jews, and many of them destitute enough to depend for their survival on meals provided by the Jewish Joint Distribution Committee and other relief organisations. There was not a free room, by all accounts, within 50 kilometres. Among the crowds, there were Americans who had been trapped in France, there were British civilians and soldiers, German émigrés and officials of the Third Reich, Central Europeans, Belgians, Scandinavians, Swiss. And there were the French. It was a bizarre and cosmopolitan collection of people, which Rougemont described as made up of 'secret agents, billionaires, fallen princes, compromised journalists, imperturbable engineers and weeping society women'.[8]

For some, the stay in Lisbon was only a matter of hours. Others would spend many weeks. It was a kind of limbo, a state of suspension between the suffocating prison they had left and the uncertainty of the exile that lay ahead. It was a world outside the war, where life retained something of its normal rhythm. The *New Yorker* foreign correspondent A. J. Liebling, on his way home, enjoyed himself swimming, playing roulette at the Estoril casino or sitting on the terrace of the bathing pavilion, drinking vermouth and eating black olives.[9] Lise and Jules Romains, leaving their luggage-filled car carefully hidden for safe-keeping in their hotel garage, would take the little train from Estoril to Lisbon and engage in friendly chats with the Maeterlincks, also on their way to New York, or with Yolande and Jacques de Lacretelle, who would decide to return to France.[10] Saint-Exupéry was at the centre of a

7. Lise Jules-Romains, *Les Vies inimitables: souvenirs* (Paris, 1985), pp. 259–61.
8. Rougemont, *Journal*, pp. 437–8.
9. A. J. Liebling, *Liebling Abroad* (New York, 1981), pp. 90–1.
10. Jules-Romains, *Les Vies*, p. 262.

group of expatriates which included René Clair and Kisling. He took time to talk to the students of a local technical school. But he also watched people playing at the casino. It was a sight that depressed him:

> a short distance from where I was living, each night, the Estoril Casino would be peopled by ghosts. Silent Cadillacs, pretending to be going somewhere, would drop them on the fine sand at the entry. They had dressed for dinner, as they used to. They were showing their starched shirt-fronts and their pearls . . .
> Then, depending on their fortune, they would play roulette or baccarat. I would sometimes go and watch them. I felt neither indignation nor a sense of irony – just a vague anxiety. The sort of thing that disturbs you at the zoo when you look at the survivors of an extinct species. . . . They were trying to believe, by clinging to the past, as if nothing on earth in the past few months had begun to crack up, that their excitement was legitimate, that their cheques were covered, and their conventions eternal. It was unreal. It was like a dance of dolls. But it was sad.[11]

On the other hand, the actor Jean-Pierre Aumont reacted quite differently. He wandered about in a happy daze, delighted by the unfamiliarity of the customs, the vitality of the bare-foot children, the swaying beauty of the women with their flat baskets balanced on their heads; and enthusing over the cheese-stands, the mountains of fruit and preserves, the cars, the coffee – all of those things of which France was now deprived.[12]

Different again, Suzanne Blum, a Jewish lawyer who had worked extensively with US film interests in France, had reached Portugal before the end of July 1940. She spent six weeks trying to turn her powerful American connections to advantage in order to obtain her US visa, which she finally got through the personal intervention of the Ambassador, William Bullitt. In the meantime, in the early days of her stay in Lisbon, she claims to have met a flood of French soldiers, who having escaped from Dunkirk, were returning to France after a stay in London. She found them very critical of de Gaulle, whom they perceived as dictatorial and anti-Semitic.[13] (Support for the famous 18 June call was obviously

---

11. Antoine de Saint-Exupéry, *Ecrits de guerre 1939–1944* (Paris, 1982), pp. 138, 329–30.
12. Jean-Pierre Aumont, *Souvenirs provisoires* (Paris, 1957), p. 124.
13. Suzanne Blum, *Vivre sans la patrie 1940–1945* (Paris, 1975), pp. 44–56.

not unanimous, even among military personnel who were already in England and could have chosen to stay on.)

For Camille Chautemps, as his unpublished journal reveals,[14] Lisbon was something of a nightmare. Chautemps was the man whose suggestion that France seek not an armistice but the *terms* of an armistice, had swung the Reynaud cabinet against any hope of continuing the war alongside the British. Ironically, it had been a suggestion typical of Third Republic compromise-seeking, and had an honourable historical precedent in a similar request from Thiers to the Prussians in 1870. Even more ironically, it was to prove the initiative that would cost Chautemps his political career. After the Armistice, he had worked for a time for Pétain, and his hope was to continue, in some way, to serve France and to keep his career alive.

He had arrived in Portugal believing that he had secured a high-ranking mission for Vichy in South America, and expected his stay to be short. But things rapidly went awry. His mission was cancelled for 'political' reasons that remained obscure, and it was not easy to develop alternative lines of action. His immediate thought was to get back to France, but Vichy did not want him: not only did he have personal enemies – among them Laval – he was also a leading Freemason, and freemasonry had been targeted by Vichy's conservative Catholic core as one of the demonic forces of France's decline that had to be destroyed. Rejecting as inadequate an ambassadorship in Rio, which was offered in compensation, Chautemps worked on hammering out, with the help of Jean Giraudoux at the French Legation, the details of a mission to the United States. He would finally accept it, though not without hesitations that kept him lingering in Lisbon for another month. During that time, he explored other avenues, including examining with German officials the implications of living in the Occupied Zone.

One of Chautemps' acute concerns was financial, since he was dependent on his government salary to support his family. It was thus important to him to retain some sort of official status. Pétain was obviously embarrassed about what to do with him, as the final agreement shows: Chautemps would get a diplomatic passport and receive a monthly allowance from the French Embassy in Washington, but he would be a private citizen, not a diplomat, and his expenses would be expected to be commensurate with those of a private citizen. On the other hand, his 'mission' would consist of

14. Access to some of Camille Chautemps' private papers, including his unpublished diary, was kindly provided by his daughter, Antoinette Samuels.

giving Americans a faithful interpretation of Vichy's policies and of counteracting misinformation being spread about the French government's reconstruction efforts.[15]

Had Chautemps been able to foresee what lay in store for him on the other side of the Atlantic, he may well not have undertaken the journey. None the less, in mid-November 1940, he and his family boarded the little American Export Lines steamer *Excambion*, heading for New York. This vessel saw its share of significant refugees. A few months later, André David, a Catholic writer who had gained some fame as the organiser of the '*Conférences des Ambassadeurs*' in prewar Paris, shared the journey with ex-King Carol of Romania and his bewitching paramour Mme Lupescu, who were on their way to a luxurious exile in Mexico. David, in his memoirs, reminisces kindly about the former monarch's love of music and his pet dogs, and about the bingo games they played during the eight-day crossing. As for Carol's reputation for having been more fascist than the fascists, David dismisses it, painting him as a man motivated by the 'sincerest wish to serve his people and keep his crown'.[16] (Unfortunately, David does not seem to have had much of a sense of irony.)

David also claims that the *Excambion*'s entire civilian crew, from the purser to the hairdresser, was in the pay of the Nazis. If so, Lise and Jules Romains had not noticed it on their crossing of the previous summer, as they lolled on their deck-chairs in the sun, trying to reassure Darius Milhaud and his wife Madeleine that the offer of work from Mills College – received by cable during the trip – would adequately solve the musician's financial predicament. On the eve of their arrival in New York, they shared their 14 July celebration with film-maker Julien Duvivier and his wife, and the Franco-American novelist Julien Green and his journalist friend Robert de Saint-Jean.[17] Three weeks later, the *Excambion* again left Lisbon, with another load of aristocrats, intellectuals and artists: René Clair and his wife, Salvador Dali and Gala, Man Ray, the American composer Virgil Thomson, the Countess du Bourg de Bozas, as well as Suzanne Blum.[18]

There were other boats and other stories. Jean-Pierre Aumont took the *Nyassa*, with 100 other passengers – French, German, Belgian, Canadian, English – and gave them a poetry recital on

15. Vichy government document dated 17 October 1940; from Chautemps papers.
16. André David, *75 Années de jeunesse* (Paris, 1974), pp. 157–8.
17. Jules-Romains, *Les Vies*, p. 265.
18. Blum, *Vivre sans la patrie*, p. 58.

board, inwardly raging at the fatuous snobbery of some of his companions and at openly expressed pro-Pétain statements.[19] Denis de Rougemont went on the *Exeter*, remarking with his usual astringency how appropriate it was that so many of these steamers had names beginning in 'Ex' (*Excalibur, Excambion, Exeter*), since most of their passengers were also ex-somethings: 'ex-ministers, ex-directors, ex-Austrians, ex-millionaires, ex-princes'. He spent the journey pondering on the future shape of Europe, worrying about whether he would find an audience in New York. Or else he joined the evening crowd pressed around the door of the captain's cabin, straining to catch the radio news.[20]

Saint-Exupéry travelled with Jean Renoir and Sido Freire on the *Siboney*. The airman-writer and the film-maker had much in common, in addition to their gregarious personalities. Both had hesitated a long time before making the decision to go to America, and both had only done so when pressured to become official participants in the elaboration of Vichy's plans for the New France. On the boat they became firm friends, and would subsequently provide each other with mutual support during some critical episodes of the exile.

The patchy, anecdotal nature of the many accounts of the exodus bears witness to its confusion. As the steamers and the *Clippers* shuttled back and forth across the Atlantic, a whole civilisation was being fragmented. But as Jean Renoir observes in his autobiography, 'great disasters are slow in showing their destructive effects',[21] and on an individual level, many refugees simply did not have access to enough information to be able to think much beyond their immediate situations.

Most of them relied on relatives or friends or personal associates to provide them with the sponsorship necessary for entry to the United States. On the other hand, many others would never have made it without more organised help. Within days of the fall of France, a high-powered group of US university presidents and media representatives had founded the 'Emergency Rescue Committee' (ERC), with the mission of saving as many as possible of those artists, scholars and politicians whose lives had been put in more acute danger by the Nazi invasion and by Vichy's hard-line internment policies for German refugees. An outgrowth of the American Friends of German Freedom, its particular focus was on

19. Aumont, *Souvenirs*, pp. 126–7.
20. Rougemont, *Journal*, pp. 446–8.
21. Jean Renoir, *My Life and My Films* (New York, 1974), p. 182.

extending the rescue of Germans that had begun with Hitler's rise to power. However, it also had a crucial part in the saving of some very significant French people, notably André Breton, Marcel Duchamp, André Masson, Marc Chagall and Jacques Lipchitz; as well as Jacques Schiffrin, the creator of Gallimard's famous 'Bibliothèque de la Pléiade', the eighty-year-old Collège de France mathematician Jacques Hadamard and the legal philosopher Boris Mirkine-Guetzévitch.

The ERC was a marvellously typical American organisation: funded by private donations but fiercely public-spirited, it was supported discreetly by Eleanor Roosevelt (and thus by the President), and it contrived to subvert the draconian immigration regulations enforced by the Assistant Secretary of State, Breckinridge Long, who was renowned for his xenophobia. Its director, Frank Kingdon, managed eventually to get 2000 'emergency visas' granted for significant refugees.

The unlikely hero of ERC operations in France was a young Harvard classicist, Varian Fry. His own account of his adventures, *Surrender on Demand* (New York, 1945), reveals how, during his 13-month secret mission, he overcame his inexperience, and outwitted or outflanked the increasingly suspicious and threatening local authorities. Under the cover of a relief organisation set up in Marseilles – '*Le Centre Américain de Secours*' – he developed a tight network of contacts and helpers, who at considerable risk to their own freedom, and sometimes their lives, eventually brought about the freedom of around 1000 refugees. But part of Fry's success was his willingness to improvise, and the ability to discern and use whatever resources arose. His French charges, for example, derived great benefit from the generosity of the eccentric and passionate Peggy Guggenheim, whose love of art was more than once entwined with her affairs with the artists. Nevertheless, her support of the surrealist group was wholehearted and constant. She not only paid the fares of the Bretons and the Massons, but would continue to pay Breton $200 a month for his first year in America.[22]

Varian Fry and the EMC were one of the avenues used by Louis Rapkine, another remarkable man, who distinguished himself through his tireless efforts to save French scientists. The son of

---

22. Peggy Guggenheim, *Out of this Century: Confessions of an Art Addict* (New York, 1985), pp. 227–50. Also Cynthia Jaffee McCabe, 'Wanted by the Gestapo: Saved by America – Varian Fry and the Emergency Rescue Committee', in Jackman and Borden (eds), *The Muses Flee Hitler*, pp. 79–91.

Russian émigrés, Rapkine had gone to France in 1911 and from there to Montreal. In 1924, he had abandoned a medical degree at McGill in order to return to France to work on basic biological research. He rapidly achieved a sound reputation in the area of cell division, and was a Rockefeller Fellow in 1926–8. A frequent visitor to Britain, he was implicated in early efforts to save scientists from fascist countries, and in 1934 took the initiative to set up an international committee to find employment and laboratories for refugees. During the '*drôle de guerre*', having become a naturalised French citizen, he was in London on a government mission, working as a liaison officer between French and British biologists. Even before the French collapse, he had been working with distinguished members of the British Royal Society (Sir William Bragg, Professor A. V. Hill, Sir Edward Appleton), devising plans to save the greatest possible number of French scientists. The original project involved bringing them to England, but this was blocked by the British attack on the French fleet at Mers el-Kébir, after which all communications with France were interrupted. Pressed by the Royal Society, the Rockefeller Foundation invited Rapkine (along with the physiologist Henri Laugier) to go to the United States for discussions about how French scientists might be saved.

Rapkine arrived in the United States in August 1940. His aims were clear: to avert French scientific collaboration with the Germans, and to put French science at the disposal of the allied war effort. But unlike Fry, he had no ready-made American connections, no direct lines to presidents of universities or to Eleanor Roosevelt. Every case had to be built up from scratch, and the task required simultaneous action on many fronts: seeking out universities that might be willing and able to offer places, finding salaries for others and travel expenses for all, contacting the government departments that might be interested in their particular fields, arranging the affidavits for the granting of visas.

He bombarded the President's Advisory Committee, the American Joint Distribution Committee, the American Jewish Congress and the American Friends Service Committee, as well as the ERC. He hounded or charmed wealthy friends and acquaintances, especially among the French-Jewish community – the Wertheimers and the Rothschilds were 'generous donors' – to create a French Scholars' Fund, which was used, in part, to subsidise the living expenses of the scientists' families. He sought and obtained the help of the Hebrew Sheltering and Immigrant Aid Society. In the end, he had the primary responsibility for saving thirty-six French scientists and their families, three-quarters of them Jewish. A small number, to be sure, especially in view of the prodigious energy that Rapkine had to expend. But his success list contained many top people, like the nuclear physicists Pierre Auger and Francis Perrin, the illustrious mathematician Jacques Hadamard, the Alsatian pathologist Charles Oberling. For many of them, like the electronics engineer Stanislas Winter, Rapkine would become a life-long friend, but he also remained the mysterious angel who had produced so many miraculous escapes. And yet an angel of keen practical sense:

> Louis' charm was in no way esoteric: when one got to know him, one discovered a strong character, an excellent evaluation of the material conditions in which he had to act, an almost clinical lucidity in his judgement of people, without that ever affecting his acute feeling for human solidarity. With all that, no austerity, a delicious sense of humour, a taste for gaity and joking, one of those rare men whose exceptional gifts did not crush out everyday life.[23]

One of the more poignant escape stories is that of Rapkine's wife Sarah and their eight-year-old daughter Claude.[24] They were in Paris at the time of the Nazi invasion, and at that time lost all contact with Rapkine. It was months before he could get them a message that he was in the United States. The first step, if there were to be any hope of rejoining him, was to reach the Free Zone. All of her first attempts to find a way across the Demarcation Line were fruitless, but in the early spring of 1941, she was eventually helped by a scientist at the Institut de Biologie Physico-chimique, where she worked as a technician. He had relatives in Biarritz, and believed that he could find them a guide into unoccupied territory.

There were risks – Sarah Rapkine had already had visits from the Gestapo, who were investigating her husband's activities and whereabouts. None the less, abandoning her job and her belongings, she and her little girl set out. In Bayonne, she was terrified by the number and unavoidable proximity of German soldiers, but she stuck scrupulously to the plan laid out by her benefactor. She took the little train to the designated village, where she was met by a member of the escape network who hid them till the middle of the

23. 'La Mission scientifique française en Grande Bretagne', in B. and V. Karp (eds), *Louis Rapkine* (Nth Bennington, Vt, 1988), p. 136.
24. Sarah Rapkine was interviewed by the author in June 1987.

night. Then there was a three-hour walk through rain and mud, with their guide weaving a path between German dog-patrols. At dawn they reached a farmhouse on the safe side of the line. The hospitable farmers gave them food, lit a fire to warm them and organised a taxi to take them to Pau. From there, it was possible to cable Rapkine in New York. The reply was soon back, one word: 'Halleluja'.

That was only the first phase. Sarah Rapkine and her daughter still needed exit permits and US visas. There were some anxious weeks. Rapkine was not prepared to risk the success of his bigger operation by trying to bring his wife in as a scientist, and chose instead to go to Canada and re-enter the United States with immigrant status, which gave him the right to bring in his family. Meanwhile, from the village near Lyons where she had found accommodation, Sarah Rapkine made daily visits to the city to check her situation with the US consul, whom she found uncongenial and unhelpful (although he had the reputation of being kind),[25] and to try to sort out her exit permit.

The French authorities were willing to give her a permit, but refused to issue one for the daughter without the father's signature. She eventually got out, not with the required permit, but with an official-looking stamp applied to her passport by an affable official at Police Headquarters. She used what had by that time become one of Varian Fry's favourite routes, on the *Winnipeg*, now converted to carry large numbers of passengers from Marseilles to Martinique.

The journey was eventful. She and her daughter travelled in the hold, two of fifteen French among over 750 people on board. Their bunks were in a section curtained off for women and children, and they would have been without sheets or blankets had Claude not attracted the sympathy of one of the sailors. Their diet was monotonous – lentils and wine – and the conditions stifling. For this reason, since the weather was fine, they often went up to sleep on the deck. It was from there, in sight of the lights of Fort-de-France, that they witnessed the capture of their vessel by a squadron of allied aircraft. The *Winnipeg* was forced to change course for Trinidad, its crew and passengers now prisoners of the British. (The British at this time were routinely screening would-be entrants to the United States, in Bermuda, and also in Trinidad and Jamaica, for intelligence information, and to intercept Nazi spies. It was a major espionage centre.)[26]

25. Cf. Jean Renoir, *Lettres d'Amérique* (Paris, 1984), p. 31.
26. Cf. William Stevenson, *A Man called Intrepid* (New York, 1977), pp. 187ff.

The touch of grace that so often surfaces in the Rapkine story revealed itself again here. While the other refugees had been taken ashore for interrogation by British intelligence officers, the fifteen French had been left on board, their fate uncertain. A forced return to France was not out of the question. But among the British officers charged with inspecting the passenger list was a man who had worked with Louis Rapkine in London, and who had kept in close touch with his activities in New York. Sarah Rapkine and Claude were taken ashore and given comfortable lodgings while arrangements were made for their passage to New York. When she was finally reunited there with her husband in mid-June 1941, it had been exactly a year since their last 'normal' communication, a letter received from London on the eve of the Armistice.

Arrival in New York produced very different impressions for different people. Jules Romains and his wife, after being fêted on board their ship by admiring and enthusiastic journalists, were whisked away by Romains' American publisher, Alfred Knopf, to the suite that awaited them in the Mayflower Hotel, overlooking Central Park.[27] Jean-Pierre Aumont, experiencing the actor's urge to conquer a new public, found his first sight of Manhattan rather daunting: 'A compact, hostile barrier. An eruption of edifices standing like petrified spurts from a crater. Phallic temples dotted with windows. Approaching this crenellated prow-shaped mass sends a shiver through the heart.'[28]

Denis de Rougemont missed the view of the celebrated skyline, being confined for two hours in the saloon, where taciturn immigration officers painstakingly interrogated the passengers, one by one. But he had been filled with wonder by the approach:

I woke in my damp cabin with the feeling that everything around me was changed. And indeed! Close-by greenery was parading past the port-hole!

Ran to the bridge. We are in the Hudson channel. A haze of tropical heat tinges the banks with blue. I was not expecting to see American nature, to see it first, and so near, before the sky-scrapers, the statue. . . . I have never had the sensation of a more foreign landscape, nor of one more strangely welcoming. All those trees, so lush, so bushy, and a bit crazy! And those colonial houses, spread out, but seeming so intimate behind their grand porticos. And how attractive is this approaching land, with the immense security of the continent one

27. Jules-Romains, *Les Vies*, p. 268.
28. Aumont, *Souvenirs*, p. 129.

imagines beyond the orange cliffs, fringed with forests, dark green like a luxurious tapestry.[29]

Ellis Island was an object of fear for many refugees, the last barrier to be crossed before entry to the promised land was assured, but a passage that was difficult for those whose papers were not in order, or who failed to answer the immigration officials' questions in quite the right way. André David, who had been sponsored by Charles Boyer, and whose visitor's visa was valid for six months, made the mistake of declaring his intention to remain in the United States until his country was liberated. This earned him a nine-day stay on the Island, while Boyer and his other friends worked frantically to get him released. His experience, all in all, while obviously disagreeable, was not painful, and his evocation of this 'prison which pretended not to be one' is worth recording:

Ellis Island was a well-kept place, not at all like other 'concentration spaces', since the Americans refused to admit that Ellis Island was a prison. Married couples were separated: the men slept in male dormitories, the women in female dormitories; if they had children, the little boys followed their fathers, the little girls their mothers. The women supervisors were strict about morality: as soon as they glimpsed a young man holding a girl a bit close in the shadow of a coat-rack in the common hall, they would rush up and separate them. Every day the sheets were changed, and clean towels were distributed night and morning. The food was copious and well prepared. Practising Jews could eat their ritual food and each race was treated according to its customs. Women and children were given milk supplements, sewing kits and games. A refrigerator provided a permanent supply of cold drinking water . . .[30]

If locked windows and bars made the atmosphere oppressive, there was nevertheless a daily exercise walk, and it was possible to have visitors. David's friends brought him regular supplies. The Island's own administration was thus reasonably humane, but it was inflexible, and it required considerable influence to make it bend – David was eventually released only through the personal intervention of Theodore Rousseau, Vice-president of the Guarantee

29. Rougemont, *Journal*, p. 448.
30. David, *75 Années*, p. 159.

–25–

Trust. Otherwise the waiting could have been very long – up to a year, renewable.

> In the common hall, several hundred people spent whole days waiting for their names to be called, with the ones who had been there longest, by order of arrival, sitting, as in the theatre, in club chairs in the front rows of the stalls; then, the later arrivals on chairs further and further from the door, and more and more modest, until one reached the simple benches at the back of the room. This room was provided with a telephone booth; people queued up, from the time they awoke until bedtime; taking turns to call their lawyers.[31]

André David, once he was released, spent two weeks in New York, dazzled by the luminous geometry of the city. Charles Boyer, who had come to fetch him, then took him back to California. Boyer was one of a number of people around whom action groups would form. David had arrived very much alone: he had one or two close friends, and various acquaintances, but he would have very little news of his own family for the next four years. Within weeks, however, he would be putting his talent and experience to work for his country's cause as the director of Boyer's 'French Research Foundation' in Los Angeles.

A similar pattern was repeated in many different situations: against the scattering effect of an exodus whose motivations were almost as varied as the number of refugees, other forces would operate to gather the dispersed individuals into social, political or artistic communities, thus transforming the nature of the exile from a multitude of individual phenomena into a series of cultural institutions.

The range of people and professions is impressive. Novelists, poets and playwrights of note included André Breton, Alain Bosquet, Maurice Dekobra, Henri Bernstein, Louis Verneuil, Jacques Deval, Yvan Goll, Julien Green, André Maurois, Maurice Maeterlinck, Jules Romains, Saint-John Perse, Antoine de Saint-Exupéry. Other significant figures in the arts were Léger, Hélion, Ozenfant, Tanguy, Dali, Lipchitz, Milhaud, Lourié, and the elite of French cinema directors and actors, from Renoir, Clair and Duvivier to Gabin, Dalio, Aumont and Michèle Morgan.

Among leading prewar political figures were Camille Chautemps, Pierre Cot, Henri de Kérillis, Fernand-Laurent, Edouard Jonas,

31. Ibid., pp. 160–1.

André Maroselli, Hervé de Lyrot and Jacques Stern, as well as previously senior public servants or officials like Alexis Léger, or the economist André Istel or Jean Monnet. There were the scientists, like Lévi-Strauss, the Perrins, Bertrand Goldschmidt, etc. There were major bankers and financiers, like the Rothschilds and André Meyer, there were academics, like Gustave Cohen and Henri Focillon, and philosophers, like Jacques Maritain. There were business people and engineers, artisans and union officials. And a very large number of top journalists: Pierre Lazareff, Philippe Barrès, Pertinax, Jacques Surmagne, Emile Buré, Michel Pobers, Robert de Saint-Jean and Geneviève Tabouis.

Tabouis, like Charles Boyer, but to a much more significant degree, would become a nucleus around whom a unification of effort would occur, lending coherence and direction to the exiles' attempts to rebuild their identity, and to turn the debilitating shock of defeat into a liberating reaffirmation of the values underlying their culture. The process was difficult and slow, and in order to measure the scale of the achievement, it is useful to note the initial state of mind of someone like Tabouis. She was an activist who had taken strong positions in support of Briand's peace initiatives in the 1920s, and against the fascist leaders in Europe: a fighter and an idealist, but her arrival in New York marked her professional and personal nadir:

Numerous reporters are on the huge pier in New York, awaiting the arrival of the boat. They all ask me the same questions at the same time. For the first time, I hear those brutal words 'The Collapse of France'. But in their pressing questions, I detect such a real love for France, such distress at its defeat, that it seems as if this immense America is somehow in harmony with my pain! . . .

That first night in New York, in my hotel room, seeing some of the photos . . . taken that morning, I looked at myself several times without recognition!

An expression of anguish has turned me into another person, and I note that in a few weeks, my hair has gone completely white.

I am haunted by longing for my loved ones: I am shamed by the attitude of the new French leaders towards Germany. The suffering beginning for the tens of thousands of French patriots, so innocent of what is happening, overwhelms me.[32]

32. Tabouis, *Ils l'ont appelée Cassandre*, pp. 15–16.

At the desk in that hotel room, Tabouis set to work, seeking to build up, from what she felt as the ashes of her sixteen-year career as an international correspondent, something that she could again be proud of, not just as a journalist, but also and above all as a Frenchwoman.

– 2 –

Settling In

Alone in the house for the past two days. I have been
out only to scrape and shovel the snow piled up on the
sidewalk and in the driveway.

Increased insomnia. All Europeans go through that, I
am told, during the first months of their stay in New
York.

Denis de Rougemont[1]

Individual reactions to exile varied greatly and often evolved
markedly with the passage of time and with changes in the circumstances of the war. Few had any previous detailed knowledge of
what it was like to live in America, and differences in everyday
behaviour patterns, as well as in social, administrative and political
organisation, were large enough to be severely disorienting for
many, especially during the early months. Even those with well-
established professional careers and who were well taken care of
locally seldom found an easy transition into American life. Not
surprisingly, most, despite a general sense of the gravity of the
events which had befallen their homeland, and the realisation that
some radical break with the past had occurred, initially set about
trying to re-establish their previous life-styles and working habits.
Only progressively did they discover that far from having been
thrown upon a desert island, they were confronted with a civilisation as vigorous and complex as it was alien to the one they had
known. Periods of adjustment for the émigrés were more or less
long, and more or less successful, depending on several factors:
individual resilience, the ability to practise their professions, willingness to take real account of American mores and attitudes, and
the capacity to adapt their social and political thinking to the
frequently unpredictable new realities created by the war.

Robert Bloch, head of La Porcelaine de Paris, thrived on the opportunities that New York offered to the enterprising businessman, and

1. Denis de Rougemont, *Journal d'une époque* (Paris, 1968), p. 467.

his young son Michel found the whole experience exhilarating, 'an extraordinary adventure'.[2] The family's arrival had been cushioned by their prewar business associates, and a cousin, who had a furnished apartment waiting for them when they disembarked, organised schools for the children, and provided initiation into American business life. Michel's mother, a painter-decorator, had brought from France samples of patterns for wallpaper and fabric design, and quickly created a niche for herself in the market, although her sales collapsed a year after their arrival, when war regulations forbade the use of the big copper cylinders needed for the printing process.

Her loss, however, proved to be her husband's gain. Robert, after serving a brief apprenticeship with his associate, a lamp-maker, had rented premises and set up his own porcelain-decorating business, helped by a French foreman, Gabriel Verneuil, who had been established in America for twenty years, and who knew all about where to buy supplies and to hire reliable staff. Table-lamps were in vogue, and with all the metal going to the munitions industry, glass and porcelain bases were much in demand. Even more spectacularly, metal buttons were replaced by ceramic ones, and Robert Bloch's workshop processed hundreds of thousands of them, painting them gold or silver for the fashion industry. According to Michel, although the family did not make a fortune, they did live well in their Waverly Place apartment, and at the peak of his business, Robert was employing fifty workers.

In the meantime, Michel was at George Washington High School on 225th Street, where for three months he was given special English lessons, along with numerous other foreign students. Many of these spoke French, being from France, Belgium or Luxembourg, or German Jews who had already spent some time in France. He revelled in the freedom of the American school system, in the relaxed exchanges between teachers and pupils, in the fact that students were encouraged to read the newspaper in class. With fellow pupils, including Niels Perrin (son of Francis Perrin the nuclear physicist), he participated in drama productions, and in the summer, like many young Americans of his age, he went off to camp. Despite the relative ease of the family's integration into American life, however, it is interesting to note that the friends of both Michel and his parents were almost exclusively French.

A quite different story is revealed in the wartime correspondence

---

2. Interview with Michel Bloit, 5 June 1987.

of Jean Renoir in Hollywood.[3] Renoir was already disenchanted with French society before the war, and his last great masterpiece, *La Règle du Jeu* (1939), in its portrayal of a world completely given over to frivolity and hypocrisy, is infused with weariness and despair. Renoir had believed in the possibility of social change, and earlier films, such as *Le Crime de Monsieur Lange* (1934), had shown this enthusiastic idealism. By the time the war broke out, he had become quite cynical, and his fundamental doubt even led him to making aberrant, reactionary statements, such as the recanting of his previous radicalism and the expression of anti-Semitic views to the Portuguese press in Lisbon.[4]

His arrival in America was like a rebirth, and he embraced the new country with adolescent eagerness. He rented a big house on Sunset Boulevard, complete with two black servants, and took to driving a Buick convertible, while his companion Dido Freire had a Packard. His highly paid contract with Twentieth Century Fox gave him enough material security to deny any refugee status. 'We are not refugees,' he wrote to his brother Claude in June 1941, 'merely people determined to follow our profession, whatever the circumstances.'[5]

None the less, for a long time in his work he was miserable or bored – a 'living corpse' as he put it. The lack of freedom, the curtailing of individual creativity inherent in the specialised and mechanised American film-making methods, were a painful shock to the man who, more than any other, had imposed an aesthetic of personal style on French cinema production in the 1930s. He had arrived with the hope of making a film that would draw American attention to the plight of children arising from the German invasion and occupation of France, and a second personal desire was to create a film version of Saint-Exupéry's *Wind, Sand and Stars*. In neither instance was he able to get the project off the ground, and had to accept to play the relatively minor role allowed by Hollywood to directors. He moved about, from Fox to Universal to RKO, and although some of his work – *Swamp Water* (1941), *The Southerner* (1944) – resulted in a certain amount of public success, he seems to have derived only mediocre pleasure from it.

He learned in due course to appreciate the professional quality and commitment of his American colleagues, to the point that by

3. Jean Renoir, *Lettres d'Amérique* (Paris, 1984).
4. Curtis Cate reports this incident in his *Antoine de Saint-Exupéry* (New York, 1970), p. 432.
5. Renoir, *Lettres*, p. 56.

the end of 1942, he had concluded that his future lay in Hollywood and that he must stay in the United States after the war. 'Europe disgusts me,' he confessed to his son Alain.[6] In fact, although he did continue to live in California, his only significant post-war films would be made in France, although none of them has the strength or depth of his prewar production. Exile did not finish him as a film-maker, but it dissipated his creative energies to such an extent that his career was very much diminished.

Renoir's withdrawal from the big social and political issues that had formed the backbone of his work in the 1930s was almost organic, a shrinking away from engagement in any kind of political thought. He wrote to Saint-Exupéry: 'I am happy to break with all the political forms of my ex-homeland. I like Mr Roosevelt, and I like neither Vichy, which tends to have a few too many people shot, nor de Gaulle, who seems just a bit too opportunistic.'[7]

He pulled out of Boyer's French Research Foundation, and frequently lashed out at his exiled compatriots, especially the gaullists, whose bellicose 'all or nothing' approach he found abrasive and dangerous. This did not prevent him from making occasional patriotic broadcasts, or from making pro-French propaganda films – *This Land is Mine* (1942) and *Salute to France* (1944). He was deeply convinced, however, that the France he had known and loved was gone forever, and it was that certainty, together with a measure of nostalgia, that inspired him to begin work on his book about his father – in order to escape from what he felt as the crushing destruction of history, and to rescue at least the memory of the 'humble, everyday values' of the times before everything went wrong.[8]

More than by his work, real or projected, and more than by his depressed reflections on the state of the world, Renoir's first eighteen months in America were dominated by his efforts to get his nineteen-year-old son Alain out of France and into America. To achieve this, he had no qualms about enlisting the help of the Vichy French Embassy in Washington, or in making a written declaration of his fidelity to Marshall Pétain.[9] It is not clear how much this involved any profound inner compromise: there are no signs that Renoir was distressed by having to keep on the right side of a system he despised. He was on good personal terms with Georges

6. Ibid., p. 126.
7. Ibid., p. 103.
8. Ibid., p. 118.
9. Ibid., p. 39.

Achard, the Vichy Consul in Los Angeles, and dropped in on him from time to time to speak French.[10]

When Alain Renoir finally arrived, he horrified his father by promptly signing up with the Free French Army in New York. Renoir talked him out of it, and was happy when his son joined the US Army instead. Had the gaullists been aware of Renoir's expedients and attitudes, there is little doubt that he would have been censured, and it seems unlikely that he would have received an invitation from the Provisional Government to make a film in France at the Liberation – an invitation he moreover turned down. But Renoir was as adept at avoiding confrontation as he was at sidestepping ideological commitment. He cared about his son and about his family in France (to whom an intergovernmental agreement allowed him to send money); he cared about his friends and, to a certain degree, about his work – all things that were personally close to him. For the rest, he showed little interest: as if, for him, exile meant deliberately taking up a position outside of history.

It is difficult to assess how much Renoir's inner withdrawal was intensified by his location in California, and in particular in the artificiality of the dream-factory studios of Hollywood. Another Californian exile, Darius Milhaud, also seems to have derived from his geographical isolation an ability to keep his links with his compatriots on a purely cultural level. He and his wife Madeleine were teaching – music and French language respectively – at Mills College in northern California. Milhaud made numerous trips east, stopping regularly in Chicago for lecture and concert engagements, but both there and in New York he kept free of politics. Even his close friendship with the writer-diplomat Henri Hoppenot remained uncomplicated, which was no mean feat, for Hoppenot's own itinerary was full of political intrigue. (Hoppenot had created librettos for Milhaud's operettas in the 1920s, but he served Vichy in Uruguay before a timely move allowed him to switch sides and go to Washington in early 1943.)[11]

On the East Coast, where the war in Europe had greater immediacy, the kind of distance that Renoir and Milhaud contrived to achieve was simply not sustainable. France was constantly in the news, and being French meant being caught in often vicious

10. Ibid., p. 57.
11. Darius Milhaud, *Ma Vie heureuse* (Paris, 1973). General Marie-Emile Béthouart, in his *Cinq Années d'espérance: mémoires de guerre* (Paris, 1968, p. 210), claims that Hoppenot received warning of the US attack on North Africa from his old friend Alexis Léger. See below for Léger's involvement in US policy-making.

cross-currents of policy and opinion. The full political dimensions of the exile will be treated in later chapters, for in the first year or so they remained in a rather nebulous, embryonic state, but the general political climate of 1940–1 needs to be recalled here, since it was part of the context in which the refugees had to make their lives.

On the American side, official neutrality in respect to the war was maintained until December 1941, and diplomatic relations with the French government in Vichy were kept up until broken off by Pétain after the Allied invasion of North Africa in November 1942. Neutrality and a strongly isolationist Congress notwithstanding, President Roosevelt was determined to help Britain in its struggle against the Axis forces. His Lend-Lease proposal, which allowed the provision of arms to the British without infringement of the Neutrality Act, followed closely upon his re-election to office in late 1940 – although it was not passed by Congress until the following March. Behind the scenes, Jean Monnet and the British Purchasing Commission were working hard to bring US power into the war, and to encourage massive increases in US arms production so that the United States could indeed become the 'arsenal of the democracies' (a phrase Monnet later claimed to have coined). [12]

Support for Britain had as a counterpart very tight control over relations with Vichy, since the US administration shared to a considerable extent Churchill's fears that Pétain, and especially Laval, might facilitate German use of French resources for the war effort against the British. French funds in the United States were frozen – a move that affected individuals as well as the Vichy government, though it was relatively easy for individuals to get access to their money, while any government requests were subject to protracted and difficult negotiation. Even to secure humanitarian relief for hungry French children was not straightforward, because of the perceived danger that any supplies would simply be read by Germany as an invitation to syphon off the equivalent from a compliant French government.

The American press was by and large vehemently pro-British, and just as vehemently anti-Vichy. Newspaper cartoons of the period showed such images as Pétain kissing the Nazi boot while the ghosts of Clémenceau and Foch look on in horror; or the corpse of France, with Pétain stabbing a pen into the back already pierced by knives marked 'Politics', 'Antique Generals', 'Reds' and

12. Jean Monnet, *Mémoires* (Paris, 1976), p. 191.

'Strikes' – with the caption '*ANTICLIMAX*'; or Hitler sitting on the belly of a dead Marianne, with a pistol pointed at Pétain, who is wearing a swastika arm-band and saying to a baleful Uncle Sam: 'How could you misjudge us so?'[13]

At the same time, there remained in the media as much good will towards France and the French as among the public at large. American admiration for French culture was deep-rooted and largely uncritical, and beyond the shabby realities of the defeated and occupied nation, with its untrustworthy government, the myth of a 'true' France was carefully nurtured and revered, vague in definition, but strong in all the virtues of liberty, courage and civilisation. Exiled intellectuals were widely solicited for interviews and articles, and provided they were not suspected of being too sympathetic to Vichy, they were listened to.

The press was also adamantly supportive of gaullism, at least in so far as de Gaulle's movement represented an effort to continue the fight against fascism: this was part of the 'true France' myth. The news of the decision by the colonial governors of Equatorial Africa and Cameroon to join the Free French in August 1940 was greeted with acclaim, and later, in December 1941, it would be the clamour of the press that turned opinion in de Gaulle's favour when he defied US policy and aroused the fury of Secretary of State Cordell Hull by his armed invasion of the tiny French islands of Saint Pierre and Miquelon, off the Canadian coast. Hull's outraged condemnation of the Free French was based on America's agreement with Vichy to maintain the status quo in France's possessions, but in his memoirs, he ruefully notes his surprise at the response:

Few actions that seemed so minor have ever aroused opposition that became so bitter. In the weeks that followed, the State Department, with myself as its chief, became the target of editorials, radio attacks, and representations from various organisations, although the President had given his full support to our reaction.[14]

If US political stances were complicated, the French ones were no less so. Shortly after the signing of the Armistice, the then French Ambassador in Washington, Count René Doyel de Saint-

13. These are reproduced in Gaston Henry-Haye's *La Grande Eclipse franco-américaine* (Paris, 1972).
14. Cordell Hull, *Memoirs* (New York, 1948), vol. 2, p. 1130. Raoul Aglion gives a lively account of this incident in his *Roosevelt and de Gaulle* (New York, 1988), pp. 61–70, well illustrated with quotations from the major newspapers.

Quentin, a career diplomat, and by all accounts a charming, cultured and highly respected ambassador, received the news that he was being recalled. His replacement was Gaston Henry-Haye, who proved considerably less than adequate to the task. In his late forties, he knew America well: he had been sent as a military adviser in 1917 and had travelled the country extensively; and again in 1931, he had been sent by Laval to prepare his US visit. He was fluent in English, and also well connected: friendly with the key US diplomats William Bullitt and Robert Murphy, he was close enough to Pétain and to General Pershing for them to have been the witnesses at his son's wedding.[15] And finally, he was politically experienced, having served in both houses of the French parliament, in the Foreign Affairs Commission, and since 1935, as Mayor of Versailles. However, a staunch anti-communist, he was a believer in Franco-German *rapprochement*, and he suffered from a fair dose of anti-Semitism and anglophobia. He was also convinced that the United States, with the goal of expanding its own interests, was happy enough to see the French empire dismantled. It is thus understandable that while he was paid – albeit coolly – the normal basic courtesies by the President[16] and State Department officials, he was unpopular with the press, which was anti-Vichy to begin with.

At the time of his arrival, Robert Murphy defended him as 'a courageous man and a patriotic Frenchman',[17] but he still had to face a barrage of hostile questions about Nazi sympathies, anti-Semitism, and the rumour that he intended to seek the release of French credits so that they could go to German sources. His denial took the form of a rather unfunny quip: 'I am pro-French. I am no pro-Nazi nor a brown-shirt man. The only shirt I wear is white!'[18] He would never escape this defensive position. Even when affecting even-handed reporting, the *New York Times* lay-out editors managed to transmit their anti-Vichy bias. On 29 September 1940,

---

15. Henry-Haye, *La Grande Eclipse*, pp. 112–13, 123, 173, 304.
16. Roosevelt did not like Henry-Haye. Camille Chaumtemps, in his unpublished diary, notes that during his interview with the President, the latter spoke of Henry-Haye with open animosity, stating bluntly that the French government would have done better not to send him, and that he had a 'bad press' (4 February 1941). Chautemps also writes that Jean Monnet had told him that Henry-Haye had spoken out about his desire to see the war end as soon as possible through a British defeat, so that Europe could be united under German direction (18 May 1941).
17. *New York Times*, 6 September 1940, p. 7.
18. *New York Times*, 7 September 1940, p. 2.

France Forever's founding was amply reported in an eye-catching column on the left of page 12, with these headlines:

SAYS FRENCH HERE REPUDIATE VICHY
'France Forever' Asserts the Pétain Government
is Obeying the Orders of Hitler

Almost lost on the other side of the same page is a much smaller article, under the headlines:

SURVIVAL OF FRANCE PREDICTED BY ENVOY
Henry-Haye and Spellman Ask Prayers of Schoolchildren

The semiotic and symbolic ironies were surely not unintended.[19]

Towards the French community, Henry-Haye adopted a hardline approach, reinforced by a network of informers who reported regularly on the émigrés' political opinions. Roussy de Sales described this surveillance as a 'kind of Gestapo', an impression that was confirmed by Alexis Léger.[20] The Ambassador was supported in this activity by his consuls – at least by his consul in New York. In Los Angeles, which had received after New York the largest number of refugees, Consul Georges Achard was popular. Renoir found his conversation charming, and he was not alone. A note on the consular region of Los Angeles, prepared by the gaullist delegation in 1941, points out that even the gaullists found Achard easy to deal with: 'he succeeds in maintaining excellent relations with all, thanks to his tolerance. In particular, no propaganda praising the Pétain government or collaboration with Germany is practised.'[21] But if Achard managed to avoid applying Henry-Haye's instructions, his New York counterpart, Viscount Jacques d'Aumale, appears to have followed them, despite expressing sympathy for the gaullists.[22] His most significant role was a form of political control, and even persecution, including recommending loss of French nationality for certain prominent citizens who had

---

19. Aglion (*Roosevelt*, pp. 121–3) reports various other telling examples of Henry-Haye's treatment of, and by, the American press.
20. Raoul Roussy de Sales, *L'Amérique entre en guerre* (Paris, 1948). Cf. also Aglion, *Roosevelt*, p. 122.
21. A copy of this document, dated 25 October 1941, was kindly transmitted to the author by Raoul Aglion.
22. D'Aumale's activities are documented in an anonymous report made by a former staff member to the gaullist delegation. Transmitted to the author by Raoul Aglion.

either left France without authorisation, or who too clearly expressed anti-Vichy views. Among the victims of this procedure were Pierre Lazareff, Henri de Kérillis, Edouard de Rothschild and Alexis Léger.

A second emanation of Vichy was Camille Chautemps, whose mission as a roving special adviser to Pétain was to lead him into progressively more open conflict with Henry-Haye. From the time of his arrival in late November 1940 until October 1941, he received a lavish stipend from Vichy,[23] which he used partly to set up residence with his wife and four children in Washington, and partly for extensive, high-prestige contacts with US officials and a wide range of his compatriots. Although his political manoeuvrings among the émigrés, which will be discussed later, were not especially effective, he was generally well liked on a personal level. His diary records frequent cordial conversations with writers like Romains and Saint-Exupéry, and diplomats and political figures (Léger, Alphand, Monnet); as well as a busy schedule of lunches, dinners and meetings, with business people like Pierre Claudel and French Chamber of Commerce president Jacques Cartier, and with important Americans, like Sumner Welles (Undersecretary of State for French affairs), Robert Murphy, Admiral Leahy (the new US Ambassador to Vichy), the editor of the *New York Times*, the owner of the *Washington Post*, and so on.

Such an expansive style could not but irritate Henry-Haye, who complained of lonely nights,[24] and whose whole approach to his mission was based on constraint and interdiction. Personal difficulties between the two were compounded too by Chautemps' flamboyant wife, Juliette Durand-Texte, a prize-winning concert pianist whose skill at bridge meant frequent invitations to play in important social circles, where her effervescent indiscretions often led people to conclude that her husband's mission was more important than the Ambassador's.[25] The Chautemps were not often invited to the Embassy.

More profoundly, Chautemps, soon after his arrival, had organised the possibility of communicating directly with Vichy through the US diplomatic bag rather than through the French Embassy, and by the advice he sent Pétain, he did in fact significantly

---

23. The transcript of his trial, a copy of which is among his private papers, gives the figure as 90,000 francs per month, i.e. about $9000 at the official exchange rate of the day, and quite a princely sum.
24. Henry-Haye, *La Grande Eclipse*, pp. 270ff.
25. Chautemps diary, 3 March 1941. Also interview with Chautemps' daughter, Antoinette Samuels, September 1989.

undermine the authority and policies of Henry-Haye. Although he never withdrew from his conviction that the Armistice was inevitable, he consistently maintained that any political or military collaboration with Germany was a 'moral monstrosity', and likewise, any hostile action against Britain or America. He moreover believed sincerely, if naively, that his views were shared, not only by the vast majority of his compatriots in France, but by Marshal Pétain himself.[26]

He would later change his mind about the latter, but when he wrote to Pétain with stern warnings about the dangers of trusting Darlan, of collaboration generally, or to criticise Vichy's anti-Semitic measures, or French actions in Syria and Indochina, it seems to have been not just to give Vichy accurate information about American opinion, but because he honestly thought that Pétain was in a position to redress the situation and would indeed do so. In supplying Vichy – with full American knowledge – with details of the growing strength of US military might, he thought that he was strengthening Pétain's hand against German pressures. Similarly, when he gave information and advice to the Americans, it appears to have been from a genuine desire to enlighten the Administration about the mentality of the occupied French, to create a better climate of understanding and to increase the provision of relief. His belief in Pétain's integrity was so complete, however, that when the Marshal broke with him and terminated his mission, he was not just disillusioned, but in the view of the intelligence agent who interviewed him, distraught.[27] His confidence in his own judgement was obviously shaken.

Tensions between Chautemps and Henry-Haye were high from the beginning, and would increase as the war proceeded, but neither had much effect on the opinions of the refugee community. As early as October 1940, the chief financial attaché at the embassy, Hervé Alphand, who was never comfortable with Vichy's policies and never quiet about saying so, proferred a broad assessment of the community's political profile. The great majority, as he saw it, were divided between those, on the one hand, who accepted the

---

26. Statement to FBI, 20 March 1942 (Document 62–4156, kindly provided by A. Samuels).
27. OSS document, dated 22 November 1941. Chautemps' sincerity and his attempts to influence Pétain are amply documented, not only in the published version of his diaries (*Cahiers secrets de l'Armistice*, Paris, 1963, passim), but in the unedited manuscript, and in such correspondence as his letter to the US official Louis Strauss (15 September 1941 – Chautemps papers), as well as in his statements to the FBI.

Armistice, believing in a British collapse and American abstention-ism, and on the other hand, the hesitators who, while rejecting Pétain as a German prisoner and puppet, were not able to accept de Gaulle because he seemed dictatorial.[28]

In the early months of 1941, as the British continued to hold on, and the Americans edged closer to involvement in the war, the first group shrank, while the ranks of the second swelled. Alphand recognised the existence of a third group, the gaullists, who were small in numbers, but whose optimism and enthusiasm were exemplified by Eugène Houdry at the charter signing ceremony of France Forever. The goal of the movement was clear – 'to perpetu-ate the principles and ideals of France as a democracy' – and its rejection of Vichy forthright: 'It has neither the legal nor the moral authority to condemn Frenchmen who are fighting for the liber-ation of their country.' And for Houdry, France Forever was also an eminently practical undertaking, oriented towards the allied war effort:

> We are trying to link petroleum resources and industrial resources, to develop a fuel that can be easily produced, a motor that can be simply made, and then we will have an airplane that can be simply flown.

At the moment when Pétain had just declared his intention to adopt a policy of collaboration, and when London was reeling under the first effects of the Blitz, Houdry declared that he was 'almost certain' that the war would be won by the allies, and that when it was, France would be fighting among them.[29] (Houdry, for his own part, did his best to make his prediction come true. By 1942, he had doubled his production of high-octane fuel, and with over 200 engineers and chemists working for him, he was making a serious contribution to the war effort.)[30]

There were not many who shared his early optimism. And perhaps most of those who did harbour some hope wondered, like the painter Ozenfant: 'whether Pétain and de Gaulle are not secretly playing a duet: the one trying to gain time and avoid the worst, and de Gaulle preparing for the Liberation and post-Liberation.'[31]

It needs to be emphasised that early forms of gaullism in America

28. Hervé Alphand, *L'Etonnement d'être: Journal* (Paris, 1977), p. 63.
29. As reported in the *New York Times*, 29 September 1940.
30. See *Pour la Victoire*, 30 January 1943.
31. Amédée Ozenfant, *Mémoires 1886–1962* (Paris, 1968), p. 464.

had no political structure, and were simply a moral and emotional affirmation of the determination to continue the fight. It would be many months before any kind of formal administration was in place. In the meantime, the small core of supporters did the rounds of the more prominent expatriates and refugees, attempting to enrol them in the cause. As well as Houdry, there was Jacques de Sieyès, head of the Patou perfume office, who was a former Saint Cyr comrade of de Gaulle's, and who had had some diplomatic experience in Washington in the 1920s. The General had contacted him in July 1940 to ask him to act as his personal representative. There were a couple of academics – Robert Valeur and Fred Hoffherr, the latter head of the French Department at Barnard College, the former an economics lecturer at Columbia. And there was the former Trade Counsellor from the French Embassy, Maurice Garreau-Dombasle. Garreau-Dombasle was a veteran diplomat, and had served in Washington for thirteen years. Ordered on the eve of Henry-Haye's arrival to return to France, he resigned:

> I shall be always ready to devote my energy and my experience to any liberated part of the French Empire, remaining one of the thousands of French unknown soldiers who hope and work for the freedom of their land. . . . I hope to have an opportunity to be of help to the cause of democracy which I served for thirty-two years.[32]

De Gaulle promptly put him in charge of handling political, economic and financial matters for his cause.

Also among the few who did make an early commitment to de Gaulle was the seventy-year-old playwright Henry Bernstein. Bernstein was a larger-than-life character, forceful and eccentric, and he enjoyed considerable prestige with Europeans and Americans alike. He gave grand receptions in his luxuriously appointed apartment in the Waldorf-Astoria, where his presence helped to make the hotel one of the more frequented meeting-places – along with the Ritz-Carlton – for the wealthier refugees. His guests there were waited on by a white-gloved valet, surrounded by the many fine works of his art collection – paintings by Toulouse-Lautrec, Manet and Courbet, and a score of Constantin Guys drawings.[33]

32. *New York Times*, 4 September 1940.
33. Jean-Pierre Aumont, *Le Soleil et les ombres* (Paris, 1976), p. 74; and *Souvenirs provisoires* (Paris, 1957), p. 130. Also Roussy de Sales, *L'Amérique*, p. 164.

Bernstein's attacks on Vichy culminated in a series of nine vitriolic articles in the *New York Herald Tribune* in June 1941, in which Pétain was denounced as the wilful destroyer of France's liberal heritage, and for deliberately fostering the illusion that his reactionary and racist policies were imposed by Germany. Bernstein – quite rightly – defended the view that Pétain's anti-Semitic and social repression measures 'were all taken spontaneously, not under pressure from the Nazis':

> The majority of the unfortunate French people see in the Marshal an old man who, deep in his heart, sees and feels as they do, who is for England, who hates the Germans.
> This is a grave mistake.[34]

His unremitting hostility earned him the honour of being considered by Henry-Haye as among the 'most formidable of our enemies'.[35] Unfortunately, his thrusts were not always as discriminating as they might have been, and some of his nastiest comments were directed against fellow refugee writers, particularly Maurois, Saint Exupéry and Romains, none of whom was really seeking to engage in political polemics.

Bernstein had always been vociferously anti-fascist and he brought with him to New York the habits of verbal brawling so common in the venal world of the Paris press between the wars. In the more constrained atmosphere of New York 1940–1, his outbursts were not always appropriate. It was more than likely that there was an element of professional jealousy involved, since Maurois and Romains were at the height of their popularity in America, and did not have to confront the same order of difficulty faced by Bernstein in his attempts to recreate his theatrical universe in a foreign climate. Maurois and Romains published prolifically in French with English translations during their American stay, while Bernstein, with his English-language play *Rose Burke*, had to suffer the blow to his vanity of seeing the actors acclaimed, and the play declared a flop.[36]

Maurois was vulnerable to attack from the first-hour gaullists. In London before leaving for America, he had taken up Vichy's defence and refused de Gaulle's offer to join him. More importantly, during

34. *New York Herald Tribune*, 27 June, 1941.
35. Henry-Haye, *La Grande Eclipse*, p. 182.
36. Aumont, *Souvenirs provisoires*, pp. 149–51.

the whole first year of his exile, he continued to promote the opinion that the Armistice was necessary, that the Vichy government was the legitimate government of France: Pétain deserved not reproach, but gratitude and pity because of the skill and wisdom with which he had managed the nation's plight, despite having 'to make painful concessions which were certainly just as repugnant to him as they are to us'.[37]

But Maurois was an archetypal survivor, and not so foolish as to try to defend untenable positions indefinitely. He kept up his personal loyalty to Pétain, no doubt in part because of the friendship that had grown up between them as fellow members of the Académie Française. However, in his lecture tours and in his published work, he progressively dropped his defence of the Vichy government, and even his critiques of gaullist sectarianism, in favour of a more positively expressed hope for the liberation of France through an Anglo-American victory. By inclination and temperament a man of conciliation, he complained bitterly about what he felt to be the sheer injustice of the attacks on him. His only desire, he later claimed, had been to 'maintain in America respect and love for France, and to show the Americans that this war was their war'.[38]

For Maurois and his wife Simone, the moral and psychological ordeal caused by Bernstein's attacks was more than counterbalanced by a life in America that was materially comfortable and intellectually stimulating. His publisher, Harper, gave him advances on his arrival, and Jacques Cartier offered him credit. Their apartment in the Ritz Tower on Park Avenue was provided free of charge. And a steady flow of books[39] and articles assured an income that was supplemented by lecturing and teaching. He gave lectures throughout the United States, from the Harvard Club and Columbia University, to Texas, Louisiana, Nebraska, Colorado and California. And, along with the Milhauds and the painter Fernand Léger, he taught at the Mills College Summer School. The Maurois also had a busy social life. They were friendly with the

37. André Maurois, 'The Case for France', *Life*, 6 January 1941, p. 68.
38. *Ibid.*, *Soixante Ans de ma vie littéraire* (Périgueux, 1966). Cf. also his *Mémoires* (Paris, 1970), pp. 335–8. This later version is purged of a number of anti-gaullist barbs, and of Maurois' more blatant errors of political judgement. See, for example, pp. 261–79 of the 1942 New York edition, where he holds Britain and the United States co-responsible for the French defeat, defends US recognition of Vichy's legitimacy and rejects de Gaulle's claim to represent France.
39. Maurois published at least ten books during the 1940–5 period, often simultaneously both in the original French and in English translation. See below.

Romains, Saint-Exupéry and Pierre Claudel, and they were often invited by American friends, including Murray Butler, President of Columbia University.[40]

Jules Romains was just as well looked after. University lecture circuits and a visiting professorship at Middlebury College in the summer of 1941 did not get in the way of an astonishing writing and publishing schedule: sixteen different titles appeared in the United States during his exile, including the first editions of six volumes of *Les Hommes de bonne volonté*. And as with Maurois, English translations most frequently came out at the same time. Liberal-minded and an apostle of pacifism, Romains had acquired great prestige in prewar Europe, and it was very much with the attitude of a European mandarin that he travelled about the country. Significantly, their best friends in New York, according to his wife's memoirs, were not French, but the old Belgian playwright Maurice Maeterlinck and his young wife Sélizette, and the German writer Stefan Zweig and his wife Lotte.[41] (The Zweigs, deeply depressed, would die in a double suicide in early 1942.)

Romains' self-important airs brought him criticism from French and American sides alike. In his first American book, *Seven Mysteries of Europe* (New York, 1940),[42] which had initially appeared as a series of well-paid articles in the *Saturday Evening Post*, he ascribed himself a critical role in a number of secret international prewar negotiations. Roussy de Sales reacted with scornful amusement, seeing the work as proof of Romains' naiveness and as 'One more confirmation of the confusion and blindness of that whole band of sentimental appeasers and pacifists.'[43] The *New York Times* reviewer Ferdinand Kuhn Jr did not hide his disappointment:

> Jules Romains came among us as a great artist, a writer of spiritual integrity, a fighter in the cause of human dignity and freedom. With this book, he has made himself a mere retailer of 'inside stories'. . . . It is hard to decide whether M. Romains has shown less respect for his readers or for his own reputation in retailing such works as these.[44]

In terms of his general political orientation, Romains was clearly

---

40. *Mémoires*, passim. Also Milhaud, *Ma Vie heureuse*, p. 227.
41. Lise Jules-Romains, *Les Vies inimitables: souvenirs* (Paris, 1985), pp. 276ff.
42. It also appeared in French under the title *Sept Mystères du destin de l'Europe*, with the Editions de la Maison Française (New York, 1940).
43. Roussy de Sales, *L'Amérique*, p. 129.
44. *New York Times Book Review*, 15 December 1940, p. 19.

– both publicly and privately – in the gaullist camp, but he was far from being an activist. Chautemps met with him on amicable terms quite regularly in New York, noting their sharply differing views on the Armistice and Pétain, but also their common rejection of collaborationism.[45] Romains accepted a position on the executive committee of France Forever, but it was a rather nominal appointment, since the so-called 'executive' consisted of almost forty members, and the real business of the organisation was managed by the much smaller group of office-bearers. Between August 1940 and May 1941, he did a series of patriotic radio broadcasts for the BBC, transmitted to London from New York. These were also published as a volume under the title *Messages aux Français* (New York, 1941).

What Bernstein reproached him with was essentially his work with the '*Comité France-Allemagne*' in the 1930s. A key role in this group was played by Otto Abetz, an ardent German francophile who was to become the Nazi Ambassador in Paris during the Occupation, and the committee was widely believed to have contributed significantly to Fifth Column sapping of French resistance to Hitler's ideas for Europe. Romains did indeed believe in greater Franco-German understanding, but he was no supporter of Hitler. When Bernstein's most public assault on Romains appeared, in long and damaging articles in the French weekly *Pour la Victoire*,[46] Romains had been in Mexico for over a year, and although he returned to New York for a few months annually, he had decided to spend the rest of his exile in the Bernstein-free hospitality of his warmly welcoming and immensely influential friend Alfonso Reyes.[47]

One of the most interesting books that Romains wrote during his US stay is his fable *Salsette découvre l'Amérique* (New York, 1942). Albert Salsette is an émigré French university professor, who is being guided on his discovery of East Coast America by Romains, the already experienced expatriate narrator. On one level, the book operates as a user's manual for refugee intellectuals, as Salsette learns how to overcome his prejudices and to enjoy the cultural differences – the eating and drinking habits, the informality

45. Chautemps unpublished diary: 8 December 1940, 8 July 1941.
46. 17 October, 1942, p. 2, and 7 November, 1942, pp. 1–2. The former piece is accompanied by a letter of denial from Romains.
47. Lise Jules-Romains, *Les Vies*, pp. 297–8. The stay in Mexico began with an invitation to teach at the University of Mexico. Romains finished up as honorary director of the French Institute and of the European–Mexican Cultural Institute.

of social intercourse, the audacious, long-legged beauty of the women, the extraordinary scale of the buildings, subway system and freeways. At one point, the professor experiences the American mind as a kind of permanent, omnipresent World Fair. It is a world full of playful joy and abundant energy that prompt the imagination-stretching creation of structures of staggering proportions, just for the sheer pleasure of it. The book reveals here a more profound awareness of the potential power and scope of a world whose youthfulness and relative innocence are both marvellous and, because of the role that history is forcing upon it, already condemned.

Salsette is changed and revitalised by America in a way that Romains was not. The honesty and sadness of the professor's growing understanding – that the failures of the old world have become the heritage of the new – perhaps mirror the purer, less sophisticated and less convoluted side of Romains' own vision, or a trace of idealism from the time before he became an urbane patrician of international literature.

Romains' choice to remain based in Mexico is a reminder that he was still a pacifist at heart, unwilling, and perhaps temperamentally unable, to cope with too close an engagement with the machinery of war. Saint-Exupéry, on the contrary, was essentially a man of action, and for him exile meant first of all being cut off from the possibility of being in the front line. He had done more than his duty during the brief period of France's fighting war in a flying group of which three-quarters of the crews had been lost, but all his own pronouncements, and all the testimony of those who had the occasion to frequent him during this period, demonstrate that his desire to return to combat was much stronger than his urge to write.[48]

None the less, it was as a writer that he was welcomed in America, where his *Wind, Sand and Stars* (*Terre des Hommes*) had won the non-fiction section in the 1939 American National Book awards. His publishers, Reynal and Hitchcock, were keen to coax him into rapid production of a book about the war. He was lodged briefly, on arrival, at the Ritz Carlton, until his publishers could move him into what they hoped would be a congenial workplace – a magnificent penthouse apartment overlooking Central Park. He duly set about his task, beginning what would become *Pilote de guerre* (*Flight to Arras*). With characteristic delight in new

48. Antoine de Saint-Exupéry, *Ecrits de guerre* (Paris, 1982), passim. See also Cate, *Antoine de Saint-Exupéry*, and Roussy de Sales, *L'Amérique*, passim.

technology, he purchased – at great expense, but he was renowned for spending money readily[49] – the latest model dictaphone, recording his text for typing the following day by a secretary. Saint-Exupéry had a quirky personality: he loved to have people around him, but was always the loner in a crowd. The grand 500-place luncheon held in his honour by the American Booksellers Association at the Hotel Astor in January 1941 was surely less to his liking than his more intimate meetings, almost every day, over a meal of coffee, with Bernard Lamotte, or Pierre and Hélène Lazareff, or Roussy de Sales, or another reliable friend, Léon Wencelius, who was teaching at Swarthmore College and at the Lycée Français. His links with Americans were considerable, though limited to francophones, since he knew no English at all and refused to learn any.

Many of his friends during this time noted an underlying sadness and weariness in him, even when he had them gasping at his array of mystifying card-tricks. There were a number of causes underlying his despondency. First, for his adventurous spirit, he was too far away from the war zones. Secondly, he was not in good health: in addition to a gall-bladder problem, he still suffered pain and debilitation from injuries sustained in his various crashes, including the most recent one in Guatemala in 1938, which had very nearly killed him. (This situation was somewhat redressed after two operations during his stay with Jean Renoir in California over the summer and autumn of 1941.) Thirdly, until the arrival of his wife Consuelo, later in 1941, after she had followed the itinerary of her surrealist friends, a certain piquancy was missing from his life.

But there were other difficulties as well. To begin with, Saint-Exupéry did not understand America very well. He saw it as a continent rather than as a *patrie*; he scorned its young people for being more interested in baseball than in higher values; and he considered its quasi-religious belief in 'democracy' as a hollow abstraction.[50] There can be little doubt that Saint-Exupéry's stubborn monolingualism led him to some fatuous judgements – even his admiring friend Roussy de Sales thought him paralysed by his too narrow, too provincial, French mind-set.[51] However, the question about democracy is a crucial one, for Saint-Exupéry's observations are enlighteningly representative about significant

49. Saint-Exupéry, *Ecrits de guerre*, p. 161. According to his friend and illustrator, Bernard Lamotte, he paid $2700 *cash* for this machine (which at the time represented more than a year's wages for a junior worker).
50. Ibid., pp. 184ff.
51. Roussy de Sales, *L'Amerique*, p. 174.

differences of perception between the Americans and the French.

The fact is that while few Americans – and certainly no policy-makers – would have questioned the fundamental acceptance of democracy (in its archetypal American expression as government of the people, by the people, for the people) as the only and necessary guarantee of individual freedom, this view was far from obvious to French people, who had lived through the vicissitudes of the Third Republic. This was a regime of notorious instability, based on a constant confrontation of cultures, social classes and ideologies. Multiple successive governments, in attempting to enact into legislative structures their interpretation of the liberty, equality and fraternity tenets of the Republican motto, had failed completely to create consensus or unity, and the nation had lurched from crisis to crisis, and had several times been close to civil war.

For many – of whom Saint-Exupéry was one – democracy in France meant a political and social fragmentation that had reached its most complete, and most catastrophic expression in the Popular Front government of 1936. Whatever its achievements in terms of social justice for workers, the Popular Front was seen as having been a disaster for the French economy. Above all, through its failure of policy and diplomacy, it had left France pitifully unprepared, morally as well as militarily, for the inevitable confrontation with Hitler's Germany. People associated with the Front Populaire, like Léon Blum, Pierre Cot and Camille Chautemps, were not just disliked, but widely loathed and reviled.

This was as true in de Gaulle's movement as it was in Vichy France. Pétain's Riom trials of the Blums and Reynauds were not intended to be just about failures of individual responsibility, but about the inadequacies of the republican form of government. And in London, de Gaulle's declarations about France never once suggested any return to the prewar political regimen. The fall of France, for a broad spectrum of its citizens, was attributable to the weaknesses of the Third Republic, and to the extent that the Republic was a self-proclaimed democracy, it was democracy itself that fell into doubt.

To equate the ideals of democracy with the experience of a democratic regime that had not worked is not logical, but it was a commonly enough shared reaction among the French, both within France, and among the expatriates. It reveals to what extent for France, with most of its history regulated by authoritarian regimes, the foothold established by the relatively new democratic ideologies and institutions was still fragile.

French reservations about democracy – not rejection of it, but a cautious questioning attitude towards it – would be significant in the confrontation between Roosevelt and de Gaulle, though it was seldom clearly articulated. One of the rare contemporary clear thinkers on the subject was Jacques Maritain. In his *Christianisme et Démocratie* (New York, 1943) he expresses the difference very succinctly:

> The very name of democracy has a very different resonance in America and in Europe. . . . In America, where despite the power of the big economic interests, democracy has reached much deeper into daily life, and where its Christian origins have never been lost, the name evokes a living instinct, stronger than the parasitical errors of thought that live off it. In Europe, it evokes an ideal that has been made ridiculous by experience, and whose soul has been half-devoured by the same errors. (p. 15)

It is doubtful if de Gaulle or Roosevelt ever saw this text. In any case, the New York gaullists did not bother with any such subtleties when they branded Saint-Exupéry as a fascist, and accused him of all kinds of treachery, including being in America to purchase planes for Vichy.[52] The charges were ludicrous, and could have been shrugged off in a climate other than the passionate and suspicion-ridden hot-house of New York's French intelligentsia. Saint-Exupéry had always been resolutely and outspokenly anti-Hitler and anti-totalitarian generally. He was not much of a political thinker, but his essential action and writing had always emanated from his firm belief in the civilised individual's right to construct his own inner empire.[53]

Unfortunately for him, his name was included among the forty members of the National Council which Pétain devised as a replacement for the old political parties. Saint-Exupéry learned of this when the announcement was published in the *New York Times*, and reacted immediately. The next day's paper carried his denial of involvement 'in any mission or other political endeavor', and his terse comment that he 'would have declined the present appointment if consulted'.[54] But it was too late, and the stigma of being a Vichy supporter stuck, and it would stay with him until his death. Although it did not prevent him, when the chance came, from

52. See Cate, *Antoine de Saint-Exupéry*, p. 445.
53. Saint-Exupéry, 'La morale de la pente', in *Ecrits de guerre*, pp. 73ff.
54. *New York Times*, 30 January 1941, p. 6, and 31 January 1941, p. 6.

taking up the fight for his country again, it did poison his enjoyment of life.

What was his real position? He was certainly pro-Armistice, because he was convinced that France needed a pause, and that to have attempted, in June 1940, to continue the fight from the colonies would have meant the immediate total occupation of France. He also believed, however, that the Anglo-US war effort would eventually lead to victory, and that this victory would bring a return of freedom to France. He respected those who, in answer to de Gaulle's call, had taken up arms beside their British comrades, but he rejected the political aspirations of gaullism, and considered de Gaulle's attacks on Pétain as fratricidal. Vichy, for him, was neither more nor less than a stop-gap bulwark against what would otherwise have been uncontrolled Nazi repression. The people in occupied France were hostages, and the task of those still able to resist was to serve them and help liberate them – and that was best achieved through supporting the Anglo-US war effort, not through attacking Pétain or Vichy.[55]

Alexis Léger arrived in New York for 14 July 1940, and must have been sorely aware of the irony of the date. He was still suffering the shock of his peremptory sacking from his post as head of the Foreign Affairs department, which the Prime Minister, Paul Reynaud, had effected just after the beginning of the German offensive in Belgium. Léger's departure was a triumph for the defeatists in the already shaky French government.

For Léger himself, who was stung by the disgrace and disgusted by the odious intrigue which had brought it about, it was the beginning of his exile. As one of France's most respected diplomats, particularly in Britain and in the United States, and as a highly regarded poet, he did not lack friends. One of them, Archibald Macleish, raised the funds necessary to create a position for Léger as a literary adviser at the Library of Congress – a post he took up at the beginning of 1941. He was also close to the Attorney-General, Francis Biddle, and his wife Kathleen, who would take him to their beach house that next summer, providing the setting and the atmosphere that allowed him to become Saint-John Perse again. Through his poetry, he could regain contact with the cosmic dimensions of his inner world.

At the same time, the act of writing was also an act of resistance.

---

55. Saint-Exupéry, *Ecrits de guerre*, passim. See especially the very moving 'Lettre à un ôtage', pp. 343–4, and the unposted letter to an unidentified friend in late 1943, pp. 426–34.

Léger would become a striking example of those whom his fellow poet Yvan Goll praised as having 'refused to bend, and to deny the spirit, dreaming and freedom': 'Today, "exile" for a poet means a virtue rather than a disgrace. Its gives him the stature of a hero. . . . The poet is the ambassador, not of his government, but of his people.'[56]

Influential and supportive friends notwithstanding, Léger was poor, and unlike the successful novelists, he had no publishers clamouring to set him up in lavish accommodation. Between the time of his arrival and taking up his position in Washington, he lived in the very modest Shelton Hotel in New York, and, as he wrote to his '*étrangère*' and long-term lover Lilita Abreu, he tried to keep a low profile, avoiding any open contact with the French émigrés.[57] He did keep in touch, however, with many of the major figures of the exile. In his long discussions with Roussy de Sales, he made detailed analyses of the men of Vichy, portraying Pétain as patriotic but weak, and likening Laval to Stalin in his dictatorial ambitions;[58] and he developed the theory that France's fall resulted from a reversal of its traditional diplomatic doctrine of giving moral values primacy over material strengths:

> For the first time, we followed the German school, which consists of measuring exactly the material strengths confronting each other and considering the moral factor as unreal. It is the English, says Léger, who are demonstrating today the validity of the French doctrine. They should have given up the struggle at the same time as us. Because of Churchill, they continued, against all common sense. The result: they are still holding on.[59]

Léger's objections to the Armistice were absolute precisely because they were based on moral grounds – in no circumstances could it be honourable to abandon an ally in the midst of battle. At the same time, he had reservations about de Gaulle, not very well defined in the early months of exile, but strong enough to make him keep his distance. Later, as we shall see, he was to become one of de Gaulle's most serious adversaries. In the meantime, he was establishing what would become his *modus operandi*: that of a man

56. 'Poètes en exil', in *Pour la Victoire*, 14 February 1942.
57. *Lettres à l'Etrangère* (Paris, 1987), p. 65.
58. Roussy de Sales, *L'Amérique*, p. 150.
59. Ibid., p. 157.

who, publicly, was practically invisible, but who was privately very active, and whose compelling intelligence, unimpeachable integrity and unparalleled knowledge commanded complete respect. It cannot have been easy. From October 1940 to January 1941, successive Vichy decrees stripped Léger of his French nationality, confiscated his Paris apartment and his goods, and struck him from the roll of the Légion d'Honneur.[60] When Camille Chautemps, who found the 'denationalisation' of Léger both clumsy and unjust, met him in December, he found him a very unhappy man.[61] Unhappy or not, he was to stand his ground, even though it would ultimately cost him any hope of return to his diplomatic career.

By way of contrast, for Claude Lévi-Strauss, the first months in New York were to be the source of indelibly happy memories. He had been sponsored by Alvin Johnson, the head of the New School for Social Research, and was due to start teaching his course on the sociology of Latin America in the autumn of 1941. Upon his arrival the previous spring, he began to draw a monthly stipend which allowed him to rent a small apartment in Greenwich Village and to treat himself to a wealth of new experience. Whether working alone in the Public Library, discussing theory with his anthropologist and ethnologist colleagues, like Alfred Métraux, Robert Lowie or Franz Boas, heading off to the Connecticut countryside to spend weekends with his artist friends André Masson and Alexander Calder, or simply wandering up and down the 'immense disorder' of verticality and horizontality in the Manhattan streetscapes,[62] Lévi-Strauss found New York immensely stimulating, a place of endless possibilities. It also excited his collector's instinct. The city appeared as a kind of fantastic warehouse of cultural artefacts from all over the world – from South America as well as Russia, from Western Europe and the Middle-East, a treasure-house of universal culture:

the whole substance of the artistic patrimony of humanity was present in New York in the form of samples; washed about over and over as the tide does with drift-wood, following the unpredictable rhythm of the rise and fall of societies, some objects still adorned living-rooms or had

---

60. The text of these decrees has been published in *Honneur à Saint-John Perse* (Paris, 1965), p. 724.
61. Chautemps, unpublished diary, 24 December 1941.
62. Claude Lévi-Strauss, 'New York Post- et Préfiguratif', in *Le Regard éloigné* (Paris, 1983), p. 345. Also *De Près et de loin* (Paris, 1988), pp. 46ff.

gone towards the museums, while others piled up in unexpected corners . . .[63]

By his own account, Lévi-Strauss was not especially inclined towards political activism, though later he would sign up as a member of the Free French Scientific mission, and we shall see in fact that he was rather more active than he cared to admit.[64] Geneviève Tabouis, on the other hand, anxious to sound out American opinion and to broadcast her own patriotic convictions about France, plunged immediately into a frenetic schedule of discussions, writing and lectures. She enjoyed some recognition as a distinguished foreign journalist, and held positions as correspondent for the *Sunday Dispatch* and for *Critica* in Buenos Aires.

She had also been with Herriot during his state visit to the White House in 1933, and that, together with the fact that she was the former ambassador Jules Cambon's niece, opened the doors for her again now. She was received both before and after Roosevelt's re-election. She had discussions with the President, and was heartened by the determination he expressed to help liberate France.

Most strikingly, considering the chronic kidney complaint that kept her permanently frail, she contracted with literary agent Colston Leigh to undertake a sweeping lecture tour across the whole of the United States. She spoke in public meetings, in churches, in women's clubs, in colleges, universities, schools. She found Middle America appallingly ignorant of Europe, but the young people self-confident and open-minded. Her own message did not vary much – that France and the French wanted to continue the struggle, but were being prevented from doing so by Pétain and Laval, and that American aid for France's liberation was essential – but her memoirs show how sensitively and intelligently she registered many distinctive features of American life. She gauged the depth of the ambient anti-communism, and pondered its links with the widespread elementary Christian piety; she was impressed by the strength and dynamism of women's organisations, and by the freedom, variety and scope of the education system; she noted American anti-colonialism, but also pockets of prejudice and racism – anti-Semitism in Chicago, pro-Hitlerism in Milwaukee. When she returned to New York at the end of that winter of 1940–1, she could claim to know America well, and with very few exceptions,

63. *Le Regard éloigné*, p. 350.
64. *De Près et de loin*, p. 68.

she was enthusiastic about what she had seen.[65] There could not have been a better preparation for the task she would soon undertake – the founding of *Pour la Victoire*, a remarkable weekly newspaper that would become a major unifying force – perhaps *the* major unifying force – for the voices of the exile.

For a long time, for most of the émigrés, the dominant mood was uncertainty. Sometimes it was because they were unclear about the shape and direction of their personal lives or their individual professions. Sarah Rapkine, for example, as soon as she arrived, had to worry about getting her young daughter into school, and finding work to supplement the $10 a day stipend her husband received from the Rockefeller Foundation. She got a job as a chemist in a cosmetics laboratory, testing perfumes, powders and lipsticks. It was hardly her field of expertise, but she did it anyway. The factory was right across town from their little apartment on West 83rd Street. There was a lot of travel. Her husband too had to move about a great deal. He came in late at night, and his face showed the strain. It was a difficult life just to keep the family together.[66]

On a more general level, confusion also resulted from the pressures of a geopolitical situation on which the French refugees felt they had little purchase. Inevitably, they identified to some degree with the humiliation of their homeland. Choices were hard. While Vichy was unpalatable for most because of the shame of the Armistice and collaborationist policies, Pétain still retained broad credibility, and besides, America's maintaining of relations with Vichy made outright rejection by French refugees a less than obvious option. At the beginning too, American isolationism could not but stifle any reasonable hope of victory, and at that stage, de Gaulle was not a significant phenomenon, especially when seen from the American side of the Atlantic. His followers in the United States were both few in number and very invasive, and it is not surprising that even the most liberal-minded and patriotic expatriates should have felt the need to see how things would develop before committing themselves. Roussy de Sales, who did in fact make such a commitment later, epitomized this kind of hesitancy:

> I am more and more criticised for my abstentionism – including by the English. People cannot understand why I don't throw myself into the

65. Geneviève Tabouis, *Grandeurs et servitudes américaines: souvenirs des U.S.A. 1940–1945* (Paris, 1945), pp. 35–52.
66. Interview with Sarah Rapkine, June 1987.

arms of de Gaulle and France Forever, along with MM Houdry, Garreau-Dombasle, Sieyès, Valeur, etc. Before the débâcle, I didn't belong to any group. Why should I join now?[67]

It is not surprising, either, that an experienced politician such as Camille Chautemps, faced with the obvious lack of success of the policies of Vichy ambassador Henry-Haye, should explore the possibilities of a middle way, between the Pétain and the de Gaulle positions, in the hope that it might provide a wider base of agreement. In the spring of 1941, he attempted to do just that, together with the University of Besançon professor, Louis Rougier (who had acted as an intermediary between Pétain and Churchill),[68] Fred Hoffherr of France Forever, and Jean de Sieyès, the brother of de Gaulle's personal representative.[69] There was nothing treasonable about such a move, though it was certainly an example of Chautemps' lack of respect for the authority of Henry-Haye: rather, it was the same kind of jockeying for influence and compromise that had typefied the affairs of the Third Republic, and at which Chautemps had been so adept.

The importance of the American position *vis-à-vis* Europe in general and France in particular should not be underestimated in any assessment of the range of attitudes and actions of the French émigrés during the first year or so in the United States. They knew that American participation in the war was a *sine qua non* of victory – they had known it since 1919. The hesitations, contradictions and ambiguities expressed by public figures and the press alike – and the natural domestic focus on the Roosevelt–Wilkie campaigns in late 1940 complicated the situation further – made for slippery ground for those in exile.

Conversely, as the United States slowly shifted its stance away from neutrality, strengthening the chances of a victorious outcome, émigré morale steadily became more optimistic. Britain's success in staving off what had appeared as inevitable defeat, earned the

---

67. Roussy de Sales, *L'Amerique*, p. 151.
68. Rougier's book, *Les Accords Pétain–Churchill: histoire d'une mission secrète* (Montreal, 1945) makes the claim that an agreement was reached in October 1940, which was to have allowed Vichy to cooperate in the allied war effort, as well as renewing assurances that the French fleet and colonies would be kept out of German hands. Almost simultaneously, however, Pétain was meeting Hitler at Montoire, and declaring his intention to collaborate more closely with Germany.
69. Roussy de Sales was invited to join, but declined: *L'Amérique*, p. 180. Cf. also Chautemps unpublished diary 24 April 1941.

admiration of all; and the increasingly open collaboration of Vichy with the Nazis diminished the support for Pétain (with or without Laval). But in the transformation of the exile from a disparate collection of generally dispirited individuals into an entity capable of regenerating national and cultural pride, and of participating in the war effort, the critical factor was America itself. The passage of the Lend-Lease legislation in March 1941 was a watershed, and Pearl Harbor, with Germany's subsequent declaration of war, marked the crucial turning-point.

With America in the war, the émigrés could begin to envisage the liberation of France as a realistic, achievable goal; they could do something more than merely comfort one another in their distress; they could organise, create institutions; they could rejoin the fight for the future. Individually, their resources were brilliant in almost every imaginable field of human endeavour. Once drawn together, they would provide glowing proof that France and French culture were worth fighting for – as well as fighting about.

Not the old France, however. Nowhere more than in the new world was it obvious that the life that had been left behind would never be reconstituted, that the débâcle had been not just a major military defeat, but the end of an era of civilisation. It would take time before the details of change were felt in the arts, in science and technology, in politics, in social structures, but the most perceptive, at least, already had no illusions about the scope of the occurrence. Roussy de Sales presents a touchingly pathetic scene of a visit to his prewar friends Edouard de Rothschild and his wife, who had just lost their citizenship, but who continued to cling, puppet-like, to the strings attaching their minds and gestures to a way of life that had gone forever:

Dined last night with the Edouard de Rothschilds, who occupy two tiny, rather moth-eaten rooms at the Gladstone. I remember Ferrières. Physical impression of exile and loss of status. We engage simultaneously in society gossip, as in France, and in talk of the war, as everywhere. Edouard pours the orangeade. Germaine offers some glazed fruit she has received from Cannes – dried and hardened by the journey. One feels that these people are waiting, can do nothing other than wait for some unexpected reversal that would allow them to return to France. 'How nice it would be', says Germaine, 'to be able to sit beneath a tree in the country.'[70]

70. Roussy de Sales, ibid.

– 3 –

Making Themselves at Home

> there is only one France, the eternal France, the one
> which for more than a thousand years has not tired of
> making new forms of art for the benefit of men, the
> enchantment of women, the progress of knowledge, the
> refinement of sensibility – life in beauty, according to
> the divine laws of the mind and the heart.
>
> Gustave Cohen[1]

With so many writers and intellectuals among the émigrés, it was
perhaps to be expected that cultural structures should be among the
first to be established. And with the identity of French civilisation
so heavily invested in its literary tradition, it was perhaps normal
that the lead should be taken by enterprising book publishers.
Nevertheless, the creation of what would become a thriving
French-language publishing industry required courage and vision,
and it provided the exiles not only with a bridge of continuity with
their past, but with a model of open-mindedness that enabled them
to live through their trials in a context of linguistic and cultural
cohesion.

New York was not the only centre for the publication of French
books on the American continent:[2] there were bigger ones in
Montreal and in Latin America – particularly Rio de Janeiro. But
Canada, with its large, French-speaking population and its long-
standing links with France, could undertake a wide spread of
publishing activities – from the republication of recent titles from
France to the promotion of native Canadian authors. Some exiles
did publish in Canada, as they did in Brazil, though in Latin

---

1. Inaugural speech for the *Ecole Libre des Hautes Etudes*, Hunter College,
   14 February 1942. In *Lettres aux Américains* (Montreal, 1942).
2. A general idea of the extent of publishing of French-language books in
   America as a whole can be derived from a 48-page catalogue published in Rio
   in 1944. It is entitled *Les Livres français publiés en Amérique de 1940 à 1944*:
   'Documents bibliographiques No. 1'. It was followed by a ten-page
   'Supplément No. 1' (Library of Congress, Washington).

America generally, French language and civilisation were nurtured as a kind of bulwark against the cultural hegemony of the United States, and the publishers in Rio emphasised a policy of maintaining a coverage of the whole range of French literary history.

In the United States, on the eve of the war, the population of French speakers was around 1,400,000, but the vast majority of these were of receding Canadian or Louisiana origins, with little of no contact with France itself. Only 100,000 were foreign-born. On the other hand, the reading of French by English speakers was limited practically to schools and universities. What made the war-time New York French-language publishing different was that it was almost entirely a product of the exile. It was above all the creative strength of refugee writers that, for five years, made of New York a vibrant centre of French cultural production. An export centre as well, since the print-runs went well beyond the needs of the 30,000 expatriates who, in the New York–Washington corridor, made up the bulk of France-in-exile.

According to the anecdote recounted by Vitalis Crespin, an immigrant from Smyrna who headed the little group of partners running the Maison Française bookshop in Rockefeller Plaza, the idea of going into publishing was born suddenly one autumn day in 1940. Crespin was discussing with André Maurois the difficulties confronting the business: the shelves had been emptied by the first waves of refugees, the purchasing office in Paris was closed, and links with French publishers were broken. The bookshop had no ready access to stock, either of books, or of the newspapers and fashion magazines that were their bread-and-butter.

> I was pointing out my problems, said Crespin, when I suddenly had an idea. 'Perhaps,' I said to him, 'you have a manuscript we could publish.' 'I do,' M. Maurois answered spontaneously. 'I was about to take it to Harpers.' 'Why don't you let me have it?' was my reply, and it was also my start as a publisher.[3]

The book in question was *Tragédie en France*. The gesture involved no sacrifice for Maurois, since Harpers published the English translation simultaneously. But it marked the beginning of a successful five-year venture, which generated considerable momentum and assured the public of a steady supply of new titles.

The history of the Maison Française went back to 1934, when

3. 'L'emf a deux ans', in *Pour la Victoire*, 23 January 1943.

Crespin and an old school friend, Isaac Molho, decided to establish a bookshop together, and made the fortunate choice of renting space in the new Rockefeller Center. Their commercial and cultural policy was energetic: with the patronage of the Paris publishing houses, they mounted stands at the Chicago and New York World Fairs (1934 and 1939 respectively), and because many of their clients, largely American, had a special interest in art books, they dabbled from time to time in the publication of books on the history of costume.[4]

With the war, publishing became their major activity. On the house's second anniversary, Crespin spoke nobly about his only ambition being 'to continue and develop the influence of French culture in the United States and in all of America',[5] but his principal goal was in fact the commercial survival of the Maison Française. The publishing operations overall, according to Molho,[6] made no real profit, and perhaps even a slight loss, but they did work well enough to keep the business alive during the hard times.

Crespin and Molho, and their other associates Amado and Lévy, soon found that they had competition, but they managed throughout the war to maintain the advantage gained from their head's start. They moved quickly to sign up most of the best authors available – although some of these later decided to share their talents around, which suggests that contracts must have been quite flexible. As well as Maurois, Jules Romains and Saint-Exupéry gave their first works to the Maison Française, as did the leading political journalists, Henri de Kérillis, Pertinax and Genviève Tabouis, and the philosopher Jacques Maritain, whose prestige was enormous. The EMF eventually published seventy-two different authors, of whom a big majority were émigrés, and more than 120 titles.

In the first instance, they encouraged the books most sought after by the refugees: books containing information about the war, or offering explanations of France's tragic collapse. Maritain's *A Travers le désastre* (1941), for example, is rich in carefully sifted evidence for and against various hypothetical causes of the disaster – German military might, English and French military errors, the general bankruptcy of the French political and social elite. It asks hard questions. Were the French decadent? Are Vichy's policies all bad? Are the French pro-German? Anti-Semitic? Should one follow de

4. Interview with I. Molho, July 1987.
5. 'L'emf a deux ans'.
6. Interview with I. Molho.

Gaulle? And it attempts to discuss them in a way that permits reasoned, balanced answers, and seeks to lay the groundwork for enlightened resolution of the issues that were uppermost in the hearts and minds of the émigrés.

It is an intelligent and compassionate book, an exemplary reflection of the best in the French intellectual tradition. And it lived up to the ideals which it exhorted the French in America to adopt as their task, namely:

> to maintain in the world as best they can France's spiritual legacy and its tradition of liberty, [and] to contribute to the preparation of the rebirth that will occur in France when nazism has disappeared from the world. [7]

A more polemical tradition was represented by Henri de Kérillis's *Français, voici la vérité* (1942) and Pertinax's *Les Fossoyeurs* (1943), which contain savage criticism of the men and manners of the Third Republic, but which, above all, gave voice to a rebellious spirit whose vigour contrasted sharply with the breast-beating resignation of Vichy discourse, and offered the reader the hope that French culture was still resilient enough to surmount the catastrophes of its recent past.

By adopting an eclectic approach, Crespin guaranteed himself the widest possible spread of readers. He published those who were reputed to be sympathetic towards Vichy (Maurois, Saint-Exupéry), as well as those who leaned towards de Gaulle (Maritain, de Kérillis, Tabouis). He published cultural and literary history (Henri Peyre's *Le Classicisme français* (1942), Cohen's *La Grande Clarté du Moyen Age* (1943); poetry and short stories (Mathilde Monnier's *Dispersion*, 1942, the six volumes of the 'Oeuvres nouvelles' series, from 1942); translations from English and German (Stettinius on Lend-Lease, essays by Emil Ludwig, Stefan Zweig on Brazil). He also enriched his catalogue with many more popular works – novels by the prolific Belgian Robert Goffin; the lightweight, witty chronicles of Michel Georges-Michel; and the more serious and sustained literary creations of a Jules Romains (volumes XIX–XXIV of *Les Hommes de bonne volonté*), or Julien Green (*Varouna*, 1941).

The print-runs were large. According to Molho,[8] whose brother-in-law did the printing, they varied between a minimum of

---

7. Jacques Maritain, *A Travers le désastre* (New York, 1941), pp. 110ff.
8. Molho interview cited.

10,000 to a maximum of 50,000. With a publication rhythm that sometimes reached a new volume per week, there was obviously considerable stock to be moved. The bookshop itself, situated in the city's most prestigious commercial area, was well placed for sales, and the group also owned another shop in Boston. But a report made at the beginning of 1943 (by Christian Belle, attaché at the Free French Delegation),[9] makes it clear that the US market was far from being big enough to assure the economic viability of the operation. In fact, only 30 per cent of the books were sold in the United States (three-quarters of those in New York), with the rest going to Canada and Latin America, through networks established before the war.

As early as the first quarter of 1941, Crespin's success drew the attention of two other businessmen: Arthur Brentano Jr, the owner of a chain of bookstores with twenty-three branches worldwide, and with annual sales of 800,000 volumes; and a certain Mr Didier (apparently unrelated to his French homonym) – an American literary entrepreneur who among other things was André Maurois' agent. Over the next five years, Brentano would set up an operation almost as large as the EMF: 77 different authors, and almost 100 titles. Didier remained on a more modest level.

In a 14 July 1945 publicity article published in *Pour la Victoire*, Brentano's described its mission in the following terms:

> Just after the 1940 armistice, Mr Arthur Brentano Jr spontaneously undertook to do in his field everything in his power to attenuate the grave consequences that the imprisonment of France would have on the influence of French language and culture in the New World, until the day when her allies could help liberate her. At a time when the study of French was under a shadow, without hesitation or delay, he committed his house to the publication of numerous unpublished French works. Thanks to the Editions Françaises Brentano's, many authors in exile who were cut off from their French publishers and would have otherwise been unable to express themselves, were able to maintain on this side of the Atlantic the vitality of the French mind and soul.

In fact, things started out rather more slowly. At the beginning of the war, Brentano's limited themselves to publishing in association with the Canadian houses Valiquette and Variétés. The first works

9. The Belle report is entitled 'Les livres français aux Etats-Unis: note sur la vente et l'édition'. The document was kindly communicated by Raoul Aglion.

published under the Brentano label came via Canada, like Prime Minister W. L. Mackenzie-King's *Le Canada en guerre* (1941). But they were not slow to exploit, in their turn, the rich vein of journalistic and literary talent among the New York expatriates. In 1941 appeared Philippe Barrès's hagiographic *Charles de Gaulle* and Pierre Lazareff's *Dernière Edition: souvenirs d'un journaliste français*. (The English translation of the latter, *Deadline*, was a best-seller in the United States.)

There was also the first French novel to take the American exile as its theme, Maurice Dekobra's *Emigrés de luxe*, which is a brilliant evocation of upper-class experience of the emigration, with wildly exaggerated characters and plot being amply compensated by satirical portraits of real-life or representative figures, and caustically etched atmospheric scenes of wit and adultery at the Stork Club or the Café Pierre. The terribly honourable and democratic duke, who first saves a 22-year-old Austrian from a French refugee camp, then marries her and succeeds in bringing her to safety in America, is a foil for parody and eroticism, and for comment on the frivolous manners of high society refugees. The Americans do not escape either: their passions for esoteric religions, for social climbing and for eating badly are teasingly ridiculed. Beyond the froth, there is a touch of genius in Dekobra: this story, like the later *La Madone à Hollywood* (published by Didier in 1943), turns and twists, with disguises, near misses, any number of grand set scenes and a very uneasy happy ending. Dekobra's *alter ego*, the Paris émigré literary agent Leo Glass, is an outrageous and hilarious character who deserves a place in the annals of comic literature.

It was only the second half of 1942, however, that Brentano's began to offer serious competition to the EMF, and this was largely through the efforts of Robert Tenger, a dynamic Paris lawyer whom Brentano engaged as literary director of his Editions Françaises. Tenger launched himself into his new profession with flair. He later articulated the four basic principles that were his driving force:

One: to neglect nothing that might help maintain an attachment to French culture, the love of France abroad, and the friendship of this continent for France.

Two: at the time when freedom of thought in France was stifled, to allow all opinions to be expressed here. People with the most diverse opinions . . . have in this way been able to make themselves heard. The culture of a country can only develop within the battle of ideas, and in this respect the United States has given the world an admirable example. In the midst of war – and restricted only by the safeguards on military secrets – complete freedom of speech, of the press, and of publishing has been maintained, not only for the benefit of citizens, but also for the benefit of the foreigners who have found refuge here. This great country has allowed only one form of censorship: that of public opinion.

Three: to encourage the diffusion of books of all kinds. That is what explains the truly extraordinary diversity of titles in the catalogue of a house that has published everything from novels to scientific works.

Four: to give the books an agreeable and attractive appearance, both through choice of covers and through the typography. (*Pour la Victoire*, 14 July 1945)

Tenger's programme in practice was very similar to that of the EMF, but in addition – and in this way he differed from Crespin and Molho – as a French émigré, he admitted to a degree of ideological commitment in his motivation. As his text shows, he was very admiring of the freedoms underpinning American life. He kept his distance from the gaullists, because he was worried about de Gaulle's dictatorial ambitions:[10] and his comments about a nation's cultural development being dependent on open debate have these concerns as a sub-text. His friendship with the Saint-Exupérys – he had been Consuelo's lawyer before the war, and invited them regularly to his country house in Connecticut[11] – did not indicate any sympathy with the Armistice or Vichy: rather that the liberal and moderate values he believed in allowed him to rise above narrow sectarian conflicts.

Like the EMF, Tenger published some of the 'standard' authors of the exile (Maurois, Saint-Exupéry, Georges-Michel), and achieved a very similar mix of novels, essays, theatre, translations and polemical works. Towards the end of the war, he brought out some exceptionally fine work, and the editions of Breton's *Le Surréalisme et la peinture* and Saint-John-Perse's *Anabase* (both 1945) will remain as monuments to Tenger's careful and enduring devotion to French culture.

Crespin and Molho seem to have attained instinctively a balance

10. OSS Archives, RG 226, Ent. 100, Box 38, FR 696. Interview with Tenger, 21 December 1943.
11. C. Cate, *Antoine de Saint-Exupéry* (New York, 1970), pp. 478–9.

between their commercial drive, and a real respect for French literature and for the writers they published. And the respect appears to have been mutual. Jules Romains and his wife, for example, often took the underground tunnel from the Mayflower Hotel to the bookshop in Rockefeller Plaza, to go and chat with the men they called their 'Angels'.[12] Similarly, under the direction of Tenger, Brentano's publications reflected a happy symbiosis between intellectual and artistic concerns, and good business sense.

Didier was less distinguished. His list was much smaller that the EMF's of Brentano's, and although he reached a total of more than twenty titles, few of them were interesting. Exceptions were Dekobra's *La Madone à Hollywood* (1942), which revived the splendid romantic heroine of his 1932 hit *La Madone des Sleepings*, and used her as a vehicle for satirising the mores of the Europeans in the Hollywood film industry; Philippe Barrès's poignant *Sauvons nos prisonniers* (1943), which exposed the success of Hitler's use of French POWs as blackmail against Pétain; and above all, Pierre Mendès-France's memoirs, *Liberté, liberté chérie* (1943).

Isaac Molho's recollection that, economically, the industry worked on a break-even basis should, ideally, be balanced against indications of how the books were in fact received by the public. Unfortunately, these are rare. Reviews in the French language press were almost monotonously favourable, although one striking exception came from Etiemble, who was rather isolated in Chicago, and who blasted the entire production as vulgar and trivial. (Admitting only Julien Green's *Varouna* as being worthy of print, he attacked Saint-Exupéry as 'impoverished', and singled out Maurois, Goffin and Georges-Michel as being among those 'who have taken advantage of the misfortunes of these times to make a noise, make money, and cut a figure.'[13])

As for sales figures, the only reliable ones are the general comparisons made by Christian Belle in his 1943 report.[14] This shows Maurois selling better than anyone else, closely followed by Saint-Exupéry. Barrès's biography of de Gaulle sold only half as well, but still much better than Maritain's essays, which most readers found too difficult. Romains' essays did not do well either. Predictably, it was by the sales of novels that the publishers compensated for their more intellectually ambitious books.

As a corpus of 250 works, the books published in New York

12. Lise Jules-Romains, *Les Vies inimitables: souvenirs* (Paris, 1985), p. 272.
13. In *VVV*, no. 1, June 1942, pp. 64–5.
14. Belle, 'Les Livres français'.

demonstrate the literary vitality of the exile. To be able to buy French books, and reconstitute the libraries that had been left behind, was to restore an element of normality to the émigrés' uprooted lives. More profoundly, the range of material available gave them real freedom of choice of cultural level and genre: light or serious fiction, poetry, theatre, memoirs, biography, essays on history, sociology, spiritual matters, literature, philosophy; journalistic works dealing with the experience of the immediate past or present, projections for the rebuilding of France and Europe. Not only was there something for everybody, but the whole phenomenon can be seen, on a symbolic level, as something larger than the sum of its parts – a context within which the émigrés could find themselves on familiar and reassuring ground, an emanation of the essence of their civilisation: France as conscience and creativity, French as the language of reflection and speculative thought.

The publishing side of the French cultural network included a number of smaller operations. Jacques Schiffrin, who had created the 'Bibliothèque de la Pléiade' in Paris, followed a similar policy of looking for 'stars' when he set up Pantheon Books. After his arrival in late 1941, he worked for a time with Tenger at Brentano's, but when he struck out on his own, it was already after the liberation of North Africa, and he showed little interest in the exiled writers, concentrating on authors like Gide and Vercors, and on art albums (Constantin Guys, Toulouse-Lautrec). In fact, the expatriate French market, for Schiffrin, was only ever a transition, since his aim, quickly achieved moreover, was to establish a permanent place for himself in the New York publishing world.

The poet Yvan Goll, on the other hand, was part of a more avant-garde movement. He ran his 'Hémisphères' publishing venture from his apartment in Brooklyn. 'Hémisphères' was a combination of two concepts. The first was a bilingual literary magazine. Goll and his wife Claire were both intensely interested in the arts in America. They joined summer arts 'colonies' – Yaddo in Saratoga, and the MacDowell Colony in Peterborough, New Hampshire, and through them, took part in exchanges with people like Richard Wright, Carson McCullers, Thornton Wilder and Aaron Copeland.[15] Goll founded his magazine with Alain Bosquet before the latter left to serve in the US Army. It produced six numbers between 1943 and 1946. Donna Kuizenga, in her study of the magazine, calls it a 'document of a world divided', and shows how its surrealist orientation favoured an emphasis on magic and the

15. Claire Goll, *La Poursuite du vent* (Paris, 1976), pp. 249ff.

occult, and an interest in Third World cultures, as a way of combatting the loneliness of exile and the sense of futility and alienation born of the mechanised world.[16]

Above all, it shows Goll's unfailing faith in poetry as a way of being, and of transcending national – and even linguistic – boundaries. Works by such American poets as Kenneth Patchen stand beside Saint-John Perse's 'Poème à l'Etrangère', setting up a strong invitation to readers to let their imaginations expand beyond familiar borders.

The other aspect of the 'Hémisphères' operation was the publication of small volumes of poetry by individual poets – Alain Bosquet, Aimé Césaire, Goll himself, Saint-John Perse. These were mostly illustrated by expatriate artists, like Masson and Léger, and they show Goll's determination to give poets and their work proper homage.

A very similar approach, and indeed most of the same writers, had found expression a year before the appearance of *Hémisphères*, in *VVV*. This review of poetry, the plastic arts, anthropology, sociology and psychology was edited by the American artist David Hare, with André Breton and Max Ernst (and later, Marcel Duchamp) as advisers. *VVV* only appeared three times (with a double number in March 1943), but it brimmed over with that mixture of confident dogmatism, unexpected leaps, challenging new thought and infuriating mystification that gave surrealism such an exciting impact in American avant-garde art circles. Bilingual and generously illustrated, it was a major outlet for Breton's writing, but included too Lévi-Strauss on Indian cosmetics and Robert Motherwell on Mondrian and Chirico. Its multifaceted spirit was summed up in the first number, in the explanations offered for its title:

– a vow, and the double victory over forces of repression and over all that is opposed to the emancipation of the spirit.
– the View around us (the external and conscious world), the View inside us (the interior and unconscious world), and the synthesis of these in a 'total view'.
– VVV which translates all the reactions of the eternal upon the actual, of the psychic upon the physical, and takes account of the myth in process of formation under the VEIL of happenings.

16. Donna Kuizenga, 'Yvan Goll's *Hémisphères*: a forgotten French-American review of the 1940s', in *The French-American Review*, vol. II, 1–2, Winter 1977 and Spring 1978, p. 25.

The creation of special structures that allowed writers to publish in French was not a problem painters and sculptors had to face. Everything was more favourable for them. A huge collection of galleries and art dealers in East 57th Street, owned by French interests or specialising in modern French art, was already in existence before the war. Many of the exiled artists already exhibited in America and had developed friendly and fruitful relationships with their American contemporaries. Julien Levy had organised the first US surrealist exhibitions as early as 1931–2, for example;[17] both Léger and Amédée Ozenfant were already in America in 1938 – in fact, the latter had set up his New York 'Ozenfant School of Fine Arts' before the war broke out;[18] and Pierre Matisse held an Yves Tanguy show in 1939. The drift from European cities towards New York may not yet have been definitive, but it was a strong movement, and in a way, many of the artists do not appear as true exiles at all, but rather as simply spending more time than expected in a congenial new centre of artistic freedom and creativity.

In July 1944, Michel Georges-Michel did the rounds of the expatriate artists for a series of articles in *Pour la Victoire*, under the general title 'De Montparnasse à la 57e Rue'.[19] From minor figures like Claude Domec who had worked as a designer at the Gobelins tapestry workshop, and who was doing restoration work in Greenwich Village, to major artists like Léger, most seemed contented and able to make a living from their work. Ossip Zadkine grumbled about the absence of bronze and at having to sculpt in wood, but he had students, and was more than delighted by the quality of his models. Ozenfant's school was, if not thriving, doing well enough. Vertès was getting plenty of work with American fashion magazines. And Léger was ebullient:

> Ah! Here I am working on the scale of the country. I've purified my tone further, simplified the volumes, but giving them more intensity. Intensity, that's the goal. To demolish a wall, and replace it with life. (15 July 1944)

Léger's exile was a particularly successful one. He painted prolifically, including murals for Nelson Rockefeller, he gave classes in

17. See Julien Levy, *Memoirs of an Art Gallery* (New York, 1977), p. 117.
18. Amédée Ozenfant, *Mémoires 1886–1962* (Paris, 1968), passim.
19. *Pour la Victoire*, 15 July, 29 July, 5 August 1944.

universities and colleges, and he was a great socialiser – whether at parties like those given by American art critic and historian James Johnson Sweeney,[20] or at his own apartment, where he had a reputation as an expansive host and a very good cook.[21]

It is true that an important aspect of Paris art life was missing in New York: the café. Tanguy regretted that it was not possible, in New York, to take a leisurely stroll and bump into his friends.[22] Kisling tried to compensate by holding weekly French–American gatherings.[23] And Julien Levy recounts a funny anecdote of Breton trying to duplicate his favourite Paris haunts in the back room of a Greenwich Village bar:

> All the surrealist exiles, and a few other painters including Chagall and Léger, crowded into the room for the first reunion. We were all enjoying ourselves, alive with great expectations and a feeling of enormous camaraderie, when Breton raised his fist and pounded on the table. 'This will be a serious meeting,' he said. 'We will conduct it in a parliamentary fashion. When you wish to speak, you will raise your hand and I will acknowledge your signal with the words *La parole est à tel-et-tel, la parole est à vous!*'[24]

But if there were no cafés, there were plenty of parties, which a puzzled Denis de Rougemont noted to be a common way for members of the American avant-garde to get together.[25] And as the memoirs of Julien Levy and Peggy Guggenheim show,[26] there were many such evenings, with gossip and argument and not a little sexual folly.

The main thing was that the artists were able to work and to exhibit. Tanguy, who married the American surrealist Kay Sage in August 1940, eventually moved out of the city to Woodbury, Connecticut, and found the rural setting perfect. Like Léger, he was stimulated by the greater sense of space in America, and found

20. Ozenfant, *Mémoires*, p. 484.
21. Guy Fritsch-Estrangin, *New York entre de Gaulle et Pétain* (Paris, 1969), p. 183. Cf. also André Maurois, *Mémoires* (Paris, 1970), pp. 352–4.
22. Interview with J. J. Sweeney, in the *Museum of Modern Art Bulletin* (New York), vol. 13, no. 4–5, 1946, pp. 22–3.
23. *Pour la Victoire*, 31 June 1942.
24. Levy, *Memoirs*, p. 279.
25. D. de Rougemont, *Journal d'une époque* (Paris, 1968), p. 463.
26. Levy, *Memoirs*, and Peggy Guggenheim, *Out of this Century* (New York, 1979), passim.

his painting gaining in intensity.[27] He had a number of one-man shows during the war, and received ample critical attention, particularly in the special issue of *View* which was devoted to him in May 1942. And his situation was not unique. His dealer Pierre Matisse ran a big exhibition in March 1942 for fourteen refugee artists, including Ernst, Masson, Chagall, Lipchitz, Ozenfant and Zadkine. At the same time, the sculptor Guitou Knoop was showing at Wildensteins. In October–November 1942, the big surrealist exhibition, 'First Papers of Surrealism', was held in the Whitelaw Reid Mansion on Madison Avenue, with strong participation by Marcel Duchamp, Chagall, Masson and Tanguy. And as a final example, in May 1943, Zadkine had a one-man show at the Valentine Gallery.

Throughout the war, in addition to the various manifestations by the émigré artists, the small gallery owners and some of the larger American galleries had an almost uninterrupted flow of French art on show. Fristch-Estrangin notes a half dozen major exhibitions in the 1940–4 period, from individual painters like Renoir and Utrillo, through period shows – 'Les Maîtres français du XIXe siècle', 'De Corot à Van Gogh' – to thematic ones: 'La Seine du Havre à Paris vue par les artistes français', 'Le Printemps à Paris avant 1914'.[28]

The art columns of *Pour la Victoire* detail many others: a 'Paris en gravures' at the Brooklyn Museum in April 1942, Degas at Durand-Ruel, Rodin at Bucholz, and Bonnard and Vuillard at Paul Rosemberg in January 1943, just to mention a few. Ozenfant's April 1941 observation, that since his arrival in New York 57th Street was practically entirely devoted to French exhibitions, could have been extended to the whole of the city, and over the whole war period. The French presence was massive and prominent, an incontrovertible reminder of the nation's artistic stature.

The most striking phenomenon remains, however, the number of working French artists who, at this turning-point in the history of modern art, made such a large contribution to the process by which American painting came of age, and New York assumed the mantle of the principal world centre of modern art production. The stage for the change had been set earlier, of course. The tension between chauvinism and European consciousness in American art was a long-standing one, but resolution had begun to shift in the direction of more cosmopolitan taste and attitudes with the arrival of German artists – Bauhaus and others – fleeing Hitlerian repressions,

27. Sweeney, interview, *op. cit.*
28. Fritsch-Estrangin, *New York*, p. 188.

and the burgeoning New York school was frank in its admiration of its European roots.[29] (The shift in America from artistic navel-gazing to a more outward-looking attitude is clearly analogous to the shift away from political isolationism to a greater sense of global responsibility. It is to art's credit that it was in advance of politics.) The later arrival of the large numbers of French artists cannot thus be said to have *initiated* any change of direction. Their inspirational impact on the Pollocks, Gustons and Rothkos had come earlier. By their prominence, however – the sheer volume of their work, their influence as teachers – they undoubtedly accelerated the process that transformed the New York school into a phenomenon of global importance, and increased American understanding of what modernism was all about.

Their effect was catalytic, rather than the result of any deep exchange. Apart from an increase of intensity of colour and form in Tanguy and Léger (reasonably explicable in terms of stronger energies deriving from increases in space, scale and freedom), there is no evidence that any evolution in the French artists' work was *caused* by their stay in America. Their sense of their own tradition remained intact, unshaken by France's political ruin, and most of them would have shared Marc Chagall's conviction that French art was not only the most preponderant influence on American art, but that it was still in the full force of the renaissance that had begun at the start of the century. Chagall told the young Alain Bosquet: 'If I could pray, I would pray that France, so tragically fallen, might continue to bring the light of her art across the world.'[30] And what was that light, if not the product of a belief in the supremacy of the imagination over the material world, and of pluralistic freedom over tyranically imposed unity?

As far as the film world was concerned, in his book on the Hollywood émigrés, John Taylor Russell concludes that the French did generally better than their German counterparts, and that they 'managed to preserve their own character in Hollywood, in but not of the American film community'.[31] To a very considerable extent, this seems to have been true. The three major exiled directors – Renoir, Duvivier and Clair – all had the opportunity to direct several films, and if for some of the exiled actors – like Michèle Morgan or Jean Gabin – there was little chance to work, others did extremely well, or at least made a decent living. Jean-Pierre

29. Cf. Jean-Michel Palmier, *Weimar en exil* (Paris, 1988), vol. II, pp. 261–7.
30. In the fortnightly newspaper *La Voix de France*, 15 May 1942.
31. *Strangers in Paradise* (London, 1983), pp. 218–31.

Aumont reached star status with a lucrative contract from MGM (which he broke to join the French Army in Africa).[32] And Dalio, the central figure in Renoir's *La Règle du jeu*, although he had problems with his diminutive size and his lack of English, was eventually able to work his way into regular work as a character actor, in small roles – porter or croupier – in various 'resistance' films, including *Casablanca*.[33]

At the same time, there was no real community of work possible for the French in the Hollywood context. With very few exceptions, French directors worked with American actors, and French actors with American directors. The official mission that had sent Clair and Duvivier to America – to establish a French film production centre – never amounted to anything, and the only gatherings of the Hollywood exiles were of an informal, social nature. In this respect Charles Boyer and his French Research Foundation were an important focus, and served a useful purpose in helping the émigrés maintain contact with one another and with some aspects of their culture. André David, who assisted Boyer in directing the Foundation, particularly appreciated the well-stocked library, and spent much of his time reading through the complete works of Michelet. His memory of the experience produced a startling image: 'To read Michelet as I did during my exile was to kiss France on the mouth.'[34] David, who was otherwise engaged in dubbing American movies for the post-war French market, was grateful to Boyer for providing a culturally stimulating milieu. Aumont also noted the importance of Boyer's activities: 'At once a consul, an ambassador, a confessor and a philosophy teacher, he patiently received all the French, who would come to plead their cause or seek justice.'[35]

Boyer was well established in Hollywood before the war, and notwithstanding a very busy acting schedule, he used what influence he enjoyed in the service of his fellow countrymen. He was not pro-Free French from the beginning, though he became a keen gaullist in 1942, and reported regularly to de Gaulle's delegate in Washington. He also became honorary president of the Los Angeles chapter of France Forever.[36]

His new-found political commitment was not shared by all those who came to his dinners – Gabin was a royalist, for example, Clair was no supporter of de Gaulle, and Renoir avoided all involvement

32. Jean-Pierre Aumont, *Le Soleil et les ombres* (Paris, 1976), p. 97.
33. Dalio, *Mes Années folles* (Paris, 1976), pp. 173ff.
34. André David, *75 Années de Jeunesse* (Paris, 1974), pp. 171–4.
35. Aumont, *Le Soleil*, pp. 95–6.
36. Interview with OSS, 28 April 1945. OSS, *loc. cit.*, Box 40, FR 1020.

– but he appears to have been motivated by tolerance and compassion as much as by political belief, and he certainly had no personal ambition for power. As Aumont expressed it, it was simply very agreeable to get together regularly with compatriots like Clair, Renoir and Dalio and enjoy the intelligent conversation, as well as having the chance to meet other artists, such as Arthur Rubenstein or the film-star Gene Tierney, and to keep in touch with the New York community through visitors like Louis Verneuil.[37]

Verneuil, along with Henry Bernstein, was France's leading playwright in exile. He had even less success than Bernstein, who was at least able to create *Rose Burke* in English. In January 1942, in *Pour la Victoire*, Verneuil announced a three-month spring season of French theatre on Broadway, with twelve plays, under the general title 'Le théâtre de Paris à New York'. By mid-March, he was saying that the season had been postponed for a year, but in fact it had been buried. Was it his choice of plays – almost all by lightweight *boulevardiers* like Verneuil himself (Porto-Riche, Raynal, Géraldy, etc.) – that made his American backers bring the curtain down on the project? Aumont believed so, and thought that Verneuil's desire to glorify French culture would have been better served by putting on Molière or Racine.

In the end, on a personal level, Verneuil did not do badly. Brentano's published his complete theatrical works (4 volumes, 1942 and 1944) and a life of Sarah Bernhardt (1942); and the EMF published his memoirs (*Rideau à neuf heures*, 1942). The French theatre of the exile, however, was in the image of those who represented it: no longer capable of offering anything to the audience of the day. Things may have been different if Louis Jouvet's touring troupe of twenty-five top actors and technicians, which began its strange and seemingly endless tour of South America in 1941, had been able to enter the United States; but despite the efforts of Renoir, Aumont and others, permission was never forthcoming from the US authorities, for reasons that remained obscure.

French musicians had no real community of their own, but a number of them integrated well into the American music world and had successful careers. Milhaud was the only really notable composer, and from his Mills College base, where he composed a large number of works – chamber, choral, orchestral – he roved the country, teaching in universities (Harvard, Princeton, Vassar), or

37. Jean-Pierre Aumont, *Souvenirs provisoires* (Paris, 1957), pp. 162–9.

conducting various orchestras.[38] Arthur Lourié, a close friend of the Maritains and principally a composer of religious music, settled in New York, where he wrote both music and essays on art. The latter show him to be of a conservative bent, convinced that art and politics were necessarily in total conflict. He also believed that American jazz was a sign of total decadence.[39] The pianists Robert Casadesus and Nadia Boulanger performed regularly, and so did the singer Claude Alphand (then married to the diplomat Hervé Alphand), whose 'delicious' voice[40] and repertoire of popular songs allowed her to create an intimate cabaret atmosphere widely appreciated among the émigré community. Juliette Durand-Texte (the wife of Camille Chautemps) also gave piano recitals (in concert, on the radio), but seems to have been somewhat impaired in her career by the interference of her husband's political enemies.[41] All in all, French music did have a presence in the American cultural scene, and in that respect it did better than the theatre, but it had neither the impact of the painters and sculptors, nor the bonding effect of the French-language publishing ventures.

By far the most powerful cultural expression of the refugee community, however, was its press. Before the war dozens of small French-language papers had been published for decades among the French-Canadian groups scattered through New England, or among those of the Louisiana diaspora, mainly up and down the California coast. By and large, these papers maintained their character. In mid-1942, the Harvard Group of American Defense, reporting on the New England papers, described them as 'completely colorless and innocuous, interested only in the social affairs of their local group, and in maintaining cultural relations with French Canada'.[42] And while papers like San Francisco's *Courrier du Pacifique* or the Los Angeles *Union nouvelle* had greater political ambitions, they had only a limited audience and influence. In New York, on the contrary, the newspapers were more cosmopolitan. They reflected the community's political trends, its cultural aspirations, its intrigues, and its sometimes raucous dissensions.

38. Darius Milhaud, *Ma Vie heureuse* (Paris, 1973), pp. 221–40. Cf. also Boris Schwarz, 'The Music World in Migration', in J. Jackman and C. Borden (eds), *The Muses Flee Hitler* (Washington, 1983), pp. 144–5.
39. Arthur Lourié, *Profanation et sanctification du temps* (Paris, 1966), passim.
40. The adjective is Ozenfant's: *Mémoires*, p. 444.
41. Chautemps singles out Henri Hoppenot, who in late 1942 replaced Tixier as de Gaulle's delegate in Washington. (Unpublished diary, Winter 1943–4, passim.)
42. OSS, *loc. cit.*, Box 27, EU-65.

At the time of the arrival of the first wave of French refugees, in the summer of 1940, there was in New York City a single French-language weekly, *L'Amérique*, which appeared on Sundays. It was essentially a family enterprise, the organ of the French Press Company Incorporated, whose president Maurice Lacoste and his wife Josette shared the publishing and editorial activities of the paper, and much, if not quite all, of the writing. They had begun the paper in September 1933 as a literary and artistic weekly, but in the build-up towards the war came to give progressively more space to the international political situation.

This shift evidently corresponded to the interests of *L'Amérique*'s public, and so did the editorial policy, which, while stressing the impartiality of its opinions, was carefully middle-of-the-road, a mixture of *bien-pensant* democratic sentiment and of an old-fashioned rhetoric, often pompous, designed to stir the readers' hearts. Anti-fascist, it attacked Franco, from the beginning of the Spanish Civil War, as an agent of disorder, violence, terror and illegality (16 August 1936). And during the 'Phoney War', it emphatically extolled the fraternity of the French and English peoples (14 January 1940).

A comment on a March 1940 speech in Paris by the nationalist *député* Henri de Kérillis – of whom *L'Amérique* could not suspect that within a few months, he would be in New York – gives a good idea of the paper's style and its instinctive quest for safe ground:

M. H. de Kérillis needed much fearlessness in his soul and moderation in his terms to denouce before the Chamber the cancer of Hitlerism, which is trying to undermine all nations. . . . The director of *L'Epoque* has given his voluminous dossier to M. Daladier. The evidence is in good hands. (17 March 1940)

When, a few days later, Daladier was replaced by Reynaud (21 March), *L'Amérique* immediately transferred its warm support to the latter, and after the débâcle and Armistice, Lacoste launched an appeal to his readers to emulate the courage of Joan of Arc and to cling to the principles of liberty laid down by the French Revolution (23 June 1940). In the confused following months, the paper seemed unable to distinguish a clear line of conduct, but it remained motivated by the need to be staunchly loyal to *something*, even when it could not determine what that something was.

Thus, in September, it welcomed the new French Ambassador, Gaston Henry-Haye, with a panegyric of Pétain by Ivy Porter (15

September 1940), while the following January, it declared its determination to avoid being partisan and its belief that de Gaulle, Pétain
and Weygand, each in his own way, 'will contribute to save their
country' (12 January 1941). *L'Amérique*'s appeal for a unified French
front was no doubt genuine enough, but its stance would rapidly
prove unrealistic.

As its name implies, the paper reflected the attitudes of a readership principally made up of people who had been ensconced in
America for a number of years, and who were accustomed to
viewing their native France through the eyes of the American press
and official US policies. The desire it expressed for French unity
soon came to mean, in fact, overt and unquestioning support for
the American position:

> the government that sits in Vichy . . . is the only French government
> and it is recognized officially as such by the American government. . . .
> So let us get used to designating in that way the government of Maréchal
> Pétain. (19 January 1941)

Adherence to this position did not altogether exclude some parallel
support for de Gaulle, but it was limited to accepting the Free
French as a strictly military operation, and was coupled with an
increasing number of ominous warnings about the gaullists' vo-
racious and underhand political ambitions.

The Lacostes and their little team were incapable of com-
prehending the intensity of feeling that came with the arrival of the
exiles – those who had experienced at first hand the political and
social rifts of prewar France, and the even more traumatic wrench-
ings of the defeat. And in this respect, they were typical of the
established French expatriates, who would not really begin to
understand the dimensions of the struggle until America herself
entered the war.

Furthermore, in strictly journalistic terms, *L'Amérique* was ama-
teurish and lacking editorial focus, and it would be swept aside
(though not without a protest, as we shall see) by the war-
toughened, top-class professionals who rolled into New York as
refugees: the likes of Pierre Lazareff of *Paris-Soir*, Pertinax (André
Géraud) of *L'Echo de Paris*, Emile Buré of *L'Ordre*, Philippe Barrès
of *Le Matin* and *Match*, Geneviève Tabouis of *L'Oeuvre*, Henri de
Kérillis of *L'Epoque*, to mention only the best known.

These were people who had witnessed and written about the rise
of Hitler, the Spanish Civil War, the feverish months of the Front

Populaire and its aftermath, the frantic peace efforts leading up to Munich, the *Sitzkrieg* and the *Blitzkrieg*, the fall of France. Many of them had met de Gaulle in London, and they arrived imbued with a sense of urgency, aware of the desperate position of occupied France, and of the mood of depression that had settled over the country as a whole. They were aware, too, that the defences of Britain, the last bastion of freedom in Western Europe, were fearfully fragile. And finally, they knew that they had a mission to fulfil in helping to combat US isolationism, and to awaken the American people to just how bad things were in Europe.

They were warriors, whose journalistic arsenal had been well stocked by experience and regularly updated. The well-meaning, but ultimately complacent attitudes of the established French community would be peremptorily dismissed, as would the often romanticised views of Europe held by their American hosts. Instead of the polite deference to Washington exemplified by the Maurice and Josette Lacostes, there would emerge a hard-nosed and uncompromising determination to muster support for the war effort in Europe.

The first initiative for the creation of a newspaper representative of the concerns of the exiles, however, came not from the major French journalists, but from an obscure and mysterious man who called himself Adolphe Demilly. In mid-1941, he acquired what had been a bulletin for teachers and students of French, and on 15 September, launched the first number of *La Voix de France*, with the Belgian novelist Robert Goffin as principal editor, and a resounding statement of intent:

> In the struggle between the powers of disorder and the powers of civilisation, our choice has been made from all eternity: France's misfortune will never alter it. We are for freedom against slavery. We are for civilisation against barbarity, we are for the understanding of mankind against the concentration camp theories . . .
>
> Previously this paper was addressed only to university teachers because the influence of French culture spoke for itself. Today, the flame has not gone out, but others have created darkness. We believe it is our duty to act in such a way that the flame does not completely die. We know that the dearest wish of the Nazis is that it should, and we wish to fight them on the ground that is given us.

For the next year, until October 1942, *La Voix de France* would pursue its goals, not so much with any kind of consistency as with erratic bursts of enthusiasm and energy. Occasionally, quite re-markable numbers were produced, but it often appeared as a rag-bag collection of disparate articles, and sometimes failed to appear altogether. Much of this irregularity can undoubtedly be attributed to the leadership – or lack of it – provided by Demilly. The paper's whole layout reflects a lack of journalistic experience, and a reliance on the inspirations of the moment rather than any clear editorial policy or solid financial underpinning.

One of the paper's regular contributors during its first half-year, poet-novelist Alain Bosquet, presents an abrasively satirical picture of life at *La Voix de France*, and of its director, in his novel *La Grande Eclipse* (Paris, Gallimard, 1952), and its more directly auto-biographical reprise *Les Fêtes cruelles* (Paris, Grasset, 1984). In the novel, Demilly (under the name of Lemille) appears as an affable rogue, a slapdash and unscrupulous improviser who protects his source of funds in London[43] by parading a certain gaullism. At the same time, he avoids offending his readership by instructing his writers to be cautious in attacking Vichy: Laval was fair game, but Pétain was to be left alone. In the autobiography, Bosquet sharpens the thrust, which he puts in the mouth of journalist Emile Buré: 'Some are three hundred per cent gaullist, others are pétainist without being against de Gaulle, and most have the opinion of their back pockets, like Adolphe Lemille' (p. 129).

Another regular contributor, Claire Goll (wife of the poet Yvan Goll), who wrote the cinema reviews for the paper, gives a similar impression of laxity at the editorial level when she claims that she rarely went to see any of the films she reviewed, but simply copied and translated snippets of other reviews from the American press.[44]

The contribution of *La Voix de France* to the establishment of a serious French-language press in wartime New York was none the less real and substantial in at least two ways. First, some of its numbers were of very high quality indeed. They provided an image of the strong bonds linking France and America and much

43. The real source of funding is not at all clear. Raoul Aglion suggests that his office might have purchased a number of subscriptions, but states that he rejected Demilly's request for direct subsidy (*Roosevelt and de Gaulle: Allies in conflict*, New York, 1988, p. 93). The OSS reports that André Mayer was a supporter (Box 35, FR-240), but must surely have meant not the Collège de France Professor, but his financier homonym, André Meyer. In a letter to the author (3 September 1987), Alain Bosquet intimates that Demilly may have disposed of funds generated by illicit trafficking, perhaps of arms. Demilly, whose real name was Finkelstein, was from a poor Alsatian-Jewish family. He died of an embolism in Paris, during a business trip, in 1954, aged 44.

44. Claire Goll, *La Poursuite du vent*, pp. 226ff.

material of a morale-sustaining kind. One good example of this is the special 24-page number that appeared on 15 May 1942, with a huge front page photograph of Roosevelt under the banner *Hommage à l'Amérique*, and with articles by Maeterlinck, Jules Romains, Chagall, Gustave Cohen, Henri Focillon, Henri Grégoire, Fernand Léger, Pertinax, Louis Verneuil and many others. Quite diverse aspects of the cultural and intellectual exile – but showing common ground and common comfort and hope in the strength and generous hospitality of their American hosts. Even if such attempts to transcend political factionism were not sustainable, they did, to some extent, come to terms with the problem of bridging the perception gap between those who had fled across the Atlantic to escape Nazi conquest and those Americans who were now preparing the eastward crossing to reconquer Europe's freedom.

The paper's second main contribution is that, for all its looseness of direction and presentation, its very existence paved the way for the one that would dominate the New York scene from the time of its appearance in January 1942 until the end of the war, the Tabouis–Pobers–Kérillis production, *Pour la Victoire*.

The success and, indeed, the extraordinarily high quality of *Pour la Victoire*, which by any criteria must be ranked as a top-class paper, need to be understood in the context of three major factors. The first is the change in America's position in respect to the war. The Americans' new status as belligerants after Pearl Harbor meant a much more detailed interest in Europe in general, and in France in particular. Beyond the network of diplomatic relations with the Vichy government, the State Department pragmatically dealt with Free French representatives, both in those territories and colonies which had declared themselves for de Gaulle, and with the General's representatives in the United States itself. Less officially, the US administration also showed willingness to listen to the informed opinions of significant refugees. In short, a space – and an audience – had been created for the expression of a French body of opinion that had the potential to influence the development of US policy, both in respect to the course of the war, and in respect to France's role in a post-war era that could already, if still dimly, be glimpsed. It was towards that space and that audience that the creators of *Pour la Victoire* were drawn.

The second major factor in *Pour la Victoire*'s success was the build-up of explicitly political structures in the Free French movement, as de Gaulle sought to extend the base of power and influence he had established in London. These developments will be treated more fully later, but as Raoul Aglion points out, the press was part of the drive from very early on. In October 1941, Aglion wrote to the National Committee in London suggesting the purchase and reconstruction of an existing French paper, or alternatively, the establishing of a new paper under the Free French banner.[45] Although *Pour la Victoire* would never be a party paper, there is no doubt that Aglion's encouragement to its founder, Geneviève Tabouis, echoed the latter's desire to serve the Free French cause, and for almost a year, *Pour la Victoire* in fact fulfilled the role of Free French mouthpiece, and did act as a significant extension of de Gaulle's London network.

Geneviève Tabouis herself was the third major factor. We have already seen examples of the prodigious energy and activity of this fragile fifty-year-old. With her experience of European politics and of life in America, her credentials for directing 'a great French newspaper devoted to strengthening Franco-American friendship'[46] could hardly have been better. And given her extraordinary collection of friends in high places, it is not altogether surprising that she managed to persuade Horace Finaly, exiled director of the Banque de Paris et des Pays-Bas, to put up the money to launch the paper.[47]

Tabouis' choice of close collaborators deserves some attention. For Vice-President of the publishing company she created – the 'Notre Paris Corporation' – she secured the services of Professor Frédéric Hoffherr. Hoffherr had been in the United States since the end of the First World War, and although he had no serious claims as a scholar, he had been very active, both as a college administrator, rising to the position of Chairman of French at Barnard College (Columbia University), and in a large number of French societies. Much decorated as a First World War veteran and as a promoter of French culture, he had been among the first to join France Forever, where he held the office of Executive Vice-President. For Tabouis, this structural link with the American system would have been important, and so would Hoffherr's previous newspaper experience as the US correspondent for *L'Echo de Paris, Paris-Midi* and *Le Journal d'Alsace-Lorraine*.[48] His actual role in the paper would be a minor one, however, and one cannot avoid the impression that Tabouis was using an established 'local' as a

45. Aglion, *Roosevelt and de Gaulle*, p. 94.
46. Geneviève Tabouis, *Grandeurs et servitudes américaines* (Paris, 1945), p. 136.
47. Cf. Aglion, *Roosevelt and de Gaulle*, p. 95, and Geneviève Tabouis, *Ils l'ont appelée Cassandre* (New York, 1942), p. 182.
48. The information on Hoffherr is drawn from the 1942–3 *Catalogue* of the *Ecole Libre des Hautes Etudes*, p. 71.

lever to place her refugee heavyweights, Philippe Barrès, Henri de Kérillis and Michel Pobers.

The first two of these were of nationalist republican leanings. Philippe Barrès was very much his father Maurice's son, and he made a conscious connection between his admiration for his father's deep attachment to the province of Lorraine, and his own prompt espousal of the cause of de Gaulle and the Free French 'Croix de Lorraine'.[49] Later, Barrès would defend his position as unavoidable rather than ideal, proclaiming de Gaulle 'a terrible person',[50] but there was no doubting the sincerity of the praise which flows through his *Charles de Gaulle* (New York and London, 1941), the book he spent the first fifteen months of his exile writing. (Not unsymbolically, it is dedicated to his father, Maurice.)

Barrès's nationalism was squarely in the anti-German tradition. As a correspondent for the French press, he had been in Berlin when Hitler came to power, and in his *Sous la Vague hitlérienne* (Paris, 1933) had sounded an early warning about the dangers of Nazism. And in 1938, after three years as editor-in-chief of the conservative daily *Le Matin*, he resigned as the paper's stance became increasingly pro-German. There is little evidence of any close prewar contact between Barrès and Tabouis, but their views on Hitler coincided, as well as their general support of the Free French rather than Vichy. Barrès's attractiveness as a collaborator would have been enhanced by his familiarity with New York, gained during an earlier period as correspondent for *Le Matin*.

Henri de Kérillis was the prize catch. This former First World War aviation ace, who had abandoned a career in industry to pursue his political ideals, was in all ways a paradoxical figure. Nationalist and Catholic, he was none the less a devoted republican, and a confirmed enemy of Maurras and the Action Française. Hostile to the left, he fought for an alliance with Soviet Russia to combat the German threat. Supportive of Franco, at least at the beginning of the Spanish Civil War, and an opponent of Blum and the Front Populaire, he took an uncompromising stand against the Munich agreements, and was resolutely against Pétain's government and the Armistice.[51] For these opinions, openly expressed, Vichy stripped him of his citizenship and his honours.

49. See Philippe Barrès, *Charles de Gaulle* (London, 1941), pp. 254–5.
50. To Eleanor Clark of the OSS: *loc. cit.*, Box 37, FR–612, 14 July 1943.
51. The most reliable sources on de Kérillis are two unpublished theses: Olivier Gaudry, *Henry de Kérillis* (Institut d'Etudes politiques de l'Université de Paris, 1966); and Christian Lovighi, *Henry de Kérillis ou le refus de la décadence* (*loc. cit.*, 1984).

As a journalist, de Kérillis enjoyed a reputation as outstanding as that of Tabouis herself, though he was also known as being a thorny character. First with *L'Echo de Paris*, and then with his own paper, *L'Epoque*, he had maintained a rigorously independent voice, that of a man who was both crusader and prophet, fair-minded, scrupulously honest, but obsessed with the powers of darkness, and always so ready to see conspiracies that his own credibility was sometimes in doubt.

The same altruistic patriotism, and the same touch of paranoia, were evident in his performances as the parliamentary representative from Neuilly, when he specialised in denouncing the shady dealings of the Cagoule and the German Fifth Column – though just how exaggerated his fears were may never be resolved, since the greatest success of those covert operations is to have remained largely covert, even years later.[52] In any case, the quirks of de Kérillis's character were no obstacle to Tabouis, who had cultivated him before the war, taking some delight in the libel suits he had to fight against the likes of Brinon and Déat, whom he had accused of working for Hitler.[53] In order to assure his cooperation at *Pour la Victoire*, Tabouis bound herself to him with a contract that she would later have cause to regret.

Just why she chose Michel Pobers as the secretary of the Notre Paris Corporation, and as managing editor of *Pour la Victoire* remains something of a mystery. Pobers (originally Poberesky) was a Lithuanian Jew, who had worked for the anti-democratic, proto-fascist *Le Jour*,[54] and had written a lot of pro-German material, which might well have compromised him in the eyes of the very republican Tabouis. Aglion reports that she gave him as her reason for engaging Pobers the latter's experience with the practical side of running a newspaper,[55] and while this is not implausible, it is obvious that both Barrès and de Kérillis were equally well prepared for such a task.

The OSS, on the other hand, noted that Pobers was rumoured to have some (unspecified) hold over Tabouis,[56] and while such speculation cannot be verified, it is not entirely idle. There could

---

52. See, for example, Philippe Bourdrel's *La Cagoule: Trente ans de complot* (Paris, 1970), and the equally tantalising *Dagore: les carnets secrets de la Cagoule*, ed. Christian Bernadec (Paris, 1977).
53. See Tabouis, *Cassandre*, pp. 323ff; and Claude Bellanger et al. (eds), *Histoire générale de la presse française*, III (Paris, 1972), p. 535.
54. See Raymond Manévy, *La Presse de la IIIe République*, Paris, 1955, pp. 177–8.
55. Aglion, *Roosevelt and de Gaulle*, p. 95.
56. OSS, *loc. cit.*, Box 34, FR–116, 27 May 1942.

well have been some scandal in Tabouis' past that Pobers knew about – either during the time that they were both working at the League of Nations, or in the more generally unsavoury activities of the prewar French press.[57] We shall see that her later actions with respect to the *Pour la Victoire* stock leave more than a little room for wondering about the nature of her link with Pobers. Certainly, there was no love lost between Pobers and de Kérillis, and the strained relations between them would be a significant factor in the ultimate decline and dissolution of the paper.

Difficulties of personality and background notwithstanding, it was with this team – Hoffherr, Barrès, de Kérillis and Pobers – together with the former diplomat Jacques Juda-Daunou (brought in after his resignation from Vichy to handle the advertising) – that Geneviève Tabouis launched the venture that she hoped would achieve the '*union sacrée*' of all the expatriate French in America. And it is to her credit that despite the rightist leanings of the principal writers, and despite the clear editorial choice of de Gaulle over Vichy, *Pour la Victoire* did in fact manage to project such a union for a considerable length of time.

The first number appeared on Saturday, 10 January 1942, with the Arc de Triomphe and the eternal flame as its logo, and with a message from Eleanor Roosevelt prominently displayed on the front page:

> To launch a new French weekly at this time is a bold gesture, and augurs well for the confidence and courage which free nations have, and which will lead us to ultimate victory.
>
> I like your name, *For Victory*, and hope that you will have the support of the democratic, free French people. I wish you every success in this effort to perpetuate the culture and ideals of the French people whom we have known and admire.

The general policies of the paper are already clear in this number: a commitment to in-depth coverage of the war effort, of Free French activities throughout the world, of news from France itself, and of the engagements of the various French communities in America; a determination to establish a strong sense of national continuity through commentaries on French cultural and political history; a desire to provide variety in content and visual presentation, with a broad range of columns, plentiful photographs, different

---

57. See Bellanger et al., *Histoire générale*, pp. 487–8.

typefaces, political cartoons, etc.; and openness to a large number of outside contributors. After a few weeks, the eight-page tabloid settled into the pattern that would make it a paper that offered something for everyone, while maintaining editorial integrity and a high intellectual level.

During the first months of operation, Henri de Kérillis wrote a series of searching articles on the dissensions and weaknesses of prewar French society, in which he saw the seeds of the humiliating defeat of 1940; Barrès presented analyses of the personality and policies of de Gaulle and Churchill; Pobers tended to deal with particular problems, such as America's use of New Caledonia as a military base, or the implications of Laval's return to power; Tabouis reserved the broad sweep for her own column '*La Semaine dans le Monde*'.

While no opportunity was missed to attack the Vichy regime and collaboration in France – with Hoffherr, for example, documenting Vichy complicity in German repression (31 January 1942), or the publication of letters of executed hostages to their families (23 May 1942) – *Pour la Victoire* held quite closely to the line of US policy and avoided any open break with the pro-Pétain factions within the United States. Thus it noted with satisfaction the resignation of five diplomats from the Washington embassy at the time of Laval's return to power in April 1942, but was muted in its criticism of Ambassador Henry-Haye himself (2 May 1942). And no '*pur et dur*' gaullist would have approved of the paper's acknowledgement, however, grudging, of the good work of Vichy diplomats Marchal and Guérin in negotiating US aid to the North African colonies (7 February 1942), since the Free French position was that any such aid could only help Vichy, and hence the German cause. Nor would the gaullists necessarily have found acceptable the concluding remarks of a Darius Milhaud article on 'L'Opéra de Paris 1939–1942':

> It is comforting none the less to think that in spite of the despair and distress, in spite of the cold and hunger, in spite of the daily dramas of the occupation, in spite of the terrible practical difficulties of life, the lyric theatres of Paris continue to fulfil their task and envisage the creation of new works to keep French music alive and assure its continuity. (7 February 1942)

It is not at all likely that de Gaulle would have been comforted by the thought of a flourishing theatrical life in Paris.

The paper's attempts to avoid factional bickering are evident in the large amount of space given to relatively non-controversial material: Héléna Rubenstein's page for women, for example, or the advice from chef Louis P. Le Gouy on how best to prepare '*choucroute garnie*' or '*poulet celestine*', or Emile Magne's entertainingly erudite series of articles on 'La Vie et les Tracas d'un bourgeois de Paris sous Louis XIII'. And even the religious column, at first weekly, and then more sporadic, maintained a balance, with Catholic monks Ducattillon and Couturier alternating with the Protestant Pastor Marcel Brun and Jewish Rabbis Maurice Perlzweig and Stephen Wise.

The bias towards de Gaulle and the Free French appears not only in the leader articles, but also in the amount of space devoted to the activities of various local organisations. While the openly gaullist France Forever and Ecole Libre des Hautes Etudes were given regular generous coverage, the Institut Français and the Alliance Française, both suspected of Vichy sympathies, were treated with much briefer announcements and reports. However, the very inclusion of such material reflects the paper's effort to come to terms with the complex and varied groups among the community of exiles. It even gave space to Camille Chautemps, perhaps the most universally shunned of the émigrés, to vent his wounded pride when his application for membership to France Forever was rejected (30 May 1942).

We already know that there was no dearth of writing talent among the French expatriates, and no lack of interesting stories to be told. Tabouis exploited this potential vigorously. The list of casual contributors to *Pour la Victoire* is long and impressive, including Pierre Lazareff, Gustave Cohen, Etiemble, Jean Perrin, Claude Lévi-Strauss, Jacques Maritain, Henri Bonnet, André Breton, Fernand Léger, André Masson, Saint-Exupéry, Alexis Léger, Julien Green, Darius Milhaud, Henry Bernstein, Pierre Mendès-France, Jules Romains – to mention only those who wrote for the paper during 1942. To be sure, many of these authors' more durable pieces were later republished, but it was through *Pour la Victoire* that readers got their first taste of Breton's *Carnet de Martinique* and Saint-Exupéry's *Pilote de Guerre*, as well as of Eve Curie's more topical *Voyage parmi les guerriers*. And with coverage of musical concerts, theatrical events, the life of the French film community in Hollywood and the French presence in the New York art world, the paper was a major cultural forum.

Pour la Victoire's push towards the creation of a unified French position in the United States was, during the first year, unwavering, and with a circulation that rose steadily, from a little over 15,000 in May 1942, to over 33,000 a year later (with an increase of nearly 500 per cent in advertising),[58] it is obvious that the endeavour was not without success. But Tabouis and her colleagues were not the only ones striving for unity. The 'other side' – that is, those who leaned towards Vichy – also preached the same goal, and although they had opposing views about how it might be achieved, there was, for a time, a definite conciliatory attitude. For example, the regular Tuesday and Thursday night lecture series at the Institut Français included de Gaulle's delegate Raoul Aglion and Free French sympathisers André Mayer and Jean Perrin, as well as André Maurois and the Vichy consul, vicomte Jacques d'Aumale. And indeed, the fuzzy nature of the concept of unity being proposed at this stage can be seen in de Kérillis's own call in *Pour la Victoire* on 25 April 1942, which for all its stirring rhetoric and its quest for a transcendent perspective, leaves questions of detail begging:

> For the French who remained faithful to Pétain in the sincere conviction that he would be able to save the national honour, and resist the conqueror's pressures in a dignified way; For the French who came to de Gaulle because he represented in their eyes the magnificent reflex of military heroism and the fierce will of the Nation to fight to its last cartridge and its last breath; For the French stranded between the two camps, unable to choose between the side of the old Marshall and that of the young General, the time has come to come together again, hand outstretched, in the spirit of fraternity.

In fact, we shall see that before the end of the year, the 'hand', if it was held out at all, would be done so with an attitude less fraternal than fratricidal. By May of the following year, *Pour la Victoire* would begin to show more mitigated enthusiasm for de Gaulle, as well as the first major signs of the inner stresses that would eventually lead to the paper's disintegration.

Nevertheless, its first ten months were a glorious period of journalistic achievement in every sense – an achievement moreover recognised by the American papers, which reprinted some of its articles.[59] Through its cultural scope, its stylistic quality, its fine

---

58. Figures quoted in *Pour la Victoire*, 8 May 1943. The OSS gives the circulation figures for 1944 as 28,000, plus a further 7000 in South America (*loc. cit.*, Box 40, 31 October 1944).

59. Aglion, *Roosevelt and de Gaulle*, p. 96.

analysis of political information, and the stress it gave to the positive, unifying aspects of the refugee community, it was – and remains – an outstanding model of intelligent articulateness and responsibility.

During the late spring of 1942, a series of six feature articles appeared in *Pour la Victoire*, entitled 'New York est-il français?' They were written by Jacques Surmagne, the exiled director of *France Presse*.[60] They are a veritable celebration of New York francophilia, and of the huge number of French associations, clubs, churches, hospitals, and cultural and educational institutions that were at the service of the 'old' and 'new' members of the expatriate community. Surmagne plays down any idea of serious division within the group, believing that: 'it should be easy for us all to conform to a mould in which, having each proclaimed our little *mea culpa*, we would think only of tomorrow's unity.' His optimism, in the light of fierce underlying conflicts, which would soon surface, was undoubtedly naive. But his research into the French community was obviously thorough, and took in the experience of ordinary people – hairdressers, chauffeurs, teachers, doctors obliged to re-sit their exams and work as waiters – as much as the more prominent people. The overall impression is that of a group whose hope was in America's strength and integrity, but whose hearts were still very much in France.

He also reminds us that although direct links with France were distended, the continuation of US diplomatic relations with Vichy also meant the continuing possibility of regular correspondence between the refugees and their families back home. More than 60 per cent of the émigrés interviewed by Surmagne were in contact with France, and the Pan American Clippers were bringing more than 15,000 letters a month – censored, of course (by the Americans and the British), but according to Surmagne, in an extremely indulgent manner.

Surmagne's articles are an interesting reflection of the mood of *Pour la Victoire* as a whole during 1942. It was, for the refugees, as for the more established French settlers, a period of relative well-being. With the Americans in the war, there was room for realistic hope for a not-too-distant liberation of the *patrie*. And the exchange of mail between families softened the sense of exile. Finally, there was enough high-quality French cultural activity to restore, very substantially, a sense of national pride. From Pearl Harbor to the

60. *Pour la Victoire*, 2, 9, 16, 23, 30 May, and 13 June 1942.

Anglo-American invasion of North Africa in November 1942 was in fact a time when it was still possible to have the illusion that perhaps, after all, nothing irreparable had occurred in French society. That is what Tabouis and Kérillis believed. We shall see how wrong they were.

– 4 –

Not Under Bushels: The French Mind Abroad

'Our intellectual world has much to learn from the French. In France the integration between life and learning is complete. . . . The French professor would never hide his light under a bushel.'

Alvin Johnson[1]

When he was looking for a way to get to America, Gustave Cohen, the great French medieval scholar whose academic life in France had been terminated by Vichy's anti-Semitic decrees, appealed to his former student, Jean Seznec, who was teaching at Harvard. But the man who was on the dock to meet him when he arrived in New York was Henri Peyre, who had secured Cohen a teaching position at Yale. Cohen was Peyre's senior by more than twenty years, and an academic colossus in France – hugely erudite, with dozens of books and editions to his credit, stretching over the Renaissance, classical and modern periods, as well as in his field of specialisation. Peyre too was already established as a fine scholar, but unlike Cohen, he was one of a number of French academics who had developed an early interest in teaching part of the time in America: after obtaining his chair in Lyons, and following three years as a '*détaché*' at the University of Cairo, he had returned to Yale as head of department in 1939.

The two men were not destined to get on well together: Cohen, in his account of his trip to the United States, fails to mention Peyre's role in his salvation;[2] Peyre, of Cohen, wrote that he was 'full of ideas and plans, full of himself, too, and often criticised here for personality reasons'.[3] The meeting was a symbolic one, however, since both Peyre and Cohen were going to make significant

---

1. Alvin Johnson, *Pioneer's Progress* (New York, 1952), p. 372.
2. Gustave Cohen, *Lettres aux Américains* (Montreal, 1942), pp. 71ff.
3. Letter to the author, 19 October 1987.

contributions to the exile, though in very different ways. Peyre, through his own teaching and through the integration into the American university system of as much as possible of the émigré talent, reached out to large numbers of American students, of whom many would become France's liberators. Cohen initiated what would become the showpiece of the exile's intellectual elite: the Ecole Libre des Hautes Etudes.

Some of the French professors in American universities had been there for a very long time. This was the case of Gilbert Chinard, whose whole university career had been spent in the United States, with posts at Brown, Chicago, Johns Hopkins and the University of California before he went to Princeton in 1937. Chinard's field was the history of ideas, and he had written extensively on Franco-American links, particularly in the eighteenth century and around the period of the French Revolution. Similarly, André Morize, who had taught military science and tactics at Harvard during the first World War, had returned there to stay as early as 1919, adding to his influence by directing the French School at Middlebury College. Jean-Albert Bédé went to Princeton in 1929, to Brown in 1935, and then to Columbia.

In the 1930s a new pattern evolved whereby American universities invited French scholars for regular visits, or even gave them positions that allowed them to alternate periods of work in America and France. Jacques Maritain first visited North America in 1933, and held dual appointments at the Institut Catholique de Paris and Toronto's Pontifical Institute of Medieval Studies. Art historian Henri Focillon, since 1933, simultaneously held chairs at Yale and the Sorbonne, as well as at the Collège de France. And the Swiss ethnologist Alfred Métraux successively occupied posts at the University of California in Berkeley and Los Angeles, then at Yale. Thus, before the arrival of the refugees, a network already existed which facilitated the wide diffusion through top American universities and colleges of some of the best thought and scholarship that the French university tradition had to offer.

This resulted in part from the enthusiastic openness of American universities to knowledge and learning of all kinds. It was this intellectual curiosity, coupled with a deep commitment to academic freedom, that motivated the American Association of University Teachers, in 1933, to condemn Hitler's assault on the German intellectuals and academics, and set in motion fund-raising activities to rescue displaced scholars.[4] Universities and philanthropic

4. Cf. Jean-Michel Palmier, *Weimar en exil* (Paris, 1988), vol. 2, p. 286.

organisations like the Carnegie Corporation and the Rockefeller Foundation were far more generous with their efforts and money than the State Department was with its immigration visas: and their conviction that the refugee scholars would be of benefit to America was in deep conflict with the xenophobic isolationism of official immigration policy. Teaching visas being easier to obtain than visas issued under the established quotas, American universities that employed refugee academics were often saving both learning and lives.[5]

The example of Yale gives an idea of how flexibly and fruitfully the best universities adapted their programmes in order to bring in interesting refugee talent. In the French Department, in addition to Cohen's position, Peyre organised numerous visits, of great diversity. The Catholic philosopher Maritain came to lecture, and so did the surrealist André Breton. And believing that the circumstances demanded a political edge, Peyre also invited Henri de Kérillis several times, although he was far from sharing his conservative nationalism. Breton's lecture was published in *Yale French Studies*, and arrangements made for the translation of Focillon's masterwork of art history, *La Vie des Formes*.[6] Yale had Focillon on its staff as well, although he went to Dumbarton Oaks as a Harvard Research Fellow in 1940–1. Another visiting professor, in the field of political science, was Pierre Cot. (Before the political career which saw him rise to Airforce Minister and then Minister of Commerce and Industry in the prewar French government, Cot had held a chair of law at Rennes.) Cot used his base at Yale in 1941 to write for a wide range of American periodicals, from *Foreign Affairs* and the *American Journal of Sociology* to *The Nation* and *The New Republic*.

The Yale example can be extended to various other universities. Columbia took legal and social philosopher Georges Gurvitch, Jacques Maritain, and two of Louis Rapkine's rescued scientists, the aged mathematician Jacques Hadamard, and the physicist Francis Perrin. Indeed, Rapkine received willing cooperation from many universities: biologist Boris Ephrussi went to Johns Hopkins; Brown took physicist Léon Brillouin; mathematician Claude Chevalley was given a place at Princeton, physiologist André Mayer at

---

5. Cf. Herbert A. Strauss, 'The Movement of People in Crisis', in J. Jackman and C. Borden (eds), *The Muses Flee Hitler* (Washington, 1983), pp. 55–6. Strauss points out that the generosity exercised towards the European professors was sometimes at the expense of American teachers, because of generalised academic overpopulation.

6. Letters to the author, 19 October 1987 and 8 November 1987.

Harvard, and so on.[7] The participating universities were mostly East Coast institutions – which reflects the fact that the exile was mostly an East Coast phenomenon. Only a few of the émigré intellectuals appear to have gone far westward: Etiemble was at the University of Chicago, while Paul Vignaux, a sociologist specialising in Christian trade unions, was at Notre-Dame.

The influence of the French academics could in no way match that of their more numerous German colleagues who, as Jean-Michel Palmier among others amply demonstrates, made an enormous contribution to all fields of knowledge, and to the methods and structures of American university teaching.[8] None the less, the French presence, here as elsewhere, was a real one, and the welcome extended to the French by American universities was more than cordial. Henri Peyre was not sure of the strength of the French impact, but he remained impressed by how admirably well he and his colleagues were treated, despite their turbulent and argumentative behaviour and their endless wrangles.[9]

Just where the first idea of founding a French university in New York originated remains unclear. Raoul Aglion claims credit for it;[10] the historians of the New School for Social Research, Rutkoff and Scott, basing their opinion in part on interviews with Pierre Brodin and his wife, believe that the idea grew out of discussions between Brodin, Maritain and Cohen;[11] Maritain publicly designated Cohen as the originator;[12] Henri Peyre recalled Cohen first airing the concept at the Taft Hotel in New Haven, with Focillon.[13] Alvin Johnson, head of the New School, certainly dealt with Cohen, and considered him to be both initiator and prime mover.[14] There are probably elements of truth in all the stories.

The New School was founded in the wake of the First World War and Alvin Johnson became its director in 1923, with the aim of making it 'an institution for the continued education of the educated'.[15] After 1933, Johnson got funding from the Rockefeller

7. Information from documents prepared by Rapkine for the OSS in 1942 (RG 226 Ent 142 Box 1). Copies kindly provided by Sarah Rapkine.
8. Palmier, *Weimar en exil*, p. 182ff.
9. Peyre letter of 19 October 1987.
10. In his *De Gaulle et Roosevelt* (Paris, 1984), pp. 129–30.
11. P. M. Rutcoff and W. B. Scott, *New School: A History of the New School for Social Research* (New York, 1986), p. 154.
12. Speech at the Ecole Libre inauguration, reprinted in *Pour La justice: articles et discours (1940–1945)* (New York, 1945), pp. 78ff.
13. Peyre letter of 19 October 1987.
14. Alvin Johnson, *Pioneer's Progress: An Autobiography* (New York, 1952), pp. 371–2.
15. Ibid., p. 274.

Foundation for the salaries of some dozens of German scholars, turning the school into a real university. Maritain had lectured there before the war broke out, and it was into that structure that Johnson invited Claude Lévi-Strauss and the Belgian philologist Henri Grégoire.

The proposal that came to Johnson from Cohen for the creation of a regular French university was attractive: Johnson had spare space, he was interested in expanding the New School into a centre of international studies, and he was persuaded that the group of exiled French and Belgian scholars would permit the creation of a permanent institution that would serve the needs of future American teachers of French, as well as create links with the French university world. It could not be *called* a university, because New York State education laws demanded a minimum endowment of half a million dollars for such an appellation. However, staffed by scholars of outstanding eminence, and with a wide array of faculties, centres and institutes, it would be in fact a more than respectable tertiary institution.

Rutkoff and Scott are correct in describing its inspiration as political as well as intellectual, since from the beginning, the intention was to create an institution that could deliver valid French diplomas. This in turn was an indirect way of reinforcing the hand of the Free French movement, by recognising its right to civil power, while denying the same power to the Vichy authorities (who were responsible for forcing most of the scholars, like Cohen, out of their jobs in France). Whether Aglion and the gaullist delegation or Cohen made the first move finally does not matter much, since they were all working towards the same end: Cohen was an unconditional gaullist, and de Gaulle's representatives were anxious to build up support, which was still, in late 1941, at a very low level.

On the other hand, there were others, like Maritain, who were still very uneasy about any *de facto* recognition of quasi-governmental powers for de Gaulle, so that Aglion's account of the difficulties of finding a name for the institution is very plausible. The '*libre*' of the Ecole Libre des Hautes Etudes was ambiguous enough to satisfy all parties, including the Belgians.[16] None the less, de Gaulle did formally commit his National Committee to recognition of the Ecole's diplomas.

The establishment of the school depended on American good will, and on that of Alvin Johnson in particular. The agreement that

16. Aglion, *De Gaulle et Roosevelt* p. 130.

was signed between its organisers and the New School is a demonstration of Johnson's extraordinary largesse, as much as of the extremely demanding and comprehensive conditions set by the French. These included complete autonomy in staffing questions, teaching and all financial matters, and the use of French as the language of instruction. In return for free class and seminar rooms (except for lighting and janitorial and clerical service), the Ecole Libre had to promise only to engage a competent bilingual (French–English) secretary, and to respect a broadly liberal educational organisation and approach, specifically binding itself 'not to propagate or favor any ideology of parties, of groups or institutions that profess or practice intolerance, violence or spiritual constraint'.[17]

For Johnson, of course, the intellectual and moral advantages that the New School – and through it, American education – derived from the agreement far outweighed the services he was providing. Besides, his belief in the universal value of French culture was as strong as that of the Ecole's organisers, who were never, despite their nation's disgrace, shaken in their sense of vocation as luminaries, or in their unquestioned conviction of their right to absolute autonomy. Was this illusion on Johnson's part, or arrogance on the part of the Cohens and Maritains? Johnson admired what he saw as the specifically French achievement of the integration of life and learning. The professors at the Ecole Libre took the superior value of their intellectual and cultural tradition for granted. They were an elite, and they assumed that they would be treated as such. They were right. Obviously they appreciated the generous spirit with which America opened its doors to them, but they would not have expected anything less.

That much having been said, there are distinctions of degree that have to be made between the underlying motivations of those who, like Cohen, were boisterously militant patriots, and those like Maritain, for whom France was essentially the 'homeland of freedom', with democratic ideals and cultural openness that were products of a Christian worldview. Cohen's discourse, as revealed in the speech he gave at the Ecole's inauguration, is full of nationalist ardour, of paternalistic pity for the suffering population in occupied France, and of his own identification as an elect member of an elite nation, which, as the authentic inheritor of Greece and Rome, 'is the surest guarantee of human progress'.[18] Maritain

17. Copy of the agreement from the archives of the New School for Social Research.
18. Reprinted in Cohen, *Lettres*, pp. 109–21.

believed that the real value of the Ecole Libre was in the model it offered of a civilisation whose genius was to gather the diversity of beliefs, ethnicities, ideas and creations brought to it from all directions, and transform them into something universally human.[19]

That Cohen was more political than Maritain is understandable: he did have a serious personal account to settle with the Vichy regime, which had used barbaric anti-Semitic decrees to drive him from his hard-earned Sorbonne position. He had fought for France in 1914–18, had been wounded in battle and cited for bravery by Pétain himself. His destitution was a flagrant injustice, and he knew that those who had pronounced it were France's greatest betrayers. Maritain, on the other hand, was more concerned to stress that France and America were involved in a common combat against Nazism:

> To continue French culture, to the measure of our power, and to participate as much as we can in the common work of the culture of this country – to work in union with the French people who reject the yoke, and to work in union with the people of this country – those are not two self-contradictory things, or even different, for today there is only one and the same combat for the salvation of all and for human dignity, as there is only one threat of slavery and degradation for all.

At the time of the launching of the Ecole, the differences between Cohen and Maritain appeared small, and their viewpoints could seem complementary. In fact, the tension between Cohen's gallocentricity and Maritain's emphasis on Franco–American links was already an embryonic form of the bitter division that would shatter the school's harmony as the conflict between de Gaulle and Roosevelt became more explicit. In the meantime, this was still the exile's golden age, and although during the build-up to the inauguration there were heated arguments about whether the professors would wear full academic regalia (Maritain's idea, rejected by Focillon and Koyré,)[20] the ceremony itself, as glowingly reported in *Pour la Victoire* (21 February 1942), was a model of unity, dignity and grandeur.

It was held in the Assembly Hall of Hunter College, and was

19. Speech at the Ecole Libre inauguration, reproduced in *Pour la Justice: Articles et discours (1940–1945)* (New York, 1945), pp. 78ff.
20. Raoul Aglion, correspondence with Adrien Tixier, 24 January and 13 February 1942. Copies kindly provided by R. Aglion.

attended by 3000 people. After Alvin Johnson's welcome, and a brief speech from the former American Ambassador to Belgium, D. H. Morris, Adrien Tixier read a message from de Gaulle, received by the standing audience with what *Pour la Victoire* described as 'deep reverence':

> On American soil, which with the British Empire is the refuge of humanity's freedoms, this institute will maintain in the world the reputation of a liberally and democratically inspired higher education in French.
>
> I am pleased to see in the collaboration you have been able to establish under the aegis of Free France between scholars and teachers of different nationalities one of the most significant manifestations of our time . . .

But if de Gaulle's mark was on the ceremony, there were others as well. The Nobel Prize physicist Jean Perrin received a standing ovation when he paid homage to Léon Blum and the Front Populaire's commitment to scientific research, and to those scientists in France who were trying to keep the flame of knowledge alive. There was of course no shadow of support in Perrin's talk for any colleagues working for Vichy – on the contrary, he clearly condemned both collaborationism and hedging of bets – but his sensitivity to the Front Populaire and to the people in occupied France evoked a body of opinion that was certainly not uppermost in the gaullists' minds.

The Belgian speakers, too, gave voice to an independent cultural viewpoint, and while the messages from the representatives of Czechoslovakia, Latin America, Poland and French Canada all recognised the centrality of French civilisation to their own ethos, it was very much in Maritain's sense of a vehicle of freedom of the spirit, and defence against tyranny. And for Maritain, as we saw, this was not the prerogative of France alone, but of Franco-American friendship.

The tone of the event was enhanced by the punctuating of the speeches and messages with the American, French and Belgian national anthems, sung by stars of the Metropolitan Opera. But perhaps the most impressive single element was the speech of the Ecole's president, Henri Focillon. Focillon was already struggling against the sickness that would kill him a year later, and was too ill to be present. His words were read by Jean Perrin – who by a sad irony would die himself within two months. The speech is full of good sense, and of the wisdom of a scholarly mind infused with love of knowledge, and above all with a will to new life and the future:

> Our Ecole is not an asylum against the harshness of the times, a retreat to some shelter from the peril. It was born of the terrible drama which is tearing the world apart. The people who founded it and who staff it know from experience that mere intellectual liberalism cannot be sufficient to save our threatened or lost freedoms. . . .
>
> Our duty is to maintain the 'eternal values', but not to take refuge in the cult of some atemporal, abstract France, somewhere beyond the harsh directions of the times. Let us take care not to treat our culture as a memory whose relevance has been dead for centuries. . . . In our eyes, the eternal values are above all the living ones; it is the living quality that we respect and love in the great testimony of the past. . . .
>
> The scourge that threatens the world is not just Servitude, it is Monotony of the mind. To think the same, to create identical machinery, to treat mankind in series, to abolish that precious touch of difference which always, from somewhere, corrects and colours the rigour of unanimity – those are the goals and techniques of totalitarianism.
>
> An infallible principle of decadence resides in distrust of unruliness. We cannot always be sure of inventing originality, but anywhere we chance to meet it, we must enfold the fragile plant with infinite care.
>
> Perhaps these reflections clash with popular definitions of the French spirit, which are based primarily on what people call our aptitude for logic – that is, our spontaneous sense of proper balance and our art of presenting it in the sparest light. In fact, there is much more in the French spirit, and it is because we accept the great diversity of races, languages and ways of thought that France has always been able to fulfil a universal role.

Focillon admired de Gaulle for the precise – and unusual – reason that he had acted boldly and against the routine thinking of the older leaders. It was not so much that he had saved French honour and freedom, but because he was driven by an inspirational and pure courage, strong enough to transform 'the methods, the techniques, and the very drawsprings of action'. Had Focillon lived long enough, he would have been dismayed by the 'rigour of unanimity' that came to characterise the gaullist movement in America. Quite apart from the problems caused within the Ecole, we shall see that even Focillon's own funeral became something of a political battleground.

As launched, the Ecole Libre's structure and theoretical offerings were extremely impressive. It had two full faculties: Arts, and Law and Social Sciences. It had a large Sciences section. It had two centres – one for Latin American studies, one for dramatic and cinematographic arts – and three institutes: Eastern and Slavic Philosophy and History; Comparative Law; Sociology. Other centres were created later. It very quickly attained a high overall activity level: by the end of the first term, over ninety professors were teaching a total of more than 200 different courses.[21]

The problem was a dearth of students. At its peak, according to a document in the New School archives,[22] there were 928 students in 207 courses, which suggests some very small classes, especially in view of the fact that Maritain had up to 180 and Cohen 160.[23] Moreover, the majority of students were not enrolled for degrees at all, but were simply attending out of interest. Mostly Americans, they preferred lectures about French literature and history, although according to Aglion, courses on French law and foreign policy were also well attended.[24]

Often, since the set-up encouraged it, ordinary members of the exiled community dropped in, for the pleasure of hearing an elegantly delivered, good lecture in French. Michel Bloit remembered going with his mother to hear Gustave Cohen lecture on the Middle Ages.[25] Nobody seems to have kept official records of the number of actual diplomas delivered. Aglion, who had a close interest in the school, and who directed one of its centres, opines that it was a mere handful – perhaps ten in Arts, two or three in Law, none in Science.[26]

Another difficulty faced by the school was financial. Apart from the teachers receiving Rockefeller money, the others were not paid at all, at least not initially. Aglion noted that the *Ecole* was launched with a $10,000 grant from the Belgians and $5000 he had raised through private donations, and estimated that it would need an annual budget of over $60,000 to function properly.[27] The London National Committee provided a small but 'useful' subsidy,[28] but for the teachers at the school, their positions offered less in the way of financial reward than in prestige and in the opportunity to further the cause of French culture. Denis de Rougemont, who gave a series of philosophy classes on the social role of games, rules and ritual, remarked matter of factly in his diary: 'First classes at the

21. Rutcoff and Scott, *New School*, p. 155.
22. It is entitled simply 'The Ecole Libre des Hautes Etudes'.
23. Aglion to Tixier 27 March 1942.
24. Ibid., 28 February 1942.
25. Interview with Michel Bloit, 1987.
26. Aglion, *De Gaulle et Roosevelt*, p. 134.
27. Aglion to Tixier 30 April 1942.
28. Aglion, *De Gaulle et Roosevelt*, p. 130.

Ecole Libre des Hautes Etudes. The pay is not enough to live on for more than a month, but it does help keep French culture alive.'[29]

One of the ways it did so was through the Centre of Dramatic and Cinematographic arts, where director Jean Benoît-Lévy not only organised acting classes, but successfully took French plays out into the schools.[30] In the end, however, as a teaching institution, the Ecole Libre needs to be judged less on the number of students it serviced and members of the public (both émigré and American) it drew in – though these numbers were quite respectable – than on the pedagogical image it preserved, and the opportunity it presented for many outstanding professors to continue to exercise their profession with dignity.

The two points are moreover interconnected, because these academics not only believed in their curriculum, they identified wholly with it. They *were* what they taught, and what they taught was a France that for all its present distress, had an irrefutable and continuing claim on the high ground of learning and invention in every field, from the Middle Ages to the most advanced nuclear physics. This point was recognised by President Roosevelt in his response to Alexandre Koyré's report on the Ecole's first term:

5 November 1942

My dear Dr Koyré:

It has given me great pleasure to read the report of the *Ecole Libre des Hautes Etudes* covering the work of its first term.

Wherever French and Belgian scholars maintain purity and the honor of French and Belgian thought, the spirit of France and Belgium is maintained.

The light of French culture has illuminated the world; so long as it is maintained, France cannot die.

France is passing through dark hours. She has done so before, and has nevertheless arisen in strength and confidence.

I believe that even now the hour is beginning to strike when France may once again have an opportunity to resume her place in the world. She will owe a debt to all her children who were not frightened into silence, or misled into assisting her barbarian captors.

French thought was not made for slaves. Those who keep it alive work for the liberation of France and Belgium.

Very truly yours,
Franklin D. Roosevelt[31]

29. Denis de Rougemont, *Journal d'une époque* (Paris, 1968), p. 506.
30. Aglion, *De Gaulle et Roosevelt*, p. 133.
31. Reproduced in *Renaissance*, vol. 1, janvier–mars 1943.

Roosevelt's timing was often exquisite, and this letter must have reached the Ecole Libre at almost exactly the same time as the news of the British–American invasion of North Africa, an event from which de Gaulle was carefully excluded. The American President's praise for the efforts of the school is certainly genuine, but so was his determination to keep de Gaulle in his place. The point would not have been lost on the General's staunch supporters at the Ecole.

Even more than the teaching activity, it was the creation of a community of scholars that gave the Ecole Libre its major *raison d'être*. The main organ of this community was its review *Renaissance*. This was intended to be a quarterly journal, but although it kept to this rhythm in its first year (1943), the material of the next two years appeared only in 1946, and under a single cover.

Renaissance was nothing if not eclectic. Each number of volume I was around 160 pages, and volumes II and III, together, ran to over 500 pages. Articles covered a huge range of intellectual activity, from science and medicine, to South American ethnography, economics, philosophy, politics, history, literature and art. Names like those of Hadamard, Francis Perrin, Laugier, Lévi-Strauss and Caillois stand alongside those of Maritain, Cohen, Focillon and Peyre, bearing eloquent witness to the universal nature of French cultural curiosity.

In addition, *Renaissance* served as a mechanism for marking the extent, and the boundaries, of the intellectual community's identity. It opened its pages to painters like Masson and Chagall, or writers like André Spire and Denis de Rougemont, and it paid fitting tribute to its dead – such as Louis Cons, Jean Perrin and Henri Focillon. Its contributors were not limited to Ecole Libre staff members, but included professors like Etiemble, Chinard and Seznec, who were teaching in other American universities. Its book review section, too, reflected the same variety of subject matter, though one cannot escape the impression, ultimately, of a certain amount of mutual back-scratching. This is especially evident in volumes II and III, where *Renaissance*'s two directors, Henri Grégoire and Alexandre Koyré, like two shepherds mustering their flock, wrote almost half the reviews between them, and where one finds Georges Gurvitch reviewing Paul Vignaux's *Traditionalisme et syndicalisme* with an admiration matched only by the Vignaux review of Gurvitch's *La Déclaration des droits sociaux*.

There was also a tendency – if not an articulated policy – to avoid any controversy that might threaten the community's solidarity. This did not mean a totally apolitical stance: on the contrary, a number of articles included direct political commentary on the situation in France and Europe, with people like Laugier and Grégoire advocating unreserved support for de Gaulle. The journal's emphasis, however, was scholarly, and its main focus was away from the here and now – on other times, on broad philosophical questions, on parts of the world other than where the war was raging. When, exceptionally, it did attack a fellow émigré, it was with the certainty that no division would be provoked. Thus, for example, it twice unleashed quite savage sarcasm on one of the exile's favourite scapegoats, André Maurois. In the July–September issue of volume I, someone writing under the name of Yassu Gauclère poured four dense pages of vitriolic ridicule over Maurois' *Mémoires*, ending with:

> perhaps there is something touching in the spectacle of this 'sensitive' man who, at fifty, still suffers at being disliked, and who, being as he himself declares sincerely modest, can believe in himself only when surrounded by famous names.[32]

In the later volumes, René Taupin dismisses Maurois' *Histoire des Etats-Unis* as flat, superficial and essentially plagiarised.[33]

Maurois was a handy safety-valve for violent passions which could easily – and sometimes did – turn against colleagues or allies. The professors at the Ecole Libre were not simple personalities, and many of them had had more than their share of difficulties in life. Some of them, like Gurvitch and Mirkine-Guetzévitch, were already exiles in France – escapees from repression in Russia or elsewhere who had been naturalised French only to lose everything at the débâcle. Others – and it was the case of Aglion and Koyré – had been engaged in outposts of French civilisation, such as the University of Cairo, with a sense of mission sometimes more fervent than that with which even the most patriotic Sorbonne professors accorded themselves. When one adds to the mix egos as giant as those of Gustave Cohen and Claude Lévi-Strauss, it becomes evident that the degree of unity and harmony achieved in the Ecole was truly miraculous.

The fragility of the balance would not become public until later, but it was always there. A poignant example of it is in the 'Prudhomme affair', which is documented in Aglion's correspondence with Tixier. André Prudhomme was a law professor, the owner of

---

32. *Renaissance*, I, iii, p. 506.
33. Ibid., II and III, pp. 511–12.

Le Clunet, an international law review. He had come to America with the help of the Carnegie Foundation, and had approached the Ecole Libre for work. His wife was Jewish, and being afraid that Vichy might take retributive action against her family in North Africa, he had asked that his name not be put in the Ecole Libre programme. Koyré bungled, and Prudhomme's name was printed – which caused a bitter dispute. Far from being apologetic, Koyré then tried to force Prudhomme to resign: 'One of those stupid personal quarrels that unfortunately happen all too frequently in our colony,' the exasperated Aglion wrote to Tixier.[34]

Many of these intellectuals had been leaders in their fields before the war, or were at least being groomed for leadership, and those whom exile forced into relative inactivity were inevitably frustrated. They wrote, they lectured, they taught, but compared to their prewar lives, their field of influence was very limited: most of them had difficulty reaching beyond the émigré community. Only those who, like Maritain and Cohen, had access to the mainstream of American university life experienced a level of personal fulfilment similar to what they had known before.

In fact, Maritain's war years were the busiest of his whole life, as his biographer Bernard Doering points out.[35] His work with fellow French expatriates went well beyond his courses at the Ecole Libre. His Greenwich Village apartment was a meeting-place for all manner of intellectuals, artists, scientists and their families. Maritain, his wife Raïssa, and her sister Vera, ministered to an endless procession: the exiled monks Ducattillon and Couturier, Louis Rapkine and his wife Sarah, novelist Julien Green and his journalist friend Robert de Saint-Jean, Denis de Rougemont, Alexis Léger and so on.

The explicitly Christian dimension of the Maritains' activity is evident in all their writing, and in others' accounts of time spent with them. In this way, they were clearly maintaining something of the liberal Catholic intellectual tradition of between-the-wars France, defending the idea of a community bound together by spiritual values rather than secular ones, but at the same time recognising the need for fundamental renewal. It was a form of transcendentalism, but one that did not deny engagement with the problems of individual dignity, social justice, and racial or political ideology as they appeared in the real-world context.

34. Aglion to Tixier, 20 January, 30 July, 2 September 1942.
35. Bernard Doering, *Jacques Maritain and French Catholic Intellectuals* (Notre Dame, 1983), p. 168.

Another significant part of Maritain's dynamism opened widely onto the American scene, not only through his professorship at Columbia and his visits to many other university campuses, but through all manner of organisations that invited him to speak – from the Union of Hebrew Congregations to the Latin-American Seminar in Social Studies in Washington. He wrote for *The Commonweal*, and also for *Fortune* and for the *Atlantic Monthly*.

It needs to be said that there was never any self-promotion in Maritain. He spoke as a philosopher, as a Frenchman, and as a Catholic, and each of these aspects reinforced the others in his quest for universality. However, what drove him was a sense of service – to his companions in exile, to his fellow Christians, to his American hosts, to the world at large. He worked unbelievably hard, and seems not to have refused any demand on his time, or any request for his participation.

Maritain's command of English was an obvious advantage, since it widened his access to the American media and public – both his reception of what they had to offer and his opportunity to participate in them. It was often a lack of English that ghettoised the French intellectuals, and constrained them to spheres of action like the courses at the Ecole Libre. It was no doubt partly to overcome this kind of frustration that Boris Mirkine-Guetzévitch felt the need to recreate in the New York of late 1942 the Société d'Histoire de la Révolution Française.

Mirkine-Guetzévitch had reaped multiple international honours as a legal philosopher in the prewar years, and had been an executive committee member of the French Revolution society at the Sorbonne. Furthermore, he really did believe in the ideals of the French Revolution, and held them up as an antidote to the betrayed revolution in his native Russia. But the skeleton organisation established in New York, with the dying Focillon as president, and with no known other members than Mirkine-Guetzévitch and his three other vice-presidents (Maritain, Cohen, Chinard), was little more than a symbol. De Gaulle subsidised it, which was a way of rewarding his American supporters, but he must have wondered what he was getting for his money. The creation of the society shows just how hard some of the intellectuals found it to keep their feeling of community alive.

One intellectual whose experience in America was immensely enriching was Claude Lévi-Strauss. Like Maritain, Lévi-Strauss enjoyed access to more than one community, and he also revelled in the pleasures offered by New York to the *'promeneur solitaire'*. Unlike Maritain, however, Lévi-Strauss, while fascinated to the point of obsession with cultural artefacts of ancient or exotic civilisations, had little interest in the traditions or underlying beliefs of his own. He had grown up in a revolutionary ethos, and although a passionate collector of the old, was utterly committed, intellectually, to new directions in thought and method. In New York, he was as pleased to be a neighbour of Claud Shannon, the cybernetics pioneer, as he was to sign himself 'Claude L. Strauss', to avoid confusion with the blue-jeans manufacturer.[36] Among the different circles in which he moved, three at least had an impact significant enough for him to recognise their formative influence on his post-war thinking.

The first of these was made up of the American anthropologists and those who gravitated around them. Lévi-Strauss's work in Brazil had led to easy contacts with many colleagues – with Métraux, with Robert Lowie, with the great Kroeber from California, with fellow refugee Paul Rivet, director of the Musée de l'Homme, and above all with the Columbia University team – the grand old man of American anthropology Franz Boas, and his disciples Ralph Linton and Ruth Benedict. Lévi-Strauss liked this company and learned from it. He also quite wickedly delighted in the epic hatred that Linton and Benedict had for each other, and in being present at the Columbia Faculty Club lunch at which Boas keeled over backwards and died.[37] The milieu was none the less one of the critical elements in his intellectual growth. It provided a forum, a laboratory, in which new concepts of culture could be evolved and discussed with a freedom and openness, and with a range of data, unparalleled by anything in the old European context.

The second group that Lévi-Strauss frequented was the avant-garde artists – Masson, Calder, Breton, Ernst. From the time that he had shared the boat journey to America with André Breton, another dimension had begun to appear in his thinking, and he would later ascribe to his American links with the surrealists the enrichment and refinement of his aesthetic tastes.[38]

One suspects in fact that the influence was deeper. First, Lévi-Strauss's aversion to the Western traditions of analysis, and his preference for 'primitive' thought that simultaneously considers several aspects of a whole, is closely related to many ideas underlying avant-garde art's emphasis on the present. The surrealist rejection

36. Claude Lévi-Strauss, *De Près et de loin* (Paris, 1988), pp. 46–7. Also *Le Regard éloigné* (Paris, 1983), p. 347.
37. *De Près et de loin*, pp. 57–60.
38. Ibid., p. 54.

of tradition and of the notion of cultural patrimony and evolution, the quest to illuminate new or buried imaginative configurations – these things cannot but have found resonances in Lévi-Strauss's emerging commitment to synchronicity as a methodology: that is, to a decision to study not the way that cultural patterns and mores have *evolved*, but rather what they *are* and how they work in the here and now. Such an approach does not *reject* the past, but it does abolish the notion of development, and it reduces the notion of past to what can be perceived in the surface of the present. The adoption of this perspective was an indispensable step in Lévi-Strauss's articulation of structuralism.

Even more important, however, was his third community, which was hardly a community at all, in that it consisted only of himself and one expatriate Russian colleague at the Ecole Libre, Roman Jakobson. Jakobson was twelve years older than Lévi-Strauss, and of a much more outgoing nature, but the two were destined to become lifetime friends. According to Lévi-Strauss's memoirs, they were introduced by Alexandre Koyré, the Ecole's general secretary. If this is true, it may well give Koyré greater claim to immortality than his work as an historian of philosophy and science, for the meeting of Jakobson and Lévi-Strauss was to revolutionise the methodology and epistemology of the human sciences.

Lévi-Strauss followed Jakobson's lectures with passionate admiration, agog at the Russian's prodigious erudition and linguistic mastery, and sensing that he was living 'a decisive moment in the history of thought'.[39] It was partly through his contact with Jakobson's brilliant analyses of linguistic structures, of phonology, and of the affinities and relationships between different languages, that Lévi-Strauss clarified two paradigmatic notions that he would transform into major principles of his own thinking. The first was a general inspiration based on the role of the mind's unconscious activity in the production of logical structures. The patterns, rules and habits of social life could thus be seen as manifestations of a deeper, less conscious organisation underlying them. Secondly came the fundamental axiom that constitutive elements do not have any necessary instrinsic value, but depend for meaning on their position.[40] This concept allowed the construction of formal models, based on detailed observation, that could serve as keys to open up the hidden structures. On these foundations, and pushed along by

39. Ibid., p. 64.
40. Ibid., p. 157.

his flamboyant new friend, Lévi-Strauss began to write *Les Structures élémentaires de la parenté*. Structural anthropology was born, and with it, one of France's major contributions to post-war epistemology.

Not many of the French émigré academics, as we have seen, were as involved in ground-breaking work as Lévi-Strauss. However, through the efforts of men like Peyre, Focillon, Maritain and Cohen, strong links were forged or maintained between the French and American university worlds, assuring continuity in the free flow of scholarship and new ideas, and reinforcing the commitment to the disinterested pursuit of truth. There was nobility in these efforts, and humility as well. Henri Peyre even found time, for example, to organise baccalaureat sessions with Pierre Brodin at the Lycée français.[41] Furthermore, the impetus given at that time to French studies in American institutions had an enduring effect, establishing a permanent network of channels through which ready access to new developments in French thought and culture was thereafter guaranteed.

Few, if any, of the expatriate professors had that explicit goal, of course, and the broadening of American perspectives was more a product of the openness and enthusiasm of the Americans themselves than in any intention of proselytizing on the part of the émigrés. The latter were more concerned with maintaining their own culture and image. Henri Peyre put it thus: 'We wanted to believe that we would return to France after the war as heroes who had preserved French culture and maintained pro-French sympathies in the United States. . . . We were drunk with illusions.'[42] Peyre, in fact, never went home at all, but remained at Yale, where he was universally admired as the doyen of French studies in America. His judgement here of the intellectuals' wartime endeavours is perhaps a little severe. Heroes or not, the professors worked hard, and their achievements were far from negligible, in their service both to the American universities and to the French community in exile. This was already a significant contribution to the war effort, and a very respectable form of resistance against the repressive ideologies that had engulfed their homeland.

41. Letter to the author 19 October 1987.
42. Ibid.

– 5 –

Making War for America

> Beneath the bleachers in the stands of the University
> football stadium was being constructed, in the greatest
> secrecy, the edifice made of graphite and natural ura-
> nium to which [Fermi] would give the name of atomic
> pile . . .
>
> Bertrand Goldschmidt[1]

Even before the United States entered the war, many refugees,
anticipating or hoping for the eventual involvement, had posi-
tioned themselves for active participation in the American war
effort. These activities took various forms. Some of the émigrés
worked directly for one of the big government agencies – the
Office of War Information (OWI) or the Office of Strategic Services (OSS). Some were involved in development of arms and of
military and political strategy. Others simply joined the US Army.
Of these, some fought out the war in US uniform, while others
were recruited into intelligence operations of one kind or another.
What they all shared was the conviction that the liberation and
future of France depended first and foremost on America, and that
the most effective way of helping their homeland was to put
themselves in American service.

One of the most striking stories is that of Pierre Lazareff. Lazareff
had made numerous visits to the United States before the war, and
as the director of one of France's leading newspapers, *Paris-Soir*,
had developed professional links and personal friendships with
many key American colleagues, such as Waverly Root, Dorothy
Thompson and Walter Lippmann – all of whom were vigorous in
their promotion of moves to increase US help to Britain. Lazareff
had his own British connections, and in addition, two of his closest
French friends in exile assured him quick access to the networks of
influence and power.

The first of these was Raoul Roussy de Sales, the *Paris-Soir* New

1. Bertrand Goldschmidt, *Les Rivalités atomiques: 1939–1966* (Paris, 1967), p. 38.

York correspondent, who had married an American and had been resident in the United States for a decade. Roussy de Sales had cultivated an enormous number of contacts, both French and American, and in all areas of public life. It was he who did the ground work to get Lazareff and his wife Hélène their visas, and he broadened their already considerable entry to New York society.

The other friend was Antoine de Saint-Exupéry, who was scorned and vilified by hard-line gaullists as being soft on Vichy, but who was none the less powerfully connected. His American translator, Lewis Galantière, was to be one of the key administrators of the OWI, and he was also close to (then) Colonel William Donovan, whose nomination as the Coordinator of Information in mid-1941 marked the birth of serious and independent US intelligence operations. From the moment of their arrival, the Lazareffs were invited to dinners, receptions, parties and private discussions that maximised their visibility and influence. Hélène Lazareff had been a top women's editor in France, and she immediately found work as an assistant editor with *Harper's Bazaar* and the *New York Times*. Her husband first took up a contract to write *Deadline*, his best-seller account of France's fall and his own escape to freedom, but at the same time discreetly developed the relations that would lead to his appointment as head of the French Section of the Voice of America – the OWI's propaganda unit.

The French Section's first broadcast took place on 25 February 1942. The beginnings were humble. Lazareff worked with a team of three, doing one fifteen-minute broadcast a day, which was relayed to occupied France by the BBC. Within two years, however, demonstrating the same energy, enterprise and ingenuity with which he was to build the post-war *France-Soir* empire, he had transformed the section into an extremely powerful instrument, with a regular staff of more than 100 working out of centres in New York and San Francisco, creating 350 fifteen-minute programmes a week, and broadcasting world-wide. Nor was the work limited to radio: Lazareff's umbrella also covered the publication of propaganda pamphlets and leaflets, and a film unit. (It was under the latter aegis that Jean Renoir helped with the production of the 1944 *Salute to France*.)

The New York office was responsible for Europe and North Africa, while San Francisco broadcast to New Caledonia, French Polynesia and Indochina. The range of programmes was vast, and the overall complexity of the operation illustrates Lazareff's extraordinary dynamism and his great organisational and managerial skills. As well as daily news programmes, covering military, political, economic and social matters, there were programmes on public affairs, religion, women's questions, labour relations, science and medicine, the Resistance, and so on. There were Flemish-language programmes (as well as French) for Belgium, and Vietnamese ones for Indochina.

A certain amount of direct American propaganda was involved. This was designed in part to familiarise the audiences with the life-style and mentality of their future liberators, but it also did something rather new, by extolling the American way of life not just as something of which Americans themselves could be proud, but as a model of behaviour for the rest of the world.

The main purpose of the broadcasts, though, was to raise the morale of the people in France, and in those other occupied countries where French was still widely spoken; so that in addition to the news broadcasts and political or economic commentaries, there were numerous cultural programmes that drew on the rich talent of the refugee community. Many of the expatriate writers did programmes, and so did Darius Milhaud, conductor Pierre Monteux, singer Lily Pons, and pianist Robert Casadesus. Actors like Jean Gabin, Michèle Morgan, Victor Francen and Annabella also participated (and for them, it provided a useful role that their lack of English had denied them in Hollywood), along with Jean-Pierre Aumont, Jean Renoir and Jean Benoît-Lévy.

Lazareff's policy, as well as to offer a maximum of variety, was also to remain above the often petty political squabbles that went on. His perspective was broad and tolerant, and it reflected the generosity of American idealism as well as some of the thorny complexities of the exile. American figures as major as President and Mrs Roosevelt accepted to speak, and Mayor La Guardia of New York. He also had the Canadian Prime Minister, Mackenzie-King, and numerous other international dignitaries, from Britain's Anthony Eden to Czechoslovakia's Jan Masaryk. It was this kind of context that allowed him to invite both staunch gaullists and those whom the gaullists, for political reasons, considered as their mortal enemies – such as Generals Béthouart and Giraud. But Lazareff did not restrict himself to prominent people: he also broadcast interviews with ordinary French sailors and soldiers, and with French people working in American factories and shipyards. And he even devised a way of sending personal messages from refugees to their friends and family in France.

In San Francisco, Lazareff's directors were René Viallant and Jehanne Salinger, and the regular contributors included Stanford University's Professor Albert Guérard. OWI archives reveal that

Viallant and Salinger did not get on at all well, and a nasty personality conflict seethed until early 1944, when Salinger was forced to resign for reasons of administrative incompetency.[2]

In New York, where Lazareff had direct managerial control, there were no such frictions. Lazareff's assistant, Robert de Saint-Jean, describes him with unmitigated praise. Able to give a frank evaluation of his subordinates' work without giving offence, he was himself a prodigious worker: Saint-Jean recounts one 14 July when Lazareff worked non-stop for eighteen hours, creating and writing no less than twenty fifteen-minute programmes for broadcast.[3] Another regular collaborator, Denis de Rougemont, portrays him as a kind of dervish, whirling through the big newsroom with its thirty clacking typewriters, a pencil perched on his ear, and his forehead stained with ink from the duplicators, handing out documents and 'maintaining a perpetual excitement, whipped up by felicitous phrases, white rages, and contagious enthusiasms'.[4]

In addition to Saint-Jean and Rougemont, Lazareff could rely on a wealth of experienced writers and journalists – among them Philippe Barrès, Julien Green, Yvan Goll, Jacques Maritain and Claude Lévi-Strauss. The painter Amédée Ozenfant, who was also on the permanent staff, noted sourly in his diary that because the team was anti-fascist, the FBI suspected them of being communists and kept them under frequent investigation.[5] There was, of course, rigorous censorship of the material being prepared for broadcast, and Rougemont pondered the long-term effects on his style of churning out, according to the given directives, twenty-five pages a day that had to be both quickly translatable (for censorship purposes) and ready for immediate broadcast. The losses he saw were the elimination of stylishness and elegance, and was not sure whether they were compensated for by the gain in directness and efficiency.[6]

André Breton was another daily worker at the OWI. He had to suffer the FBI investigation, but he avoided any danger of contamination to his style by refusing to write. He simply lent his resonant voice to the texts of others. According to Saint-Jean, the FBI's interest had been aroused by the omnipresence of the word 'revolution' in so many of Breton's titles (*Révolution surréaliste, Surréalisme au service de la révolution*),[7] and whether or not this is literally true, it

2. OWI archives: RG 208, OWI, NC-148, ENT 523–525.
3. Robert de Saint-Jean, *Passé pas mort* (Paris, 1983), p. 314.
4. Denis de Rougemont, *Journal d'une époque* (Paris, 1968), pp. 515, 527.
5. Amédée Ozenfant, *Mémoires: 1886–1962* (Paris, 1968), p. 498.
6. Rougemont, *Journal*, pp. 533–4.
7. Saint-Jean, *Passé pas mort*, ibid.

certainly corresponds to the spirit of the Bureau at that time. There was a huge gap between the intellectual sophistication of the European cultural adventure of the century's first three decades, and American officialdom's often painfully rudimentary attempts to come to terms with the forces in conflict in the European war. Breton bore the indignity with his customary pride and distance.

He was in a sorry emotional state at the time. Alain Bosquet spoke with him in the early summer of 1942, while preparing his special 'Hommage à l'Amérique' number of *La Voix de France*, and Breton confessed 'his solitude, his lack of understanding for this city he hates and refuses to consider objectively'.[8] Anna Balakian describes him as a 'powerful man trapped in a cage, muzzled by a language he could not speak, circumvented by a society he could not understand, caught in economic obligations to a wife and small child he did not have the means to support'. And she points out how this personal alienation was rendered even more painful when his wife Jacqueline left him, taking their daughter Aube, to live with David Hare, the sculptor with whom Breton had launched *VVV*.[9] Amédée Ozenfant often shared the same working hours as Breton at the OWI, but found him absorbed and detached: 'uprooted, lost, sterilised, idle, he took refuge in an imaginary world'.[10] This was confirmed by Denis de Rougemont, who on the other hand enjoyed the opportunities to chat with Breton. Each evening, they spent time together talking, often dreaming up fanciful ceremonies:

> There was one, for example, which was to last for three days, in a huge mansion whose doors had been bricked up, where each guest would bring a person unknown to the others, with everyone in disguise and masks, with verbal exchanges following a rigorously prescribed style, with time regulated, and with the slightest sign of lapse in attitude or language bringing immediate punishment. The idea was to revitalize the meaning of words, gestures, dress, and through them, the meaning of Surprise. . . . An introduction to hieratic life . . .[11]

Rougemont saw this as a compensation-dream – a way for fellow poets to transcend the mechanical limits of their work as propagan-

8. Alain Bosquet, *Les Fêtes cruelles* (Paris, 1984), p. 162.
9. Anna Balakian, *André Breton: Magus of Surrealism* (New York, 1971), pp. 173ff.
10. Ozenfant, *Mémoires*, p. 503.
11. Rougemont, *Journal*, p. 515.

dists, but it looks more like a direct projection of the inner torments of the exiled intellectuals. Breton, in particular, suffered from real distortion of his thought. By the end of December 1944, he was convinced that America would become a fascist state within six months of the end of the war.[12]

Lazareff's colleague at *Pour la Victoire*, Michel Pobers, wrote a ringing leader article on the occasion of The Voice of America's second anniversary. Stressing that it was the American entry into the war that had given the French resistance movements their confidence in ultimate victory, he went on to declare that The Voice of America allowed the French people to establish direct, human contact with the nation that would guarantee their salvation.

> The immense merit of Pierre Lazareff, placed at the head of the French section of the Office of War Information, and of all his collaborators, is precisely that they understood from the beginning the importance of their mission for morale. Psychological warfare? No doubt. Propaganda? Of course. . . . But above all, the 350 weekly broadcasts of *La Voix d'Amérique* have been, and will remain a superb school of friendship, a course in confidence, an example of democracy at work.[13]

Pobers' subtext here, which was brought out by his editorial on the same day, is that he did not believe de Gaulle to be a democratic leader. Even without emphasising that, the dominant message is obvious: without America, French resistance would have been largely futile. However correct that view, it was far from congenial to the gaullist cause. It was none the less closely shared by Lazareff himself, who when he turned up in London at the Liberation, paraded about not in Free French garb, but in the uniform of a US Army colonel.[14] Lazareff's view was that the French in America represented 'a hundred times nothing'.[15]

The major differences between working for the OWI, and working for the Coordinator of Information (and later, the OSS) was that the former was more or less above board and relatively well remunerated, whereas the latter was clandestine and it paid very little. The OSS archives in Washington show a prodigious

---

12. Ibid., p. 551.
13. *Pour la Victoire*, 26 February 1944, p. 5.
14. André Gillois, *Histoire secrète des Français à Londres de 1940 à 1944* (Paris, 1973), p. 330.
15. Expressed to OSS agent Eleanor Clark on 14 February 1944. OSS RG 226 Ent. 100, Box 38, FR 746.

effort on the part of the Americans to take command of their own intelligence operations – the British 'friends' remaining none the less a strong presence throughout the organisation and for the duration of the war. William Donovan's closest American associates in the area concerning France were Allen Dulles, De Witt Poole, John Hughes and John Wiley, but various other agents, such as Philip Horton and Eleanor Clark, would play a crucial role in the flow of information from the French community.

On the French side, distinctions need to be made between various levels of participation. There were those who were unwittingly spied upon or milked for information; those who knowingly and willingly cooperated from time to time with American agents; those who were regular contributors of intelligence without necessarily being paid; those who accepted payment for their regular contributions; and finally, those who were actual agents for America. Of the five categories, the last remains difficult to document, because secrecy has been maintained around the area, although there are tantalising indications that a few very prominent French figures were in this situation.[16]

As for the first group, all significant expatriates underwent scrutiny, even when – especially when – they themselves were informants. Reliability of opinion was checked and cross-checked constantly. One of the startlingly evident tendencies in the almost universal willingness of the émigrés to cooperate with the OSS was their desire to talk about each other, to spread frivolous or malicious gossip, to try to convince the American authorities that their particular viewpoint was the one to be heeded, and that others were consequently suspect in one way or another. Pierre Rodrigues, a journalist on the staff of the paper *L'Amérique*, was an especially unrepentant rumourmonger and purveyor of information that was often unsubstantiated or inaccurate. In early 1942, for example, he claimed that a member of *France Forever* stole a gaullist mailing-list and sold it for 10 cents a name to Mme Lacoste, the co-publiser of *L'Amérique*; he presented the seventeen-year-old son of Philippe and Ethel Barrès as being 'mentally deranged' (Claude Barrès later died a hero's death);[17] and he claimed Pierre Cot to be married to a Venezuelan (while he was in fact married to the daughter of an American who lived in Venezuela).[18] Less wildly, but still with plenty of venom, one finds de Gaulle's delegate Adrien Tixier

16. Files that have not been released by the CIA to the Washington archives include those of Pierre Cot and Pierre Lazareff.
17. Suzanne Blum, *Vivre sans la patrie 1940–1945* (Paris, 1975), p. 55.
18. OSS, *loc. cit.*, Box 34, FR 5.

trying to gain political advantage via the OSS by attacking Gene-viève Tabouis and *Pour la Victoire*, while Tabouis hit back by criticising Tixier's strong-arm tactics and lack of judgement.[19]

Roosevelt had established the Foreign Nationalities Branch of the OSS in December 1941:

> to provide a new field of political intelligence by organising contact with political refugees and with those important groups in American citizenry which were of recent foreign extraction and retained therefore distinctive ties with their country of origin.[20]

From the well over 1000 files devoted to them, it is obvious that despite internal conflicts, the members of the French community, in their overwhelming majority, collaborated in an open-spirited and even enthusiastic way in the OSS's efforts to keep itself up to date with the activities of the key individual émigrés, their news-papers, and the organisations they formed.

Thus Raoul Aglion, for example, who was in charge of de Gaulle's New York office, held regular briefing sessions with Allen Dulles and other OSS agents, and did not hesitate to consider the broad American interests as having primacy over some of the policies promulgated by de Gaulle. Of the gaullist officials, Aglion was probably the most sensitive to the motivations of US policies, and the most circumspect about some of the more strident aspects of gaullism. In particular, he was a firm supporter – in direct contradiction to the Free French position – of the United States' maintaining its relations with Vichy, and he told Allen Dulles, who passed it on to Donovan, that the collaborationists in France would have a freer hand if the Americans were out of the way, and that the US presence was a serious and effective deterrent.[21]

Aglion was not the only gaullist to respond to the OSS's calls for information and advice. Henry Bernstein, Henri Torrès, Philippe Barrès, Robert Valeur, Emile Buré and Tixier himself, all of them

19. Ibid., Box 35, FR 153–154.
20. OSS Foreign Nationalities Branch, Box and Folder List preamble.
21. OSS Entry 142, New York Secret Intelligence, Folder 10, Aglion file, 16 April 1942. In a private letter of 15 February 1988, Mr Aglion states that his position was based in part on the conviction that the Americans were determined to stay in Vichy anyway. To support them allowed him to make positive suggestions about downgrading the US presence from Ambassador to Chargé d'affaires, and about keeping the Vichy Embassy in Washington under careful surveillance.

'unconditionals', were all in contact at one time or another, many of them frequently. And so were Etienne Boegner, who was part of the original gaullist delegation but later fell away, and Jacques Maritain, who was very diffident early on, but gradually became a firm enough supporter of the General to be given the post of first post-war French Ambassador to the Vatican.

Other regular informants, apparently unpaid, were Tabouis and Kérillis, from *Pour la Victoire*, Alexis Léger (who, as we shall see, used every possible channel to convey his negative assessment of de Gaulle's political ambitions), Louis Rapkine (part of the gaullist team, but universally admired for his integrity and selfless devotion to his beliefs), and Suzanne Blum, who gave much energy to Jewish causes and to trying to help the defendants at the Riom trials in France.

Henri Bonnet, future French Ambassador to Washington, expressed his views generously and clearly. For a start, he was one of the few pro-gaullists not to condemn Saint-Exupéry, understanding that the aviator-poet was not to be judged in the narrow terms of party politics. And more importantly, with his background of a decade at the League of Nations, and another in the promotion of world reform in higher education and international cultural interchange, he worked carefully, with the Americans, towards the establishment of a new direction for Europe. He presided over the French Study Centre of International Relations, which was set up in early 1943 as a vehicle to promote democratic and liberal ideas. Bonnet actually approached John Hughes with the request that America might send its recent scholarly and scientific journals to North Africa, so that the intellectuals there might feel less starved of up-to-date knowledge.[22]

As principal agents, Dulles, Poole and Wiley worked directly and closely with those among the French expatriates who had the greatest political, economic and military knowledge: Léger, Aglion, Chautemps, André Istel, Guy de Rothschild and General Robert Odic, former head of the French airforce in North Africa. Among the other agents contributing to the thousands of pieces of information flowing in, many are not identified by name. One especially intriguing one, presumably a female, designated herself only by her fluctuating weight: 'Agent 119 lbs', 'Agent 121 lbs', etc.

However, the person who had the greatest overall contact with members of the French community, especially during the critical

22. OSS, *loc. cit.*, Ent. 100, Box 37, FR 564–568, April 1943.

1943–4 period, was Eleanor Clark. Clark conducted literally dozens of interviews, often several in a day, and her reports stand out by their intelligence and naturalness. Even fifty years later, they reveal a spirit of observation and a gift of depiction that make her work the most reliable – and the most readable – set of insights into the people and situations of France-in-exile. Clark's reports will be drawn on extensively in later chapters, but it is worth citing a couple of examples here. The first is an excerpt of her 12 July 1943 meeting with Paul Vignaux, the Catholic trade union specialist, who was speaking, among other things, of Alexis Léger:

> to whom I gather Vignaux as being quite close, at least ideologically. According to him, Léger has become the bête-noire number one of the De Gaullists, who imagine he exerts a fantastic amount of influence in Washington. They call him a 'traitor', etc. Vignaux said Léger might have political ambitions of his own, but would not try to build up a situation for them; if a situation were presented to him, he would probably take advantage of it. Vignaux said that Léger was absolutely a patriot; he was also profoundly liberal.

The second is extracted from a 16 July 1943 talk with General Odic, just back from a trip to North Africa to prepare General Giraud's visit to America. Clark was astonished by:

> the rather pathetic picture of Giraud which he has built up. Odic is absolutely loyal to Giraud, yet the conclusion left by his testimony was that Giraud is no match for the Fighting French leader, and that he has fallen helplessly between the camps of de Gaulle and Vichy.[23]

Among the French who were in the employ of the OSS were journalists Albert Grand and André Géraud (Pertinax). The latter was also active as a journalist in the American papers. He was syndicated with the North American Newspaper Alliance, and had regular by-line columns in the *New York Times*. Joseph Botton, who had been the General Secretary of the Catholic French Metal Workers Union, was also on the payroll, as were the social commentator Boris Souvarine, who worked with Vignaux on radio messages to be transmitted to the workers in occupied France, Vignaux himself, General Odic and Camille Chautemps. Because

23. Ibid., FR 605, 617.

of his political prominence, Chautemps makes a particularly interesting case-study.

Chautemps met John Wiley in March 1941, through William Bullitt, the former US Ambassador in Paris. Although the two discussed political affairs, it is apparent from Chautemps' diary that in the first months of their acquaintance, Wiley did not reveal his OSS link, preferring to keep the relationship on a more informal, friendly basis. Towards the end of the year, however, when Chautemps' allowance from Vichy was abruptly cut off, Wiley came up with an offer for Chautemps to collaborate with Donovan's team, and with enough money attached to help the Frenchman through his difficult financial straits. By December, he was in full swing: 'Regularly, about twice a week, I send Wiley notes on the most recent topics of European politics that seem to interest him. And each Tuesday, I go to have lunch with him, and we exchange our political impressions'.[24]

In this apparently innocuous fashion, Chautemps became a paid agent of the US secret service. The US motivations in drawing him in were, to say the least, ambivalent. An OSS memo of 22 November 1941 establishes that they were less concerned with the information he might provide than with the embarrassment and destabilisation he might cause if his financial distress and acute sense of futility were not remedied. An alternative to putting him on the payroll was to send him out of the country 'to somewhere he could do little or no harm'. This itself was of course an implicit recognition of Chautemps' potential importance, so that the $500 per month he was given for his services was a sensible insurance policy to keep him on the American side.[25]

What of Chautemps' own motives? It is true that he was desperate for money. Eugène Houdry had already helped him out,[26] but the sudden change of fortune obliged the family to resort to all kinds of cash-raising activities: Chautemps' wife gave piano lessons, one of his sons took on a newspaper round, and he himself drove a school bus![27] It would be wrong, however, to infer that Chautemps was pushed towards the OSS only by financial need. When his Vichy mission ended, he was never quite reconciled to the idea of being a mere private citizen, and could not believe that

24. Chautemps diary, December 1941.
25. Document kindly transmitted by Chautemps' daughter, Mrs H. Samuels.
26. OSS, *loc. cit.*, Box 35, FR 262.
27. Transcript of Chautemps trial, Jules Romains' testimony. Copy kindly transmitted by Mrs H. Samuels.

his political knowledge and experience should simply be ignored and be wasted. Although he did not believe that France could act independently, and indeed that its fate would be decided by the relative strengths of the two conflicting external forces – Germany and the Anglo-American allies – once the Americans entered the war, he was humiliated by the Vichy decision to remain neutral, and from that point on he was openly pro-American.

His decision to serve the OSS was thus in accord with his convictions. Furthermore, when it became uncertain for a time, in March 1942, whether the OSS payments would continue, Chautemps did not hesitate to continue his regular reporting to Wiley. (Ironically, his work for the OSS seems to have been unknown to the FBI, which considered Chautemps as a case of extreme importance, and kept him and his family under permanent, detailed surveillance, with the Washington Field Office instructed to submit weekly reports covering their investigations. They found nothing suspicious.[28]) Chautemps was anxious to serve his country, and like many others, he believed that working for America was the best way to do it.

One group that found it difficult to create a niche in the US war effort was the scientists – those who had been brought in through Louis Rapkine's rescue campaign, or those like Bertrand Goldschmidt who had found their own way to the United States. Rapkine was an early and wholehearted supporter of the Free French cause, and had worked hard to secure a complex agreement between the US authorities and the Free French so that the scientists could work in war-related research. It was an ambitious plan. The idea was first to group the individual scientists under the wing of the Free French delegation, and to this extent Rapkine succeeded. In December 1941, de Gaulle approved the creation of a '*Bureau scientifique*', and accepted the principle that certain French scientists be placed at the disposal of the US services. At the same time, however, he demanded the right to vet each proposal, and this insistence on autonomy would prove to be one of the main causes of the scheme's failure.[29]

In the meantime, on the American front, Rapkine had initiated discussions with the Office of Scientific Research and Development, and the National Defense Research Committee, attempting to get security clearances for the members of his group. And in

28. FBI document of mid-1942, kindly transmitted by Mrs H. Samuels.
29. Telegram of 11 December 1941. Document kindly provided by Mrs S. Rapkine.

February 1942, he drew up an eight-page memorandum[30] addressed to the various US National Defense forces, reviewing his group's history, and proposing his plans for cooperation. The scientists, he said, were:

> psychologically and morally unhappy just to be allowed to go on with pure scientific research on personal research work. *They desire intensely to be put to work on problems of National Defense* . . . with the sole purpose of continuing the fight for democracy alongside the Americans and the British.

He tried to turn to advantage the Free French demand for autonomy by portraying de Gaulle's control over proposals as:

> a sort of military guarantee . . . every one of the scientists would have to be approved, after close scrutiny, by the only French military authorities which are still fighting alongside the democracies.

But there could be no hiding the fact that the memo was an attempt to get the US authorities to give an explicitly gaullist organisation a real and direct role in the American war effort. This in turn would have entailed a *de facto political* recognition of the Free French. This was impossible, since in early 1942 America was still very much committed to its recognition of Vichy's legitimacy.

Rapkine's offer was a rich one, as the outlines of his protégés' competencies reveal. The list includes specialists in aeronautics, nuclear physics, radioactivity, economic warfare, cartography, psychotherapy and wound-healing. And the fact is that although Rapkine's overall plan was not ever realised, some of the scientists, at least, did make substantial individual contributions to war-related research and development in the US. Engineer Robert Alkan worked for the Army and Navy on various aspects of aerial armaments: automatic gunsights, an automatic computer for ballistic deflection, aerial torpedoes. Francis Perrin, later to become High Commissioner of the French Atomic Energy Commission, did weapons-related research at Columbia. The Planiol brothers, André and René, worked on superchargers for aircraft engines. In the medical field, W. Liberson was engaged by the research laboratory of the Hartford Retreat Hospital in Connecticut, to apply his

---

30. Copy kindly provided by Mrs S. Rapkine.

knowledge of electroencephalography to would-be pilots. And more mundanely, Leonide Goldstein taught pre-medical subjects to future American Army physicians at Amherst.

If Rapkine's dream of a united Free French scientific participation in the war was made difficult to achieve by America's Vichy policy, there was an even greater impediment, as Bertrand Goldschmidt discovered. Goldschmidt was a chemist who had been working before the war with André Debierne and the Joliot-Curies on the development of a nuclear chain reaction. As he tells the story,[31] on his arrival in New York in May 1941, he offered his services to the British Embassy, where an arrangement was initiated for him to work at Columbia University, in a team led by the Italian Nobel Prize physicist, Enrico Fermi.

Fermi too was working on the production of a chain reaction, and could see Goldschmidt's potential value to their work. They anticipated using him to explore the purification of uranium. However, the US officials, keenly aware of the significance of the project, were already increasing security, and after a four-month wait, Goldschmidt, on the grounds that no more foreigners should be recruited to the team, was refused the necessary clearance. Goldschmidt was furious about his exclusion, the more so because the three main team leaders – Fermi (Italy), Szilard (Hungary) and von Grosse (Germany) – were all from Axis nations, while he, as a Frenchman, was not acceptable.

The British were more accommodating. Goldschmidt, after his rejection by the Americans, joined Rapkine's Free French group, and was detached to the British Department of Scientific and Industrial Research. The intention was that he would join Hans Halban and Lew Kowarski in England, but instead, after a brief stay in Canada, he was sent to Chicago, at the end of June 1942, as one of the *British* scientists chosen to work under Arthur Compton on a joint Anglo-American atomic project. Fermi and Szilard were part of the group. Goldschmidt's mission was to become an expert on plutonium chemistry.

He worked in Chicago for four months, but despite good relations with the other scientists, the British group could make no progress in terms of achieving an autonomy in their work, and a decision was made to set up an alternative joint Anglo–Canadian project in Montreal. When Fermi's atomic pile began to function, in December 1942, the Americans suspended their collaboration with the British, cutting the Montreal group out of the information exchange.

31. In *Les Rivalités atomiques: 1939–1966* (Paris, 1967), passim.

During an 'informal' visit to Chicago to explain their disappointment, Goldschmidt and his colleague Pierre Auger were told by Compton that the American leaders were now convinced that they were going to possess a weapon that would not only allow them to win the war, but to control the peace. However, Auger and Goldschmidt did not return to Canada empty-handed: Auger had the basic plans of the atomic pile, and Goldschmidt some test-tubes containing the results of his work, including a few micrograms of plutonium. A theft? Goldschmidt admitted that it was a 'political act', and it was certainly one of the critical factors in what would become France's development as an independent nuclear power, and hence in many significant aspects of the geopolitical evolution of the post-war era.

It is something more than a metaphor to say that America's mastery of nuclear power brought with it political ambitions that profoundly and permanently altered its sense of its own identity, its conception of its role in the world, and the climate of trust that had characterised its relationship with its allies – especially Britain, but France as well. Henceforth, the European nations, which had been struggling to free themselves from Nazi domination, would have to fend off another danger, unexpected and paradoxical: namely, potential domination by the friend to whom they had turned to help them regain their freedom and independence.

The behind-the-scenes political machinations to which a few French scientists were privy – Goldschmidt, Auger, Henri Laugier, Francis Perrin were the main ones – were largely unknown to the French émigré community as a whole. Because of his friendships with scientists and with William Donovan, Saint-Exupéry knew about the development of the atomic bomb. During 1942, he was working on *Le Petit Prince* and *Citadelle*, but during his late-night chess-games and conversations with Max Ernst and Denis de Rougemont, discussions sometimes turned around the implication for the future of the 'secret' experiments.[32] Saint-Exupéry also made a personal and significant contribution to American intelligence. As the Anglo-American invasion of North Africa was being prepared, he provided General Spaatz with detailed information on local airports, installations and flying conditions.[33]

One Free French organisation did collaborate with US authorities without problems, but quite probably only because its background and its modest size meant that it fitted better into the

32. Antoine de Saint Exupéry, *Ecrits de guerre* (Paris, 1982), pp. 345–6.
33. Curtis Cate, *Antoine de Saint Exupéry* (New York, 1970), pp. 472ff.

American scene than into the frame of de Gaulle's geopolitical vision. This was the Free French War Veterans organisation. One of its founders, Alfred Jodry, has recounted[34] how this organisation was brought into being in November 1940, when the committee of the existing Federation of French War Veterans decided to break relations with their American counterparts. Jodry himself, although born in Belfort, had been in the United States since 1913, a residency broken only by his service in the French army in the First World War. Like him, all the other members of the Free French War Veterans had fought in the Great War, and all of them continued to think of themselves as French, but as French indissolubly tied in with their American comrades. The organisation was welcomed by American Veterans organisations, and took part in parades alongside them.

After Pearl Harbor, New York Mayor La Guardia was looking for volunteers for an auxiliary police section to patrol the piers of Manhattan and Staten Island at night. Twenty-four members of the Free French War Veterans, led by Henri Laussucq, offered their services. Laussucq, at that stage, was already 60, but that did not prevent him, two years later, from training as an OSS agent for demolition work in France, where he was parachuted in late 1943. He was hugely successful, and in 1945 was decorated with the Silver Star by Truman's own hand, in the presence of General Donovan. Only later did the French award him the Legion of Honour.

Laussucq's choice to serve as an American rather than as a Frenchman was not uncommon. It did not spring from any lack of French patriotism, but resulted rather from the conviction that it was less problematic to serve France through America than by selecting one of the rival factions seeking to represent France. Future Yale Professor, Georges May, followed this path. He and his family had escaped from the South of France in the summer of 1942, and although he contemplated joining the Free French, the bickering within the French community caused him to turn towards the American Army. After basic training, he was recruited into the OSS, where he served first in the Map division, then on the Indochina desk.[35] To choose de Gaulle as a symbol of France's honour was one thing; to join his army could mean fighting against other Frenchmen. Not many were willing to take that position.

For those who had immigrant status, there was in any case an

34. Correspondence with the author, August 1987.
35. Interview and correspondence with the author, September 1987.

obligation to serve, if called upon, in the US military services, though many pre-empted the draft by volunteering. When Michel Bloit finished school in 1942, he was almost eighteen. In December that year, he joined the American Army. His story[36] is that of an 'ordinary' person – that is, someone who had no obvious political or social significance – but as well as offering the excitement of the adventures and dangers he encountered personally, it also allows various insights into the workings of America at war. It will be remembered that Bloit had arrived in New York with his parents, porcelain manufacturers, in March 1942: a Jewish family that had managed to slip out of France just ahead of anti-Semitic persecutions.

Bloit began his military service with three months basic training at Fort Dix. It was tough. (Geneviève Tabouis, during one of her investigative tours, chatted with some young French volunteers, and noted their surprise at the vigour of the training and the rigour of the discipline.[37]) He was still a private when he was sent onto the next phase, which was several months of interpreting and intelligence training at Camp Ritchie in Maryland. Groups were being groomed there for the invasion and occupation of Europe, with intensive language classes and lessons in the history and geography of the various countries. Among those preparing the invasion of France, Bloit encountered the Belgian poet Alain Bosquet – who moreover has given his own characteristically acerbic account of the experience in both fictional and autobiographical forms.[38]

Bosquet found the American approach to this kind of training as naive as it was enthusiastic – which did not prevent him from extracting a lot of enjoyment from it, including frequenting the burlesque shows of Baltimore during his leaves. One of Bosquet's companions was a Bourbon, whose response when asked about his family's occupation was: 'In our family, we are monarchs.' Bosquet's assessment of the value of the training is corroborated to a certain extent, at least, by one of the instructors, the novelist Julien Green, who spent the last four months of 1942 teaching French language and civilisation to officers and under-officers – mainly to avoid having to do the physical exercise programme.[39]

For his part, Michel Bloit, younger and less experienced, took everything as it came. Interpreting was followed by the Signals

36. As recounted in interviews in May 1987.
37. Geneviève Tabouis, *Grandeurs et servitudes américaines: souvenirs des U. S. A. 1940–1945* (Paris, 1945), p. 124.
38. In *La Grande Éclipse* (Paris, 1982), pp. 120ff; and *Les Fêtes cruelles* (Paris, 1984), pp. 173ff.
39. Julien Green, *Journal*, in *Oeuvres complètes* IV (Paris, 1975), pp. 680–98.

Corps, and then, after a promotion to corporal, he was integrated into a batallion due to participate in the Normandy landings and sent by troop-carrier to Londonderry, Ireland, to wait for the day. It was almost exactly a year since he had joined the army.

One night he was called before the batallion commander to meet a captain who asked him if he would volunteer to be parachuted into France for a spying or sabotage mission. He would be in civilian clothes, and if caught would not be covered by the Geneva agreements concerning prisoners of war. Bloit seized the opportunity. It was more than an escape from the barren camp life and the Irish winter, it was the chance for action and adventure that he had been hoping for.

A small group of them, ten in all, were taken to London to be assessed for their aptitude to serve in the OSS, and underwent ten days of intensive physical, linguistic and psychological tests. Bloit was still a corporal, but during that time, they were treated like officers: they were given nice clothes, travelled in taxis, were lodged in good hotels. Through one of his aunts, who worked with the Free French, he had some marginal contact with de Gaulle's London milieu, but was far too absorbed in his own experience even to be aware that his enlistment in the American service might be viewed by some fellow French as less than laudable.

Having passed the OSS selection test, he began training in earnest: in weapons – particularly the bazooka – in sabotage, in espionage. He learned how to drive trains, how to make counterfeit keys, how to open safes. One of his simulation exercises involved spying on a factory in Liverpool, which led to his arrest by the English police, interrogation, and a night in jail – all of which, without his previous knowledge – had been programmed by the OSS.

By the time his training was complete, the Allied landings had already taken place, and when Bloit was finally parachuted into central France, at the beginning of September 1944, it was as part of the mopping-up operations. He had by now been promoted to second lieutenant. Being dropped 40 kilometres from the designated arrival point provided some excitement, but once he had made contact with his commander, his tasks turned out to be disappointingly mundane: acting as an adviser and weapons instructor for a *Maquis* batallion, and helping coordinate the resistance fighters' efforts with those of the American forces.[40] Fate had reserved for him, however, a sweet and ironical triumph.

40. The details of this mission are recorded in the OSS archives: Entry 91, Box 20.

The group with which he was working was surprised by the sudden appearance of a large and powerfully armed column of Germans – about 20,000 men – who were retreating towards Dijon. It seemed appropriate to try and secure the town of Sancoins, but the Germans were far too strong. Communications within the French batallion were poor, and even worse between the French group and the US Army; but they were evidently no better among the various sections of the German column, either. It later transpired that the German General in charge of the column had in fact already surrendered to General Bradley, of the US Third Army, and that the column was following a route, designated by Bradley, to a POW camp site north of the Loire. However, the German colonel in charge of the 5000 or so men around Sancoins sent a message to the Resistance batallion saying that they wished to surrender not to the *Maquis*, but to the Americans. (Whether, as Bloit believed, this was because of the *maquisards*' reputation for brutal treatment of prisoners is moot. It seems far more likely that the Germans would have seen less shame in surrendering to the overwhelmingly superior American forces than to the 'terrorist' representatives of a nation they had scornfully occupied for four years.)

Bloit was the only US serviceman in the area, and an arrangement was made for him to meet the German colonel. By the time the meeting occurred, Bloit had in hand Bradley's text, and the German knew that the surrender had already been agreed to by his superior. None the less, Bloit went through the motions of making the colonel accept Bradley's terms, point by point. Was this excessive zeal, or the sheer exuberance of a twenty-year-old second lieutenant who suddenly finds himself wielding power over an enemy colonel and 5000 soldiers? His real contribution was not the surrender, but his role in cooling the frayed tempers of the freedom frighters, who were keen to engage the Germans in combat. Not only did he prevent what would have been futile bloodshed, but he played a useful part in speeding up the process of the German surrender. On these grounds alone, his mission was a success.

But there was a more important point, and if Bloit himself showed no awareness of it in his official report, it is something that his parents would not have missed when he returned to New York on leave in October: namely the immense, if hidden, justice that allowed a young French Jew, driven from his homeland by Nazi oppression, to return to that homeland and pronounce the terms of surrender to a representative of the spent Hitlerian forces. The German demand of surrendering to the Americans rather than to

the French resistance fighters makes the irony all the more tren-
chant, since the 'American', being both French and Jew, incarnated
realities that the German Army held in the lowest esteem, peoples
consigned to total exploitation or total extermination.

There is a very real sense in which Michel Bloit, and those
compatriots who joined the American Army, can be called French
resistance fighters. Not only, like the members of the *Maquis*, were
they struggling to liberate France from German control, but they
came from families that from the time of the débâcle had refused to
give up or give in, and had continued to assert the democratic
values that had made their French identity meaningful. Under this
broad notion of resistance, moreover, it is possible to group not
only the actual soldiers – the Michel Bloits, Alain Bosquets,
Georges Mays and Henri Laussucqs – but also people like Lazareff,
Breton, Ozenfant and Saint-Jean, the organisers and drivers of the
OWI French section; or those who worked in the OSS to keep the
information flowing, or in the scientific and technological laboratories of America.

It might even be argued that someone like Camille Chautemps,
who so strongly believed in the necessity of the Armistice, and who
was actually for some time in the employ of Vichy, also contributed to French resistance when he became disillusioned by Vichy
policy and turned his efforts towards the allied cause. Did it really
matter that all these people were working under the American
banner, or even in American uniforms?

From a gaullist perspective, it mattered a great deal. Geneviève
Tabouis makes a nice distinction between 'territorial patriotism'
and 'political patriotism'.[41] De Gaulle was not interested in the
ordinary concerns of French people wanting simply to live in peace
in their homeland. Determined that France should not lose its
international prestige and its independence, he at all times maintained the policy that French participation in the war effort had to
be marked as explicitly French, and had to be conducted in a
climate of fully recognised autonomy. This attitude was exemplified in the telegram he sent to Rapkine agreeing to the creation of
the *Bureau des Scientifiques français*: 'The services rendered by
Frenchmen to the United States must be capitalised in the interests
of France instead of being represented as mere individual acts
Stop.'[42]

De Gaulle's position emanated from his vision of France as a

---

41. Tabouis, *Grandeurs et servitudes américaines*, p. 57.
42. Telegram of 11 December 1941. Copy provided by S. Rapkine.

transcendant reality. His own identification with that reality, in the context of France's defeat and obvious powerlessness, was not, initially, taken seriously, either by the US authorities, or by the French expatriate community. His persistence and single-mindedness, however, applied by some of his supporters among the refugee world with ruthless and unforgiving zeal, created bitterness and serious division, while on the wider political stage, he became, for President Franklin Roosevelt, an irritation that would not go away.

– 6 –

Franco-French Struggles

New York has become the *Café de la République* of the
transplanted French. As in Saint-Brieuc or Montauban,
they are divided, even in their misfortune.

Maurice Dekobra[1]

The Vichy Embassy in Washington never enjoyed very congenial
relations with the US authorities, either with the President, or with
the State Department. It was tolerated rather than welcomed, and
the Ambassador, Gaston Henry-Haye, was widely disliked. The
US attitude is implicit in Secretary of State Cordell Hull's justifica-
tion, in his memoirs, of the US Vichy policy, which he builds
around five points:

1 It was a policy common to the President and the State Department.
2 It was privately supported, if publicly criticised, by Churchill.
3 It ensured a steady flow of information from within France, and
   kept pressure on Vichy governments not to submit to German
   demands.
4 There was no credible alternative (de Gaulle not being considered sufficiently 'pre-eminent').
5 It allowed preparation, in North Africa, of the ground for the
   Anglo-American invasion, saving time and many lives.[2]

Although the last point is retrospective, it is clear that pragmat-
ism and expediency were the underlying motivations in the maintaining of relations, and that there was never any hint of approval of
any of Vichy's policies. The Embassy in Washington, as strongly as
the Vichy government itself, was under constant suspicion of
collaboration with Germany, and indeed, its security had been
penetrated by British intelligence even before America entered the

1. *Emigres de luxe* (New York, 1941), p. 330.
2. Cordell Hull, *Memoirs* (New York, 1948), vol. 2, pp. 1192–3.

war – with incontrovertible evidence unearthed of Henry-Haye's zealous support of Vichy's collaborationist efforts.[3]

The 'insider' in the Embassy who betrayed Henry-Haye, and Vichy, to the British, was Charles Brousse, a former French Airforce Intelligence officer who was acting as Press Secretary. Brousse was playing a complicated game. He spied on Camille Chautemps,[4] who was convinced that Brousse worked closely with the Ambassador's aide, Bertrand Vigne, and Henry-Haye himself, to sustain a pro-collaborationist position. Other staff members – including First Secretary Baron James Baeyens and attaché Etienne Burin des Rosiers – had a rather different perception. Henry-Haye was given to womanising, including with wives of his staff, and tended to neglect his official duties, leaving much of the work to Brousse, who communicated directly with Vichy without Henry-Haye's knowledge. For Baeyens, Brousse was 'the most evil element in the embassy'.[5] Henry-Haye acknowledged, in his memoirs, that he had little support from his staff, and his bitter complaints about one in particular, whom he identifies only as 'Tripe', was surely directed against Brousse.[6]

Whether or not, or to what degree, Brousse was a double agent remains impossible to determine. Whatever the case, his underhand activities typify the duplicitous, hypocritical atmosphere that reigned in the Embassy and that had many of the career foreign service staff in constant difficulties with their consciences. A few of these resigned early on: Maurice Garreau-Dombasle on the eve of Henry-Haye's arrival, François Charles-Roux shortly thereafter, and then the top financial adviser, Hervé Alphand, in the second half of 1941. Alphand was a cultured man, who had brought with him to America his collection of Pléïade classics, and the cool, incisive mind of a highly competent career professional. His special task – tidying up contracts made with the United States before the war – allowed him to live in New York, where he frequented liberal, pro-English society, together with people like Roussy de Sales, Charles Boyer, Robert de Saint-Jean and the Rothschilds. He also kept up friendly relations with Camille Chautemps and Saint-Exupéry. He was open about his disdain for Vichy, and entertained fellow dinner guests with his imitations of Pétain and Laval.[7]

3. William Stevenson, *A Man called Intrepid* (New York, 1977), pp. 337–76.
4. Chautemps diary, 27 May 1941.
5. OSS RG226, Ent. 100, Box 35, FR 262, 16 December 1941.
6. G. Henry-Haye, *La Grande Éclipse franco-américaine* (Paris, 1972), pp. 168–9.
7. H. Alphand, *L'Etonnement d'être: Journal* (Paris, 1977), passim. Also R. Roussy de Sales, *L'Amérique entre en guerre* (Paris, 1948), p. 169.

Alphand first began to talk about resignation in early May 1941, in the context of the Syria campaign, in which it seemed that Vichy was moving towards a policy of actual military collaboration with Germany. Without a clear American commitment to join the fight against Hitler, however, he saw a British surrender as still possible, and believed that resignation in those circumstances would be futile. After Roosevelt's 26 May declaration of an unlimited state of national emergency, he made his move, and submitted his letter of resignation to Henry-Haye. When he finally left his post in August, it was with a public declaration of considerable force to the American press:

> It is because I am certain that the very existence of our nation is imperiled that I took the step of severing the ties which bound me to those who are today administering the French State. The duty of Frenchmen who are outside their country and can act is clear: they should join those who are getting on with the fight.[8]

At the time of Laval's return to government in April 1942, US–Vichy relations took a sharp turn for the worse, for Laval was seen as the most pro-German of the entire Vichy political field. The US Ambassador, Admiral Leahy, was recalled, and President Roosevelt, in a radio address of 28 April, made his dissatisfaction clear:

> Recently we have received news of a change of government in what we used to know as the Republic of France – a name dear to the hearts of all lovers of liberty – a name and an institution which we hope will soon be restored to full dignity.
>
> Throughout the Nazi occupation of France we have hoped for the maintenance of a French government which would strive to regain independence to re-establish the principles of 'liberty, equality and fraternity', and to restore the historic culture of France. Our policy has been consistent since the beginning. However, we are now concerned lest those who have recently come to power may seek to force the brave French people to submission to Nazi despotism.[9]

No fewer than five members of the Washington Embassy resigned at this point: they were the first and third secretaries, Baron James

8. *New York Times*, 20 August 1941, p. 18.
9. ibid., 29 April 1942, p. 1.

Baeyens and Etienne Burin des Rosiers; the trade counsellor, Léon Marchal; the code clerk Charles Benoît; and a vice-consul, Henri Fiot.

The case of Marchal is especially interesting in that he had been the man most closely involved in trying to negotiate a US relief programme to help feed and clothe the people of France, whose severe shortages because of the German occupation were generally acknowledged. The British – and the gaullists – opposed any such relief, on the grounds that any supplies would inevitably end up – directly or indirectly – in German hands. In his memoirs, Henry-Haye makes much of this issue, accusing the US authorities of subordinating humanitarian considerations to 'the real or supposed imperatives of a global strategy'.[10] Saint-Exupéry too was incensed by the objections raised to feeding hungry children, and particularly by the likes of Henry Bernstein and Eve Curie, who advocated rigorous application of the British blockade, while living themselves in absolute luxury.[11]

Marchal, in a book written shortly after his resignation, provides a first-hand insight into just how hard it was to get any serious guarantees from Vichy that American goods sent to relieve the French population would *not* serve the German war effort. He himself was anti-Nazi and pro-British from the start, but had been torn between two viewpoints on Vichy: one was that US policy held Vichy to keeping the fleet and colonies out of German control; the other was that the Armistice was Hitler's way of neutralising the fleet and colonies that he could not easily conquer by force. Laval's return marked the end of a year of hestitation, with Marchal concluding that to serve Vichy was, *necessarily*, to serve Germany rather than the allies.[12]

Most of those who defected from Vichy joined de Gaulle, though not all, and it is a measure of the weaknesses of the gaullist movement in the United States at that time that only two of the major defectors, Consul François Charles-Roux and the ageing code clerk Benoît, decided to work for the gaullist delegation in America. (Garreau-Dombasle had acted as a representative for de Gaulle in New York from September 1940 to July 1941, but after fierce squabbles with another of the General's agents, Jacques de Sieyès, he had retired to California to await another call. It eventu-

10. Henry-Haye, *La Grande Eclipse*, p. 232.
11. See Curtis Cate, *Antoine de Saint-Exupéry* (New York, 1970), pp. 443ff. Also Antoine de Saint-Exupéry, *Ecrits de guerre* (Paris, 1982), pp. 205ff.
12. Léon Marchal, *De Pétain à Laval* (Montreal, 1943), pp. 207ff.

ally came, in the form of an ambassadorship to Mexico.[13])

Many of the émigrés, as we have seen, did not find de Gaulle a convincing alternative to Pétain, and even when, in the spring of 1942, the Vichy government began to lose whatever credibility it had had, de Gaulle's movement was in no position to attract any substantial support from the expatriate community. It is now time to examine in more detail just why that was so.

Raoul Aglion describes the painful confusion that existed at the time of his arrival among de Gaulle's supporters and would-be representatives. Garreau-Dombasle and Sieyès were unable to agree on the boundaries of their respective responsibilities. Sieyès was supposed to limit his activity to recruitment, health and welfare, but as de Gaulle's designated 'personal representative', he tended to stray into the political and economic spheres that were Garreau-Dombasle's domain. The two men derided one another, watched by the affable and optimistic – but powerless – Eugène Houdry.

De Gaulle was far from happy about the situation. In April 1941, he sent René Pleven a telegram from Brazzaville:

Where are we in the US? Has Sieyès been able to begin his mission of organising our committees? Has Focillon rallied to our cause? Can't we get Saint-Exupéry on side? What has our air mission achieved? Where are our liaison and health aircraft?[14]

He eventually decided, in May, that he ought to formalise relations between the Free French and the United States, and he sent Pleven on a mission to try to realise that aim. Instead of the basis for the strong organisation he hoped to forge, however, Pleven found himself confronted with the least desirable of situations: the distinguished people he approached to lead the Free French delegation all turned him down, while among those who eventually accepted, none had the stature or the connections to assure any serious level of contact with the Americans. Furthermore, not only did they not get along with one another, their commitment to de Gaulle was less than wholehearted.

In principle, Pleven was an excellent choice for the task. Like Jean Monnet, and often together with him, Pleven was a high-level businessman whose private affairs often led him into doing work for the government, and he had been particularly active, just before

13. See Raoul Aglion, *Roosevelt and de Gaulle* (New York, 1988), pp. 24–5.
14. Charles de Gaulle, *Lettres, notes et carnets* (Paris, 1980–8), vol. III, pp. 303–4.

the war, in helping assure the supply to France of American aircraft and military equipment. In addition, he had been the European head of an American telephone company, so that his personal contacts in the United States were very considerable. And in fact, he was a plausible enough emissary to be able to achieve, in his discussions with the State Department, *de facto* American recognition of Free French control over those parts of the French Empire which had rallied to de Gaulle, and a quasi-diplomatic status for the Delegation that he was trying to establish. He had less success with his fellow countrymen.

His first choice for chief delegate was Alexis Léger, but the diplomat-poet declined, for the same essential reasons that he would maintain his distance from de Gaulle throughout. Although he had considerable admiration for de Gaulle's refusal to accept the Armistice and determination to continue the fight against Hitler, he doubted too deeply de Gaulle's commitment to democracy to lend any support to the General's quest for political legitimacy.[15] In addition, there was probably some truth in Aglion's assessment that Léger was resentful that de Gaulle had been Paul Reynaud's man:[16] it must indeed have been difficult for him to dissociate entirely the General from the politician who had so treacherously dismissed him, on the eve of the débâcle, from the headship of Foreign Affairs.

The English scholar Julian Hurstfield has rightly pointed out that there were deep differences in political vision between Léger and de Gaulle, with the former a committed Atlanticist and the latter more a continentalist.[17] But that is not sufficient to explain the growing passion with which Léger, through his contacts with the State Department, the Administration and, above all, the OSS, would fight de Gaulle to the very end. His real fear was that de Gaulle was reactionary, authoritarian and dictatorial, and that his leadership could only result in the establishment of a totalitarian regime in post-war France. It was that fear that drove him.

Léger's distaste for public appearances was not feigned. He was a solitary, and discreet to the point of being secretive – qualities which even without his political convictions would surely have hindered him from taking up Pleven's offer. At the same time, he

15. Léger made a statement to this effect to the OSS: *loc. cit.*, Box 34, FR 116, 18 May 1942.
16. Aglion, *Roosevelt and de Gaulle*, pp. 186–7.
17. Julian Hurstfield, 'Alexis Léger, Les Emigrés français, et la politique américaine envers la France', in *Espaces de Saint-John Perse 3* (Aix-en-Provence, 1981), pp. 189–200.

was a man of great determination and persistence, and his 14 July 1942 message to his fellow exiles – '*L'An III de l'exil*'[18] – as well as being a carefully worded expression of faith in the French people, calls upon the expatriates never to compromise or forget. It is this attitude that characterised the intense political discussions he held, usually with individuals, and often in the intimacy of his tiny Georgetown apartment, throwing the whole weight of his immense experience, knowledge, and verbal persuasiveness into his effort to help shape a democratic and liberal future for his lost homeland.

After Léger's refusal, Pleven turned to Jacques Maritain, who also enjoyed great prestige in America. The philosopher was more willing than Léger to collaborate, but he was just as firm in his rejection of any direct role, let alone a leading one. Maritain's position would evolve over the period of exile, but throughout 1941 and 1942, although he occasionally accepted to speak publicly in the name of the Free French (he did so, for example, at the funeral of Jean Perrin, who was buried under the French flag and the Cross of Lorraine),[19] he repeatedly avoided any endorsement of political fealty to de Gaulle, on the grounds that de Gaulle's movement had, and should have, no governmental status. In his 1941 *A Travers le désastre*, he made his position explicit:

> De Gaulle's determination has relieved many consciences; at a moment of general political débâcle, he acted like a man. . . . However, it is not after all in one man that we have our best hope, but in the people of our country.

And he goes on to state that if de Gaulle had not acted, and if there were no Free French Committee, the political problem would not be changed.[20]

What Maritain did accept was to serve on a council that would act as an advisory group to the gaullist delegation, and indeed he consulted with Pleven about how such a group might be constituted.[21] Privately, however, he continued to worry about de

---

18. Published in *Pour la Victoire* 18 July 1942, along with many other messages, including those of Roosevelt, Lord Halifax, and . . . de Gaulle.
19. See *Pour la Justice: articles et discours (1940–1945)* (New York), 1945, no. 14.
20. *A Travers le désastre*, (New York, 1941), pp. 116–17.
21. Raoul Aglion has kindly provided documentation of these contacts in August 1941.

Gaulle being a 'new Bonaparte',[22] and in fact, the proposed council never materialised.

As for Jean Monnet, Pleven's third choice, he had not approved of de Gaulle's setting himself up as the head of a French National Committee under British protection, and had told him so in London before going to work for the British Supply Council in Washington. In his memoirs, he acknowledged retrospectively that he and de Gaulle were pursuing separate paths to reach the same ultimate goals, but his decision to devote himself wholly to bringing American might into the war meant that the concerns of the Free French were of limited interest at that stage. He steered clear of both Vichy sympathisers and gaullist supporters in the United States.[23] He was not a personally abrasive man, and when he met with Chautemps in May 1941 – at a time when Chautemps was still in the employ of Vichy – the former prime minister found him amiable. However, he also very firmly rejected Chautemps' advances.[24] He did the same with Pleven, and later, after the allied invasion of North Africa, his advice to Roosevelt was not to recognise the claims of any of the French factions to being a legitimate government.[25]

Pleven toiled valiantly over a number of months, and eventually cobbled together a delegation composed of five people: Jacques de Sieyès, Etienne Boegner, Raoul Roussy de Sales, Adrien Tixier and Raoul Aglion. Of these, only de Sieyès was an 'unconditional' gaullist. Boegner, the son of Pastor Marc Boegner, head of the French Protestant churches, was a close friend of Alexis Léger, and shared his grave reservations about de Gaulle's democratic principles. Like Léger, he was well received by the US authorities, and tended to place more importance on American opinion that on de Gaulle's. He was also a personal friend of Lord Halifax. On the other hand, although he had numerous attachments with top-level banking and industrial interests, he did not fit in easily into American society.[26] Roussy de Sales resisted Pleven's overtures for a long time, and when he finally accepted, it was with a marked lack of enthusiasm: ' . . . because there is nothing else to do, and if I can be useful – as is claimed, though I am far from sure of it – how can I refuse? It's a question of working for France despite the French. A

22. OSS, *loc. cit.*, Box 35, FR 209–210.
23. Jean Monnet, *Mémoires* (Paris, 1976), pp. 171ff, 200.
24. Chautemps unpublished memoirs, 17 May 1941.
25. Monnet, *Mémoires*, p. 219.
26. OSS, *loc. cit.*, Box 34, FR 86.

curious problem.'[27] As a leading journalist and a man of good social standing, he knew the US political scene as well as anyone. He also had the respect of enough of his compatriots to make Pleven's choice seem reasonably sensible: if he could not in any way be classified as a 'gaullist' – and he held the proponents of *France Forever* in contempt – he had at least taken a strong anti-Vichy stand. On the other hand, he was in poor health: Aglion describes him running meetings in his dressing gown and even from his bed.[28] (He was to die of tuberculosis in late 1942, aged 46.)

Aglion himself, because of his diplomatic experience – he had been an attaché in the French Legation in Cairo – was expected to play an important coordinating role. His resignation from his post in Cairo had been based on his rejection of the Armistice and on his loyalty to the Franco-British alliance, as well as on his disgust at the overtly pro-German sentiments of some of his colleagues[29] – so that there was no doubt about his pro-Free French commitment. However, his openness with the British and with the OSS (he reported regularly to the latter) corresponded to a liberal vision of the gaullist cause that was not shared by all, and especially not by Adrien Tixier, who was to become Aglion's *bête-noire*.[30]

De Gaulle, in a telegram sent to Pleven in September 1941, explained the reasons leading to the choice of Tixier as chief delegate:

> He is reputed to be a loyal and solid man. In addition, the French unions – the former CGT as well as the Christian ones – have an excellent attitude in France. Finally, the social question is the big question for tomorrow.[31]

Tixier deserves special attention because he was a bizarre and paradoxical figure: one who flaunted his differences with de Gaulle quite openly, but who also ran his delegation with a brutal determination that angered his fellow delegates as much as it offended the US President and the State Department. Nobody liked Tixier, but many feared him, and he stands out as a person who, by his own example and action, contributed substantially to de Gaulle's

27. Roussy de Sales, *L'Amérique*, p. 216.
28. Aglion, *Roosevelt and de Gaulle*, p. 38.
29. Aglion resignation letter: copy of document kindly provided by R. Aglion.
30. See Aglion, *Roosevelt and de Gaulle*, pp. 72–8.
31. Charles de Gaulle, *Lettres*, vol. IV, p. 80.

anti-democratic reputation in the United States, while at the same time building the machine that would ultimately guarantee de Gaulle his success.

Tixier was a hard-core union man, and at the outbreak of war he was a director of the International Labor Organisation. He had lost an arm in the First World War, and had also suffered head wounds, the after-effects of which made him sometimes erratic, irascible, forgetful. He believed de Gaulle's choice of him was based on purely political calculations: his function was to help gain the support of the trade unions in France to the movement, and also *vis-à-vis* the Americans, to stand as evidence that de Gaulle was not as anti-democratic as he appeared. At the same time, he made no attempt to conceal, in private conversations, his willingness to break with the de Gaulle if the latter proved to be inimical to labour. He saw the heart of French resistance as being not with de Gaulle's National Committee, but with the working classes in occupied France. His service to de Gaulle was predicated on the idea that the Free French movement could be one vehicle to help ensure significant political reforms in the post-war era.[32]

Pugnacious, contentious, Tixier bullied his fellow delegates quite mercilessly, maintaining among them a high degree of anxiety and peevishness. Boegner and de Sieyès found it difficult to work with him at all, and the Aglion–Tixier correspondence covering official business between the New York office and Washington is suffused with suspicion, sarcasm and complaint. Tixier often seemed dreadfully ignorant of what was happening in the New York community, and indeed did not appear to care, but he never missed an opportunity to assert his authority, sometimes in nastily petty ways. When it suited him, he even by-passed the New York office altogether to handle New York business himself. Roussy de Sales, in his diary, marks his distance while bemoaning the personal quarrels and wondering how he got talked into joining in the first place.[33]

In March 1942, Tixier went to London to try to talk de Gaulle into adopting a more comprehensive and realistic political approach, and was disheartened enough by his reception to air serious reservations about de Gaulle with the US Embassy in London. In citing H. Freeman Matthews' report on this conversation, Aglion concludes that Tixier was essentially disloyal to his leader, more interested in his own prestige and authority and in engineering a

32. OSS, *loc. cit.*, Box 34, FR 39, 86; Box 35, Fr 124, 201, 222.
33. Roussy de Sales, *L'Amérique*, p. 262.

post-war revolution in French society than in representing de Gaulle's interests to the Americans.[34] An OSS report is similarly damning: 'His [Tixier's] peronal ambitions are limitless, and he is ruthless in his methods of attaining them'.[35]

It could be argued, however, that Tixier, while convinced enough by the strength and dynamism of de Gaulle's movement to commit himself to its service, simply wanted to bend it more in the direction of the working-class interests and values he represented. To try to exercise pressure to achieve those ends, both by direct approaches to de Gaulle and indirectly through lobbying US policy-makers, seems like normal politics. In any case, in the longer term, however unpleasant and uncouth he was, he proved to be precisely the kind of blunt instrument de Gaulle needed in order to impose his leadership.

At the time of Laval's return, then, in April 1942, when opinion among the French expatriate community massively abandoned support for Vichy, the state of the gaullist delegation was still too chaotic, too fraught with dissension and personality clashes, to constitute a viable alternative for the majority. But it was not just the inconsistencies and tensions within the movement that held people back. The reasons given by Léger, Maritain and Monnet for refusing their participation were expressions of a more widely felt malaise about the nature of de Gaulle's political ambitions. Was he trying to install a dictatorship? Was he trying to set himself up, against the constitution of the Republic, as a government-in-exile? Was he, in any case, really relevant to the struggle against Hitler?

When Jacques de Sieyès returned from a visit to de Gaulle in 1941, he reported to the New York faithful the General's disappointment that of 150,000 French residents in America, only about 5000 had joined France Forever.[36] But at that time, as during the whole of the following year, many of the expatriates, even if they rejected what Vichy stood for, were in the embarrassing situation of being financially and legally dependent on what were, after all, the *only* operational French government services. Institutions like the Lycée français, with nearly 200 students, and the Institut français, directed by Pierre Bédard, could not function without French government subsidies, and of course there were as well all sorts of individuals – veterans, widows, retired people – whose only access to their pensions was through the Vichy Embassy or

34. Aglion, *Roosevelt and de Gaulle*, pp. 74–6.
35. OSS, *loc. cit.*, Box 35, FR 222, 6 May 1942.
36. Documents kindly provided by Raoul Aglion.

Consulates. To make a declaration for de Gaulle was to jeopardise pensions, passport renewals, and so on – the whole range of guarantees of security that France, despite all, continued to offer to its citizens. (It was easier in principle for those whom Vichy had stripped of their citizenship to become gaullist supporters, though Léger's case demonstrates that it was far from an obvious choice.) It is thus not especially surprising that by October 1942, six months after Laval's return, fewer than fifty people had actually registered at the Free French Delegation office in New York.[37]

The Alliance Française presented a different problem. The President of the Federation of Alliances Françaises, Frank D. Pavey, was a staunch isolationist and a fervent admirer of Pétain. Winning him over to the Free French cause was impossible from the start. In New York, the president was Jacques Cartier, the jeweller, who was also head of the French-American Chamber of Commerce. Although of a conservative, and even reactionary bent, Cartier, like his close associate and son-in-law Pierre Claudel (son of the poet Paul), tried to choose a 'neutral', 'non-political' stance, no doubt to keep the trust of their American clients, who would have been largely anti-Vichy; but his conception of maintaining the influence of French culture (through the library and lecture programme of the Alliance) did not require any affiliation with gaullism. And he was apparently right, for the numbers of readers and people attending Alliance lectures remained quite steady throughout the period.[38]

In addition to doubts about de Gaulle's own ambitions, there was a certain generalised ambiguity and inertia that would last as long as the United States kept up its relations with Vichy – that is, until the Anglo-American invasion of North Africa in November 1942. Emigré opinion was always most strongly influenced by official US positions. However, still another set of difficulties grew out of perceptions that de Gaulle's *entourage* in London included dangerous and unacceptable elements.

One of these surfaced in 1942, with the publication in London of a book by Lt.-Col. Pierre Tissier, *The Government of Vichy*, which among other things appeared to be violently anti-Semitic, and to advocate eugenics. Tissier was the comptroller of the Free French movement, as well as the general secretary of the National Coordination Commissariat. The angry response of the New York émigrés, of

37. Aglion–Tixier correspondence, 21 October 1942. Documents kindly provided by Raoul Aglion.
38. ibid., 13 February 1942. Also OSS, *loc. cit.*, Box 34, FR 116, 5 March 1942.

whom a large proportion were Jewish, had Aglion sending a worried letter to Tixier: 'it would be a mistake to underestimate the importance of the reaction that is currently taking place in the New York Jewish communities'.[39]

Did de Gaulle, in fact, have anti-Semitic tendencies? There is no evidence of it, but one of the still-festering wounds of the immediate pre-war period was the violently irrational anti-Jewish polemics of the Léon Blum era, a xenophobia conflated by Céline and others into the racist myth of the Jew as all that was anti-France and pro-war. De Gaulle, who sought the widest possible identification with the ideal of an eternal, transcendent France, did not, certainly, wish to be seen as being too close to his supporters among the Jewish Agency for Palestine, or American Zionist organisations. On the other hand, the taint of anti-Semitism – even as a suspicion – was a powerfully negative force, not only for French or American Jews, but for people like Jacques Maritain,˙ who saw in Nazi persecutions and in the Vichy discrimination laws the epitome of dehumanisation.

Just as telling were the rumours that de Gaulle was being manipulated by members of Eugène Deloncle's *Comité secret d'action révolutionnaire* (the infamous Cagoule), the clandestine proto-fascist paramilitary organisation born in reaction to the rise of the Popular Front, and accused of terrorism, political assassinations and all sorts of occult manipulations of power in the pre-war period. The person most taxed by this fear was Henri de Kérillis. De Kérillis had been an unqualified supporter of de Gaulle's refusal to accept the Armistice, and a man who through patriotism and loyalty continued to write strongly pro-gaullist columns in *Pour la Victoire* long after he had begun to have doubts about the integrity of the gaullist movement. Before the war, he had taken a keen interest in the Cagoule, and having an irresistible fascination for conspiracies, he may well have been the originator of the accusation that de Gaulle was under the sway of former cagoulards. He certainly expressed this view, and by 1945, when he published his *De Gaulle dictateur* (Montreal, pp. 40–6), he was totally committed to it.

He may also have contributed to the OSS dossier which proffers the theory that at the collapse of France, there was a three-way split of the Cagoule, with most staying linked with Vichy, but with some going to become active collaborationists in Paris, and some others going to join de Gaulle in London.[40] The theory is unverifiable, since

39. Aglion–Tixier, 13 October 1942.
40. OSS, *loc. cit.*, Box 36, FR 340, September 1942.

despite the post-war inquiry into the Cagoule and various attempts to lay the nagging questions to rest,[41] the essential secrecy of the organisation has been preserved.

Some of the facts and coincidences are none the less intriguing, and even chilling, for it is indeed true that there were ex-cagoulards not only in de Gaulle's entourage – and notably his Second Bureau chief, Colonel Passy (André de Wavrin) – and not only in Vichy (Joseph Darnand, who was to found the *Milice*; Colonel Georges Groussard, head of the *Groupes de Protection*), but also, and perhaps most importantly, in North Africa, where Jacques Lemaigre-Dubreuil was to be one of the key figures in the organisation of the Anglo-American invasion. There was also Henri d'Astier de la Vigerie, who would be arrested for complicity in the assassination of Admiral Darlan, but released on the orders of his brother Etienne, who was one of de Gaulle's closest associates.[42]

We shall return in due course to some of these figures, and particularly to Lemaigre-Dubreuil, whose activities cut across aspects of the French exile in America. But it is important to stress that among the cagoulards there was never any systematically sustained doctrine or policy. Some were royalists, hard-liner off-shoots of the Action Française (and as such, generally anti-German and anglophobic, but not necessarily anti-American). Some were fascists, supporters of Hitler and Mussolini and a jackboot conception of law and order. Some were reformers, some adventurers, some essentially little more than lovers of clandestine plotting for its own sake.

In other words, the idea of a cagoulard underground masterplan, mapping and controlling all of the major French wartime activities, from London to Vichy and Paris, Algiers and New York, is not a very convincing one, however entertaining. The fact that there were ex-cagoulards in all of these places does not constitute an argument for a coherent plan. On the contrary, their vastly different activities could serve to illustrate the degree of fragmentation within a group that, after all, had only ever come together in opposition to the threat of communist and socialist revolution.

None the less, it would have naive to deny that there was something of a network that crossed the commonly accepted public

---

41. See for example, Joseph Désert, *Toute la Vérité sur l'affaire de la Cagoule* (Paris, 1946); Philippe Bourdrel, *La Cagoule: trente ans de complot* (Paris, 1970); Christian Bernadec (ed.), *Dagore: les carnets secrets de la Cagoule* (Paris, 1977).
42. Yves Maxime Danan, *La Vie politique à Alger de 1940 à 1945* (Paris, 1963); and Renée Pierre-Gosset, *Expédients provisoires: le coup d'Alger* (Paris, 1945), passim.

barriers. Was de Gaulle aware of this? Was he party to it, or manipulated by it? It is not possible to answer these questions categorically, even today. He did, over the course of the war, increasingly select known democrats to advise him and work for him, and he took pains to be seen to be doing so, but it cannot be determined to what degree he was responding to the anxieties of people like de Kérillis.

What is certain is that in 1941–2, in New York, the anxieties were very real, whatever their basis in fact. They grew out of the memory of the hidden corruptions of the Third Republic, and the sense that perhaps the greatest danger for the future of France would come from that troubled past. It is now well known that de Gaulle, more than anyone else, was determined to put the Third Republic behind him; but to the French expatriates in America that message was as yet far from clear.

The absence of any compelling choice meant that much of the community, during 1942, adopted a wait-and-see attitude, not exactly politically neutral, since there was total confidence in the American ability to win the war, and hence a great deal of deference to that power, but on the whole, while sharing the American press's enthusiasm for de Gaulle as a symbol of resistance, the émigrés became more diffident about him the more de Gaulle sought to give his movement a political dimension and an exclusive character. It was a kind of stalemate.

Camille Chautemps, for the preceding twelve months (from April 1941), while still on the Vichy payroll, had been casting around for ways to create a more viable path than what he saw as being represented by Vichy on the one hand, and de Gaulle's supporters on the other. He saw,˙quite rightly, that Vichy was fast losing whatever little prestige it had had, and that the gaullists were no more than a noisy, disorganised minority. There appeared to be a large middle ground to be occupied, and for a politician as well-practised as Chautemps was in finding the centre of gravity of unwieldy political masses, it was a worthy challenge – the more so in that at that stage, he was still very much interested in securing a political future for himself. His failure to do so is a striking illustration of how radically, if perceptibly, the rules of the political game had changed.

Like those of many of his Third Republic colleagues, Chautemps' career had thrived on backroom deals and compromise: it was a basic condition of political survival to have a high tolerance for almost constant changes of government. It was such a survivor's attitude that Chautemps had brought with him to his exile. His personal charm was legend, and his ability to regain lost leadership had been demonstrated over and over again. He made extensive contacts with the exiles, without regard to their political tendencies: he saw Romains, Maurois, the Claudels, the Cartiers, Hervé Alphand, the Maeterlincks, Fritsch-Estrangin, Saint-Exupéry, Léger, Tabouis, Jean Monnet, fellow politicians Pierre Cot and Jacques Stern, Henry Torrès, Gustave Cohen, Louis Marlio, and so on. He also saw leading Americans: Sumner Welles, Robert Murphy, William Bullitt and Roosevelt himself. His idea, which he shared with Professor Louis Rougier, his only really devoted supporter, was that Pétain, with adequate American encouragement, would deliver the French people to the allied cause. It was based on two premises: first, that Pétain had the following of the majority of French people (undoubtedly a correct assessment up until November 1942); secondly, that Pétain was essentially anti-Nazi – a proposition much more difficult to defend, and one indeed that Chautemps himself abandoned when Vichy declared itself neutral at the time America entered the war.

Chautemps' early defence of Pétain, which did not win him many friends, was not the major weakness of his position, however, His real problem was that he, along with a few others – but very few – insisted on defending the Armistice as necessary and salutary. This was the sticking point, and it led Chautemps into sharp arguments with most of the émigrés, even those who, like Tabouis, Léger and Monnet, did not support de Gaulle.

Perhaps one of the best arguments in favour of the Armistice was put forward by Saint-Exupéry, who was personally against it and even stole a plane and crossed over to North Africa in an effort to continue the fight. Once the Armistice was signed, however, he recognised its legitimacy, as he recognised the legitimacy of Pétain's government – while having no respect or admiration for it. (Saint-Exupéry described Vichy as an 'arsehole with the function of excretion', which France had created for itself in its time of disaster.[43]) But he came to be convinced, like Chautemps and Rougier, that had France tried to carry on the war, it would have meant the lost of another two million men, of North Africa and the fleet, the deportation of millions of prisoners and Jews, the complete destruction of a nation and its people. 'Something like the genius of the species rebels against such a futile haemorrhage'.[44]

Jacqués Maritain, when he was writing *A Travers le désastre*, was

43. Saint-Exupéry, *Ecrits de guerre*, p. 430.
44. ibid., p. 431.

not yet a gaullist. However, while he did not question the patriotism, realism, or apparent reasonableness of the political and military leaders who had pressed for the Armistice, he completely rejected that solution. His belief was that the French government should have accepted Churchill's extraordinary last-minute offer of a fusion of the two empires, and continued the fight from North Africa. The essence of French identity, for Maritain, was engaged in the alliance with Britain, and although he acknowledged the fragility of England's military position, he could not countenance France's unilateral decision to withdraw from the combat. This was no simple question of defeat, but a tragic dishonour for the very identity of France.[45]

What Chautemps could tolerate in a context of political realism was for Maritain the cause of deep shame. What Chautemps defended as national survival, Maritain condemned as the destruction of the basic values – liberty, independence, democracy, integrity – without which there could be no worthwhile national identity at all. And perhaps most importantly, where Chautemps was attempting to perpetuate the political process that he had so long and so effectively worked with – a process of shifting coalitions based more on expediency and the management of conflicting forces than on any principles or values – Maritain and the great majority of the exiles were convinced that it was precisely that process, so typical of the Third Republic between the wars, which had led France to its state of inner turmoil, political demoralisation and military unpreparedness.

The Armistice thus became the emblem of that whole recent past, of social division, of political irresponsibility, of the 'peace-at-any-price' attitude that had led to the appeasement of Munich – a past that had to be left behind in order for France to construct its future. The 'middle ground' that Chautemps perceived and tried to occupy during that first year in America was in fact a mirage. His inability or unwillingness to make a clean break with the past – and he did wait until Vichy sacked him, rather than taking the initiative[46] – seems to have sprung from an almost instinctive reluctance to make clear and firm commitments. In so far as he had built his long career on keeping open as many options as possible, and because this involved a large measure of what he frequently called 'discretion' – and his grand mastership in the Freemasons is surely part of the same secrecy syndrome – his course of action in the

---

45. Maritain, A Travers le désastre (Paris, 1942), pp. 65–93.
46. Chautemps diary, 8 July 1941.

United States is quite understandable. Nor is there any reason to doubt his patriotism. But from the point of view of most of the émigrés, Chautemps incarnated everything that had gone wrong, so that although he continued to enjoy friendly relations with many on a personal level, politically, he was an untouchable.

This was made dramatically clear when at the time of Laval's return, Chautemps tried to join France Forever. It has to be admitted that there was no element of gaullist conversion on his part:

> In response to Kérillis's call for unity, I am requesting to be admitted to *France Forever*, not in order to play any role in this band of hotheads, but only to make a gesture of unity in the face of Laval's treason.[47]

None the less, he prepared his approach carefully, through a correspondence with Henri Laugier, effectively the leader of the executive committee. He also wrote to Fred Hoffherr, who sent an approving reply, promising his support when the matter came before the executive committee. The application was rejected by both the political committee, chaired by Torrès, and the general committee, on essentially the same grounds: nobody who had been party to the Armistice could become a member of Free France.[48] Chautemps responded to the rejection with a letter to *Pour la Victoire* that rather poignantly summed up his situation: 'In my isolation, I shall continue to serve as best I can a cause over which nobody has a monopoly.'[49]

Six weeks later, in a hard-hitting Bastille Day speech, Adrien Tixier stated flatly that, on the contrary, there *was* a monopoly: de Gaulle's programme, being anti-Vichy, committed to a republican form of government and to the unification of the internal and external resistance movements, was the *only* one able to represent France, and no other views were acceptable: 'We must gather around General de Gaulle and the French National Committee. Reticence, hesitation, and abstention are incompatible with true patriotism.'[50]

---

47. Chautemps diary, April 1942.
48. ibid., May 1942. There was, in fact, little chance of acceptance, since de Gaulle himself had directly refused to have any dealings with Chautemps: 'We don't want Chautemps at any price. He was absolutely disastrous in Reynaud's cabinet. He is the epitome of the finished politician' (*Lettres*, vol. IV, p. 80).
49. *Pour la Victoire*, 30 May 1942.
50. ibid., 25 July 1942.

To Chautemps and many others, such a claim was outrageous posturing, and indeed, in mid-1942, Tixier had little more than faith and determination to back his grand bid. For that reason, Chautemps can be understood for seeing the gaullists as no more than a 'band of hotheads', and for not realising that Tixier's speech contained the seed of a political death sentence for all those failing to enter the gaullist fold, and especially for those who, like Chautemps, were *ex cathedra* excluded from it.

This also became the fate of Etienne Boegner, who in May 1942 went to London to meet de Gaulle personally, in an effort to clarify the General's policies and the situation of the US delegation. On 3 June, he wrote to Roussy de Sales:

> My first contact with the General was of a rare violence. I was insulted as never before in my life. . . . For a whole hour I was showered with abuse, of me and of those for whom we are working [the Americans]. . . . In this storm, the man appeared not as a soldier, not as a politician, not as an administrator, but as a phenomenon of patriotism, who as soon as one touches on anything French, instantly strikes you with a violent electrical discharge . . .[51]

Convinced that he had been undermined by Tixier, Boegner resigned from the delegation,[52] and thereafter linked up with his friend Léger in opposition to de Gaulle, whom he had come to see as 'an inhuman and impossible leader'.[53]

People other than Chautemps tried to create political groupings broad enough in scope to escape the conflicts that so many found sterile and infuriating. One was the Free World Association, a pro-democratic movement which had grown out of the prewar International Peace Campaign, and in which the principal leaders were Pierre Cot, the former Air Minister of Léon Blum's Popular Front government, and Louis Dolivet, a Romanian Jew who had been naturalised French, and who between the wars had been a communist activist, engaged not only in organising, but in espionage and even terrorism. Neither Cot nor Dolivet were popular with the bulk of the exiles – the former because he was identified with one of the key areas of France's failure to make adequate preparations for war with Germany (namely the airforce); the latter

51. Roussy de Sales, *L'Amérique*, p. 269.
52. Aglion, *Roosevelt and de Gaulle*, p. 46.
53. OSS, *loc. cit.*, Box 38, FR 430.

because, although he had left the Communist Party in 1939, he had acquired a reputation of brutality and unscrupulousness.

The Free World Association, throughout the war, appears to have received massive subsidies from the Chinese government,[54] and this obscure situation was made all the more paradoxical by the fact that both Cot and Dolivet were members of the executive committee of France Forever. It was their prominence there – particularly Dolivet's – that made Maritain, Barrès and de Kérillis steer clear of the organisation,[55] and was one more element in the confused attitudes persisting around de Gaulle. (It also needs to be said that at that stage – during 1942 – France Forever, despite doctrinaire members like Torrès, was not yet entirely part of the gaullist political machine, and tolerated a fairly wide range of opinions. Cot, for example, although he considered de Gaulle as a national hero and the 'living symbol of the resistance', did not accept the ambitions of the London Committee to claim itself as a provisional government, and was extremely critical of de Gaulle's more fanatical supporters.[56] In most ways, in fact, Cot's position was identical to that of Léger, except that the latter decided to remain entirely outside the movement.)

Maritain, for over a year, accepted the position of French representative on another group, Count Coudenhove-Kalergi's Pan-European Union. Coudenhove-Kalergi was a quaint figure, quixotic and idealistic, but a persistent and untiring worker for the creation of a United States of Europe. It was he who organised the March 1942 memorial service for Aristide Briand at New York University, at which Alexis Léger made his one public pronouncement of the entire war. It was an impressive occasion, by all accounts, and in some ways quite prophetic, in that it not only paid homage to Briand's vision of a European federation, but looked forward to realities that would not materialise until a half-century later. French economist Louis Marlio, in one of the major speeches, had particularly far-reaching ideas about the desirability of supra-national thinking in terms of commerce and industry – concepts that strongly reinforce those that Jean Monnet would develop later.[57] None the less, Maritain eventually withdrew from the movement, because he was worried by the number of reactionaries and royalists

---

54. ibid., Box 28, EU 75, EU 384, Box 38, FR 329.
55. ibid., Box 38, FR 306.
56. See Pierre Cot, *Le Procès de la République* (New York, 1944), pp. 365–86.
57. See Louis Marlio, *La Révolution d'hier, d'aujourd'hui et de demain* (New York, 1943), *passim*.

that it attracted: for some, a European federation could only be achieved through widespread restoration of the ancient monarchies.[58]

The Free World Association and the Pan-European Union contained in embryonic form the two essential poles of the debate that would dominate the evolution of the European idea over the next decades. The first was internationalist in orientation and inspiration, and involved the renouncing of national sovereignty as an absolute value. The second had a more traditionalist, more static notion of the nation state, with union being achieved and peace guaranteed through a federal system. The two groups were rivals, but in so far as they were both based on a global vision, rather than on the narrow internecine feuds of France, they did offer a context for some to think creatively and positively about the post-war period.

Most of the émigrés, however, remained within the limits of their national prejudices, and if they did allow their minds to wander beyond their French disputes, it was to adopt the American viewpoint – or rather, to vie with one another for American approval of their positions, and to seek American condemnation of the views they opposed. The conflicts reached all levels of social life. There were restaurants frequented by the gaullists, and many more favoured by the anti-gaullists. An OSS report of March 1942 gives a colourful picture of the French eating scene, with a review of a dozen New York restaurants that catered to everyone from Free French bootleggers, through a couple of pro-Nazi racing-car drivers, to Vichy Ambassador Henry-Haye.[59]

Similar problems occurred with churches. The main French church was Saint Vincent de Paul, on the west side of Manhattan, where the parish priest, Father Piccirillo, an Italian, was hostile to the Free French movement. His two French curates, Fathers Mathiot and Galtier, were given to preaching stirring praises of Pétain. Raoul Aglion, in one of his reports, noted that Father Piccirillo was 'in open conflict with France Forever, and on very poor terms with M. Jacques Maritain, Father Ducattillon and Father Couturier, whom he reproaches for their "political attitude"'.[60]

Like Maritain, the two Dominicans had been trapped in America by the war. Ducattillon had preached at Saint Vincent de Paul for the 11 November 1940 service, and again during Lent in 1941. His

---

58. OSS, *loc. cit.*, Box 28, EU 169.
59. ibid., Box 34, FR 116.
60. Document entitled 'Fête de Jeanne d'Arc à New York' (9 May 1943). Kindly provided by R. Aglion.

major area of interest was the relationship between Christian doctrine and political ideology, and his discussions of Marxist-Leninism and Fascism were both aggressive and intellectually challenging. His November 1940 sermon is a remarkably enlightened, and enlightening, analysis of the war as being essentially about the future reconstruction of Europe: and it urges the French to keep fighting for the liberty of all peoples against the totalitarian tide.[61] It is easy to see why Father Piccirillo did not want him back. In due course, the gaullists of the parish gradually drifted away, transferring their attendance to a French-Canadian church.

There were even rival relief organisations. The Coordinating Council of French Relief Societies, which had started out as a straightforward 'French War Relief' organisation, was run by an energetic American philanthropist, Ann Morgan. She had begun her work in the wake of the débâcle, picking up from the Quakers, who had been very prominent in the early period,[62] and then progressing towards a sensible and efficient coordination of the dozens of groups that sprung up to raise funds for French prisoners, orphans, wounded and so on. Under her sponsorship, and in collaboration with the American Red Cross, large fund-raising events were held – concerts by expatriate French musicians like Robert and Gaby Casadesus, for example, or the highly significant *First Papers of Surrealism* exhibition of October–November 1942. Because she worked harmoniously with the Vichy Embassy, she was branded by the gaullists as being blindly devoted to Pétain, but Tabouis liked her, and so did Maritain, and the 'tireless generosity' she displayed in raising hundreds of thousands of dollars received the unreserved praise of Jacques Surmagne, who certainly harboured no pro-Vichy sentiments.[63]

The Free French Relief Committee grew out of a limitation in the charter of France Forever which prevented it from being used as a fund-raising organisation. Under the chairmanship of Marian Dougherty, it was created in February 1941 with the explicit goal of aiding de Gaulle with money for recruiting and supplies. Within a few months, it had twenty branches, mainly on the East Coast, but also in California. It had opened shops and organised bridge parties, concerts, exhibitions and lectures – and had raised enough cash to buy hospital supplies and refrigeration equipment for Equitorial

61. Reprinted in *La Guerre, cette révolution* (New York, 1941), pp. 279ff.
62. The OSS reports (Ent 106, Box 25) that the American Friends Service Committee, from its six offices in Occupied France, provided 34 million francs worth of help to over 80,000 children.
63. *Pour la Victoire*, 13 June 1942, p. 6.

Africa, and enough donations of material to set up the Brazzaville hospital.[64] A direct window onto the committee's operations was assured by the presence of René Pleven's wife as assistant treasurer. Anne Pleven also worked closely with her husband in developing the structures of the gaullist movement in America. According to Aglion, by 1943 and 1944, the committee was raising around half a million dollars a year.[65]

By that time, with France back in the war, the situation had changed, and even if rivalries had not died away – far from it – there was at least a much more marked sense of common goals, and the two groups worked together on major projects, such as the creation of the field ambulance group *Rochambeau*, which saw nineteen ambulances and fifteen volunteer women drivers sent to the battle zone in North Africa.[66] In 1942, however, feelings were raw, and the divisions still sharp. Camille Chautemps noted with some delight, for its rarity as much as for its irony, a successful benefit evening at the Comtesse de Lémur's, where Claude Alphand, guitarist and singer, entertained both the Vichy faithful and those who had recently resigned from the Embassy.[67]

When the Anglo–American forces invaded North Africa in November 1942, the Vichy government broke its diplomatic relations with the United States. The Embassy in Washington and the Consulates were closed. The diplomats were given the choice of resigning, putting themselves at the disposal of the Americans or internment. In the beginning, about a hundred, including wives and children, took the last course, and they were placed out of harm's way, in the Hershey Palace hotel, in Hershey, Pennsylvania. Henry-Haye, in his memoirs, notes that despite material comfort, the limits placed on their movements made the experience morally trying. So much so that many of them changed their minds and trickled out.[68]

They did not, as a rule, join the gaullists. Robert Lacour-Gayet, Vichy finance inspector for the United States, got himself released on a visitor's visa in exchange for advice and information given to the US authorities. Others, like Charles Lucet, joined his colleague Guillaume Georges-Picot in going to work with General Béthouart's

64. Reports of 9 May 1941 and 6 July 1941. Kindly provided by R. Aglion.
65. *De Gaulle et Roosevelt: la France libre aux Etats-Unis* (Paris, 1984), p. 96.
66. See General Marie-Emile Béthouart, *Cinq années d'espérance: mémoires de guerre* (Paris, 1968), pp. 216–17. Also Suzanne Massu, *Quand j'étais Rochambelle* (Paris, 1969), passim.
67. Chautemps diary, April 1942.
68. Henry-Haye, *La Grande Eclipse*, pp. 311ff.

military mission in Washington. The Air Attaché, Michel Dorance, who would go on to become an important French airforce general, rejoined the African Army under General Giraud.

The few who were left – eighteen by Aglion's count[69] – included Henry-Haye himself, who remained stiffly loyal to Pétain. They were eventually exchanged for US diplomats caught in France and interned by the Germans at Baden-Baden. It was the undistinguished end of an undistinguished mission. (After the war, Henry-Haye set himself up in Portugal, to wait out the *épuration*, and to distill the resentments that would later find their way into his memoirs.)

In a rather burlesque episode, the French-American Chamber of Commerce offered itself as an interim consular service, and sought official US acceptance of this status. There was a certain amount of mischief on the part of Jacques Cartier and Pierre Claudel, since although there was obviously a genuine need to escape the limbo in which the refugee community suddenly found itself, one of their main motivations was to block any claim to consular status by the Free French delegation – which was in all ways better equipped to handle such work, and which had, on a limited basis, been quietly carrying out some consular functions for many months.[70] The State Department cautiously bided its time, declining the offer of the Chamber of Commerce, and not extending further the authority of the Free French.

Saint-Exupéry responded to the success of the North African invasion with an explosion of boyish enthusiasm, in a text entitled 'D'abord la France'[71] – which appeared in the *New York Times* of 29 November (as an 'Open Letter to all Frenchmen'), was broadcast on the radio, and also published in North Africa. Excited by the prospect of being able to rejoin the fight alongside America and Britain, he pronounced Vichy dead, and appealed to his compatriots to forget the past, and to throw themselves wholeheartedly into the liberation of France.

Jacques Maritain responded with an article in *Pour la Victoire* (19 December), entitled 'Il faut parfois juger . . .', in which he criticised Saint-Exupéry of taking a simplistic approach to a complex problem. Unity and reconstruction could not be achieved, he argued, without the clear rejection of those who had espoused the Armistice and the Nazi cause. It was a view that he would express

69. Aglion, *Roosevelt and de Gaulle*, p. 127.
70. ibid., p. 126.
71. Saint-Exupéry, *Ecrits de guerre*, pp. 263–87.

more and more firmly over the following months, as he moved towards becoming a gaullist. In *The Commonweal* of 30 July 1943, he put it very bluntly: 'There is no hope for unity in the French people . . . until the responsible men and the ideology of this [Vichy] regime have been eliminated.'[72]

In the meantime, the polemical encounter between Maritain and Saint-Exupéry was a painful reminder that the deep causes of dispute among the French would not simply disappear because Vichy had ceased to be relevant. Saint-Exupéry's vision was indeed facile, but he was a man of unimpeachably pure heart, and he was hurt by Maritain's intervention: upset personally, because he admired Maritain, and stung by the injustice of the implication that he was sympathetic to Vichy. Had the attack come from a fanatical gaullist, it might have been shrugged off. Coming from the always reasonable Maritain, it produced confusion and a doubt verging on despair.

In retrospect, this clash between two of the good and gentle souls of the exile appears as a watershed. As a personal conflict, it was sad, because two equally likeable and distinguished writers not only made a public spectacle of their disharmony, but were unable even privately to salvage their previously cordial relations. More importantly, in a symbolic way, the falling-out was a sign of the irrevocable diversion of two paths. Maritain, slowly, was beginning to align himself with the direction that history would take. Saint-Exupéry, no less patriotic, could generate no image of a future with which he could identify. He was prepared to fight – he *needed* to fight – but he felt, profoundly, that history was passing him by.

In the short term, he was right. De Gaulle, imperturbable in his certainty that he represented France's permanent interests and that the people of France were behind him, would settle for nothing less than absolute control over events affecting the nation's future destiny. When hindered in the realisation of his aims – whether by the Anglo-American conspiracy to invade North Africa without his knowledge, or by individuals like Saint-Exupéry who dared express doubt or disagreement – he reacted with uncompromising harshness. He was not forgiving, and in what he saw as his most urgent battle – to gain international recognition of his leadership and exclusive right to speak for France – he had no tolerance for dissenting voices among his compatriots.

The machine which he had been carefully building since June

72. Quoted in Maritain, *A Travers le désastre*, pp. 286–87.

1940 was, by December 1942, almost ready to function. Few of the émigrés were aware of its sophistication or its power. Most continued, with the US administration, to think of gaullism as one alternative among others, and not a very attractive one at that. In this respect, Saint-Exupéry was something of an exception. He did sense the awesome might of the gaullists' resolve, and he did understand that in de Gaulle's vision of the future, there was no place for the whimsical idealism of dreamers like himself.

– 7 –

The Gaullist Juggernaut

> . . . there is no French political unity at the moment.
> Why? Because the politicians in power in Algiers do
> not want to reach an understanding with de Gaulle.
>
> H. Alphand[1]

According to Robert Murphy, who was the central American operator in the planning of the North American invasion, the main reasons for not including de Gaulle in the project were fears of leaks in London, and virulent opposition to de Gaulle among French naval and airforce officers, particularly after Dakar and Syria.[2] (The issue was de Gaulle's willingness to engage his soldiers against fellow countrymen, not his success or failure: Dakar had been a fiasco, while the Syrian campaign succeeded.) De Gaulle was enraged, but America's real problem came from its decision to deal with Admiral Darlan, commander of the Vichy forces in North Africa, and a consistently outspoken advocate of collaboration with Germany.

Darlan's overnight change of position, which stopped resistance to the invasion and brought the French North African forces into the allied camp, was not in itself surprising: it was simply a pragmatic and typically unprincipled shift towards where the strength now lay. The American move, however, provoked a furore in Britain and the United States alike, and despite Roosevelt's attempt to calm the situation with assurances that the measure was only a temporary expediency, the anger and confusion would not go away.

Among the exiles, who did not want to offend America, especially now that liberation of their homeland was in sight, there was embarrassment and discomfort. In *Pour la Victoire*, Henri de Kérillis tried an impossible balancing act, proclaiming his full support for American policy, in which he saw France's deliverance,

---

1. H. Alphand, *L'Etonnement d'être* (Paris, 1977), p. 143.
2. Robert Murphy, *Diplomat among Warriors* (New York, 1964), pp. 107–8.

and playing down any idea of tension between Roosevelt and de Gaulle.[3] Even the Free French Press and Information Service (under Robert Valeur), although very reserved about Darlan in its bulletin, was not overtly negative.[4] And as we have seen, Saint-Exupéry's attempt to diffuse the awkwardness brought Maritain's righteous ire upon him.

Without the timely assassination of Darlan, on Christmas Day 1942, it is hard to imagine how resolution might have been achieved. The trial and execution of the young royalist assassin, Fernand Bonnier de la Chapelle, were very expeditious. He was in his grave within eighteen hours of his crime. This speed shocked journalists and the public, and raised a slew of suspicions, but it had the advantage of preventing blame from being laid at the feet of any of the parties who benefited from Darlan's disappearance. Vichy revenge, gaullist skulduggery, a power play by Giraud, or an American plot with Cagoule or royalist assistance? Any explanation was plausible, since all parties gained, rather than lost by the death. A well-planned miracle indeed.

It allowed the Americans to return to their original projection, which was to support General Henri Giraud as the man to lead the liberation army into France. Giraud had become something of a popular hero through his dramatic escapes from captivity in Germany, and since he was out of favour with Vichy, he was free of political taint. His discussions with Eisenhower had been slow, however, and agreement was reached too late for him to be able to establish his command over the French forces before the invasion took place – hence the need for the 'temporary expedient', Darlan.

The American choice of Darlan was of course a choice *against* de Gaulle, and it obliged the latter to engage in political battles on two fronts simultaneously: one that would lead to establishing his primacy over Giraud; the other that would gain him recognition by the US president. Roosevelt's dislike and distrust of de Gaulle had been well prepared by advice received from people like Alexis Léger, and it was intensified by his meeting with André Philip, de Gaulle's emissary, in late November, and his first direct encounter, in January 1943, with de Gaulle at Anfa, in Morocco. Long after de Gaulle had established his leadership among his compatriots, Roosevelt would continue, almost spitefully, to withhold recognition of his legitimacy.

3. *Pour la Victoire*, 19, 21, 28 November, 19, 26 December 1942.
4. *Free France*, vol. 2, no. 12, 16 December 1942. Collection held by the Institut Charles de Gaulle, Paris.

Giraud quickly set up a mission in Washington, led by General Marie-Emile Béthouart. Béthouart was an obliging and practical man, whose primary task was to work out the details of equipping and supplying the reborn French Army, but inevitably he acquired something of an ambassadorial status, since Giraud, as well as being Commander-in-Chief, had been given *de facto* American recognition as the representative of French interests.

Equally inevitably, as long as there were frictions between Giraud and de Gaulle, they would be reflected among their representatives in the United States. With Vichy out of the way, the potential for understanding was obviously much greater than before, and the desire for a unified front among the exiles grew dramatically now that France had once again taken its place as a combattant in the war. For the gaullist machine in America, however, unity meant only one thing: complete and exclusive control of as many elements of the exile community as possible, and the elimination of those organisations or individuals who could not, or would not be brought into line. It is time now to look at that machine in more detail.

Adrien Tixier ran it from Washington, with a slippery tongue and an iron hand. By the end of 1942, only two of the original delegates selected by Pleven remained: Tixier and Aglion. After Boegner's resignation, de Sieyès left to join de Gaulle, and Roussy de Sales finally succumbed to his long illness. Tixier had succeeded, in the meantime, in having himself nominated as sole Delegate, and had organised the Delegation into three offices: the head office in Washington, where Tixier was assisted by Philippe Baudet for affairs of state, and where the military mission was situated; a skeleton office in San Francisco, where the Counsellor, Boris Eliacheff, rapidly fell out with Paul Verdier, the local president of France Forever and natural leader of the French community, and appears to have played no significant role;[5] and finally, a large office in New York, headed by Raoul Aglion as Counsellor, and with extensive activities in purchasing, treasury matters, press and information and most matters concerning the émigrés.

As has already been intimated, there were sharp differences of philosophy and style between Tixier and Aglion. The former operated according to an inflexible approach based on centralised and authoritarian decision-making, and he was uncouth enough to offend almost every US official with whom he came in contact. Indispensable, because of his strong union links, to de Gaulle's

5. OSS RG 226, Ent 100, Box 38, FR 621, 26 July 1943.

dealings with the internal resistance movement in France, he was not hesitant about bending, or even contradicting de Gaulle's own policies if, in his view, it strengthened the movement's position in America. He handled his work like a tough union boss pushing a log of claims, rather than as a diplomat.

Aglion brings up a number of instances where he considers Tixier to have been actually disloyal, by altering de Gaulle's messages to the US authorities or delaying their delivery; and he suggests that Tixier may have been protecting his options in case, at the liberation, de Gaulle was rejected by a revolutionary upsurge from within France.[6] On the other hand, Hervé Alphand, who had to deal with Tixier over various weighty matters – from gaining US Treasury support for Free French operations to seeking Free French admission to the United Nations – clearly respected him and his work.[7] That he was a difficult man and a ruthless politician, almost everyone seems to have agreed. But that he was in any significant or general way unfaithful to de Gaulle is harder to believe.

For his own part, Aglion, with his diplomatic background and more generous spirit, had a conciliatory attitude that projected gaullism as something inclusive rather than exclusive. He was irritated and embarrassed by Tixier's gaucheness, and infuriated by his unannounced incursions into the territory that he, Aglion, had been charged with administering. In fact, much of Aglion's work went well beyond New York, since his brief included relations with the expatriate community and its various associations and institutions, and supervision of the press and information service, in addition to the administration of what were virtually full consular services. By early 1943, the staff of the New York office numbered over fifty.[8]

Before the collapse of the Vichy-controlled structures in America, it was sometimes a question of wooing some of the more conservative elements in the expatriate group into the gaullist orbit – of establishing friendly working relations, for example, with the Alliance Française, the Institut or the Lycée. More often, it meant encouraging, through advice or financial help, initiatives friendly to the Free French, like the creation of the Ecole Libre des Hautes Etudes, or cultivating individuals like the gallery-owner Paul Rosenberg, who not only gave a hospital plane and $6000 to Free French

---

6. R. Aglion, *Roosevelt and de Gaulle* (New York, 1988), pp. 72–8.
7. Alphand, *L'Etonnement d'être*, pp. 141, 144.
8. Staff list kindly provided by R. Aglion.

Relief, but had his whole family working in one way or another for the cause. There were plenty of problems: one was the 14 July celebrations in Chicago, where the Vichy Consul was warmly fêted by members of France Forever; another was the good will of those like Colonel Longin-Spindler, who in September 1942 was attempting to raise a French Legion in New Orleans to fight with the Americans:

> I consider, the Colonel proclaimed, that there is at present only one useful way to serve France: 'killing some Krauts' as Foch used to say. And because America has the intention of killing some Krauts, we must help her do so.[9]

New York was not just where most of the refugees lived, it was the major cultural and social centre of the nation, and much more pivotal in terms of availability of information in many ways than Washington. Aglion was however obliged to report to Tixier, which he did almost daily and in exemplary fashion. He moreover adopted a broad interpretation of his tasks, and frequently made attempts to get Tixier to do likewise. But Tixier was not interested in advice: he wanted control, and an uninterrupted flow of intelligence.

In order to achieve the control he desired, he used the classic methods of limiting Aglion's access to information about what was going on in London and North Africa, he cut across the New York lines of command, and he kept a cripplingly strict hold over Aglion's movements and disbursements. Aglion complained about this treatment, both to Tixier and directly to London, but he and his staff none the less played the game according to Tixier's rules, and the carefully detailed reports and commentaries on all aspects of the office's work were regularly dispatched to Washington. It must have been extremely frustrating for Aglion, given the real importance of much of his own work, to have his status so constantly and so blatantly undermined by the bullying Tixier, and it must have been annoying to be often reduced to the role of mere messenger-boy: as, for example, when Claude Lévi-Strauss would come to ask him to arrange meetings with Tixier so that he could transmit confidential intelligence about Vichy sympathies in South

---

9. Aglion–Tixier correspondence 20 September 1942. Documents kindly provided by R. Aglion.

America.[10] And indeed, Aglion's correspondence with Tixier occasionally reveals an underlying testiness.

As a representative of de Gaulle, however, Aglion presented a human face that the movement would have been hard-pressed to do without. He was liked and respected by his staff, by the members of the exile community, and by the US officials with whom he dealt. He played a vital role in finding grounds of harmony and unity in the Ecole Libre and France Forever, as well as among the always fractious high-profile individuals among the émigrés – Tabouis, de Kérillis, Maritain, Cohen, etc. He was, in fact, a paradoxical complement, on the level of grass-roots contact, to what Tixier was trying to do among the leading politicians: namely to persuade Americans and exiles alike that de Gaulle was neither marginal nor dictatorial, but a committed republican leader genuinely representative of the French people. In short, Aglion was a reassuring presence. When, in late 1943, he was forced to transfer to Washington, a number of New York intellectuals – Maritain, Mirkine-Guetzévitch and Koyré – cabled de Gaulle to request that he remain in New York.[11]

The arrival of the Béthouart mission provided a channel through which the Americans could officially encourage French recruits to join Giraud's forces in North Africa. A small number of infantrymen were formed into a US-trained legion at Fort Benning, a couple of contingents of about a hundred each. They wore American uniforms with French badges on the shoulder. Béthouart paid them an official visit with considerable pride, seeing in them symbols of the restoration of France's honour as a fighting nation.[12] Airforce and navy collaboration were on a larger scale. Over 2000 French airmen were brought to America to train on the new planes that the United States was producing for their use, and a significant number of French naval vessels were repaired and rearmed for combat in East Coast ports. (Fritsch-Estrangin notes how popular the sailors were – there were a hundred Franco-American marriages in 1943. But the French ships were also responsible for the organisation and escort of 140 convoys in the first five months of 1944.[13])

Among the émigrés, some availed themselves promptly of the opportunity to demonstrate that their refusal to join de Gaulle had

10. Ibid., 23 January 1942, 26 January 1942.
11. Cable of 4 October 1942. Copy provided by R. Aglion.
12. Marie-Emile Béthouart, *Cinq Années d'espérance: mémoires de guerre* (Paris, 1968), p. 203.
13. Guy Fritsch-Estrangin, *New York entre de Gaulle et Pétain: les Français aux Etats-unis de 1940 à 1946*, Paris, 1969, p. 215.

not been motivated by an unwillingness to fight for the allied cause. André Maurois took up his captain's commission again, serving as a liaison officer with the expeditionary corps in Italy. General Odic headed to Algiers to report to Giraud, and as soon as he could get a passage, Saint-Exupéry also went to North Africa. At 42, Saint-Exupéry was over-age for fighting missions, but as well as courting Béthouart, he used all his influence with prominent American military figures, like General Doolittle, to get around the rules. Later, after he had demonstrated in several near-misses how dramatically his flying competence had fallen away, he called on his old friend William Donovan to get the ban on his flying lifted.[14] Camille Chautemps did not have such powerful contacts. He, too, tried to join Giraud, but was turned away because of his age – though at 47, he was the same age as Maurois.

None of this activity was satisfactory to the gaullist camp. It had its own recruiting office in New York (Béthouart had opened his just a few doors further along Fifth Avenue), and it was moving determinedly to strengthen its power base. Béthouart tried to get Tixier to create a united front, but there was no denying the competition, or the clear partiality of the US administration. Even Béthouart notes that his side – Giraud – was favoured: his man got a plane to fly to Cayenne when it decided to join Algiers, for example, while Tixier's military attaché was refused one to mark Guyane's joining the Free French.

One of the noisiest affairs of this period was the *Richelieu* scandal, in February–March 1943, when over 300 sailors deserted their recently arrived ship to sign up with the Free French recruiting office. The question was: did they do so of their own free will, or were they lured? Béthouart's representative, Admiral Fenard, claimed that Aglion's office in New York had bribed them to make the change with payments of $600 each,[15] a story that was somewhat refined by Béthouart himself, who blamed Robert Valeur, of the Press and Information Office.[16] Aglion painstakingly refuted these accusations in a long report for London, in which he detailed interviews with many of the sailors concerned, and built up a case of long-repressed revolt of the men against their pro-Pétain – even pro-Nazi – and anti-British officers.[17] (To understand the level of passion on board the *Richelieu*, one needs to remember that the ship

14. Antoine de Saint-Exupéry, *Ecrits de guerre 1939–1944* (Paris, 1982), pp. 350, 397.
15. OSS, *loc. cit.*, Box 37, FR 541, 4 March 1943.
16. Béthouart, *Cinq Années*, pp. 190ff.
17. Aglion, *Roosevelt and de Gaulle*, pp. 156–64; also his report 'Enquête sur le

was a survivor of the British naval attack on the French fleet at Mers el-Kebir in 1940, and that it had been part of the defence against the abortive Anglo-Free French attempt to take over Dakar.) Aglion's version of events is the more believable, because it is carefully documented, whereas the other side's story is little more than accusation. It would not, however, have been beyond Tixier to bypass Aglion and directly order Valeur to offer enticement to the sailors. The official policy of de Gaulle was that volunteers were not to be turned away, and in the tense struggles of early 1943, the gaullists needed all the volunteers they could get.

The US authorities, here as elsewhere, supported the Giraud case. The Departments of Justice and of the Navy coordinated an action against twelve of the 'deserting' sailors, who were arrested and interned on Ellis Island. In a statement to the press, Navy Secretary Frank Knox declared that the friction between the French factions was an impediment to the war effort, and that the US government would not tolerate it. The incident caused a flurry in the American media, where the Free French had a good share of sympathisers, but the *New York Times* sternly recalled that there was, after all, a war on, and that the offending sailors were not helping to win it.[18]

In the end, the gaullist Delegation hired a lawyer, and got the sailors off as conscientious objectors. This was not really much of a victory for the Free French, especially since it was followed by a US-enforced agreement between Tixier and Béthouart that every sailor wishing to join de Gaulle would have to present his case to a tripartite commission of officers, and that authorisation would be rare.[19]

The gaullists' greatest ally in their struggle against the giraudists was Giraud himself. Giraud was essentially a soldier, of a traditionalist military mentality made up of fiercely loyal patriotism and a good dose of anti-democratic prejudice. He had none of de Gaulle's political vision or acumen, and once he accepted to engage in negotiations with de Gaulle – which was inevitable, partly because both Britain and America wanted a united French front, but also because de Gaulle had built up overwhelming support within mainland France – he found himself constantly obliged to surrender more of the high ground on which the Americans had placed him.

---

ralliement des marins à la France combattante', April 1943. Copy kindly provided by R. Aglion.

18. *New York Times*, 17 March, 1943.
19. Ibid., 24 April 1943.

He was outwitted again and again, and by mid-1943, when 'unity' was finally achieved with the formation of the French Committee for National Liberation, Giraud had to accept de Gaulle as co-president and his equal. For de Gaulle, it was only one further step towards assuming total command.

One precise example of Giraud's political weakness was his March 1943 decision to abrogate the so-called Crémieux Decree, which under the Third Republic had guaranteed the Jewish minority in Algeria the right to French citizenship. To be fair to Giraud, one needs to point out that the abrogation occurred within the context of an attempt to achieve democratic reform, and at the same time as he was rejecting the validity of Vichy laws in North Africa, including the various pieces of anti-Semitic legislation that had been in effect. Furthermore, the rights of the Jewish population were something of an affront to the Moslem majority, whose suffrage position was inferior. None the less, Giraud's action was subject to loud criticism from Zionists in New York, and from the gaullists, who were quick to seize the opportunity to brand as anti-Semitic the man they had already dubbed '*le général nazi*'.

In truth, the United States knew from early on that its support of Giraud would not bring it much joy. Two of its most respected advisers among the émigrés – Alexis Léger and Jean Monnet – were less than warm in their assessment. In March, in a long interview with the OSS, Léger dismissed Giraud as a conservative nationalist whose regime was creating a backlash swing towards de Gaulle and communism. (Léger, at this time, was obsessed by de Gaulle's negotiations with the internal communist resistance movement, and was convinced that it would lead France into the Russian sphere of influence.) Nor could he see any benefits in a union of Giraud and de Gaulle, for he believed (quite accurately, as it turned out) that cooperation would be entirely superficial, and that de Gaulle would continue with his own game-plan. Any administration formed by the two would be neither representative of the French people, nor able to care for France's international interests. The only real solution would be to broaden the North African regime, and to introduce some widely publicised social reforms.[20]

Since December, Monnet had been giving Roosevelt a similar assessment, and in late February, he had been sent to Algiers by Harry Hopkins, ostensibly as a member of the Munitions Assignment Board, but also to exert some calming civilian influence over the turmoil created by the squabbling generals. Monnet won

20. OSS, *loc. cit.*, FR 557 18 March 1943.

Giraud's confidence, and he managed to get him to introduce a more democratic tenor to his speeches, by pointing out that such an approach would make it easier to secure allied arms. Throughout the spring, he struggled to find a way of reducing the tensions between the two major protagonists, and to delineate a broad enough area of common ground for the creation of a unified structure that might truly represent France's interests.

The eventual result was the formation of the French Committee of National Liberation (FCNL), whose first official communiqué, on 4 June 1943, was a ringing declaration of the Committee's own authority and of France's sovereignty, but also of its pledge to hand over power as soon as possible to a representative provisional government, and of its total commitment to democracy and to the liberties and laws of the Republic.[21]

Monnet recognised that de Gaulle and Giraud would continue to 'dispute possession of a power they were not wise enough to share'. At this time – in late May – Béthouart was in Algiers for consultations, and from his own observations of the struggle, concluded that de Gaulle had already won.[22] But the real victory occurred during Giraud's official US visit in July.

In accordance with the advice proffered by Léger and Monnet – though not necessarily *because* of it, since Roosevelt held his own strong views on the matter – Giraud was welcomed only as Commander-in-Chief of the French Army, and not as co-president of a Committee of National Liberation whose authority the United States did not wish to recognise. And indeed, much of his visit was taken up with purely military matters. If it was certainly not a fiasco – as Fristch-Estrangin described it, and as it was treated in the gaullist press[23] – Giraud once again proved to be the least helpful element in his own cause. His lack of English, coupled with a deeply ingrained repugnance for self-expression, gave the American public the impression that this man of rather colourless personality did not have the qualities of an international leader. Simultaneously, his absence from Algiers afforded de Gaulle time to move relatively unhindered to put in place his winning moves, reorganising the Committee in such a way that would assure him effective control.

When Giraud resigned his presidency in October, leaving de Gaulle in exclusive command, it was because he had been out-

---

21. Jean Monnet, *Mémoires*, Paris, 1974, pp. 218–45.
22. Béthouart, *Cinq Années*, p. 92.
23. Fritsch-Estrangin, *New York*, p. 92.

manouevred. His own account of events asserts that he was never really interested in politics anyway, and was glad to be able to devote his full attention to what he knew best: organisation of the reborn French Army, and its participation in the battle for liberation. This is patently at odds with the energy he put into trying to gain ascendency over de Gaulle, but perhaps, on a deeper level, there is none the less truth in it. He was, in a way, projected by US policy into a role that he had neither the temperament, nor the training, nor the talent, to play.[24]

At a meeting organised by the Union Départementale des Syndicats Confédérés d'Alger on 10 October 1943, the principal speaker made the following points:

> Currently, General de Gaulle, responsible for the direction of government action and for the coordination of the Commissions, is playing a role that is getting closer and closer to that of a head of government.
>
> General Giraud, after the creation of a Commission for National Defence, can and must devote himself more and more to his duties as a military leader. When he takes up effective command of operational troops, he will cease to be president of the Committee. . . .
>
> It is the growth pains of French unity that are perfecting its organisation.[25]

The author of this text was Adrien Tixier, who had been called to Algeria by de Gaulle to take up the position of Commissioner of Labour. His sanguine analysis here was based on the knowledge of a battle won, and it did not reflect the aggression with which he had conducted his mission in the United States – or indeed, the dominating influence he continued to exert from afar on the American exiles for many months after he had left the Delegation in Washington.

One of Tixier's obsessions, while he was still Delegate, was to have a newspaper that would say what he wanted said. We have seen that he was not satisfied with *Pour la Victoire*. Since early 1942, he and Henri Laugier (of France Forever) had been calling Genviève Tabouis into frequent conference, reproaching her with giving insufficient coverage to the French Left, and failing to attack the old politics – in particular Chautemps – with enough vigour. They wanted her to dismiss de Kérillis and replace him with the ardent socialist lawyer Henry Torrès.[26]

24. See General Henri Giraud, *Un Seul But: la victoire* (Paris, 1949), passim.
25. Adrien Tixier, *Un Programme social* (Alger, 1944), pp. 14–15.
26. OSS, *loc. cit.*, Box 35, FR 153, 26 June 1942.

Tabouis had manoeuvred quite well in the early months of the struggle. It was true that she did not accept copy from Pierre Cot: she gave as grounds for refusal that he was 'not suitable for the American climate', but the fact was that both Barrès and Hoffherr were so resentful of the Popular Front government that they had threatened to resign if Cot were allowed to write for the paper.[27] But she could demonstrate that her columns were at least as open to the Left as to the Right: Laugier himself had written (10 January 1942) and so had Tixier (30 May 1942). More significantly, *Pour la Victoire* enjoyed a direct relationship with de Gaulle's London people, which had the effect of outflanking, at least temporarily, Tixier's moves. Although de Kérillis was having private disagreements with de Gaulle, his public support for him only rarely faltered. And Tabouis had made a contract with François Quilici to reproduce sections of the London gaullist newspaper, *La Marseillaise*.

Tixier none the less pressed ahead with his plan to gain control of a newspaper, and by October 1942, he had worked out a deal with Demilly's *La Voix de France*, placing Torrès and another committed gaullist, Emile Buré, as editor-in-chief and lead writer respectively. The appearance of the first number of the new-look *Voix de France* coincided with the invasion of North Africa, and while in *Pour la Victoire*, de Kérillis tried to play down the internal French conflicts and joined with Barrès in a measured prediction that de Gaulle and Giraud would reach an understanding on how to work together, both *La Voix de France* and Lacoste's *L'Amérique* immediately took up a much more polemical stance. The strength of the Pobers-Tabouis management lay in the fact that high-running passions – such as those that emerged in the Maritain–Saint-Exupéry debate – could find expression in a civilised and intelligent form. At *La Voix de France* and *L'Amérique*, however, it was more of a petulant and pompous verbal brawl. Irritated by the clamour and inflexibility of the gaullist agitators, Lacoste published an article by Georges Cannet (8 January 1943) in defence of Giraud: 'Can't one take up a rifle to defend one's country unless one has signed up in the party of those gentlemen? It's utterly grotesque!' This was followed shortly by a finger-wagging scolding by Lacoste himself (24 January 1943): 'The opposition . . . shown by this noisy, conniving, activist minority to Washington's policies in North Africa cannot but damage the harmony of the allied efforts. A foreign political clique has no place in the United States.'

27. Ibid., also Box 34, FR 84, 24 April 1942.

In the meantime, things were falling apart for Torrès and Buré, who having barely established themselves in *La Voix de France*, were confronted by the sudden announcement by Demilly that he no longer had funds to publish the paper. However true this may have been, there was another motive, for even as the gaullist staff were scambling to find other sources of finance, Demilly was negotiating with Pobers an amalgamation of *La Voix de France* with *Pour la Victoire*. The amalgamation took place in May 1943, amid gaullist accusations that *La Voix de France* had sold to Jacques Lemaigre-Dubreuil for $35,000. Lemaigre-Dubreuil, an industrialist whose dealings with the Germans had given him great freedom of movement through occupied France, was one of the conspirators who ensured the success of the allied invasion of North Africa. He had come to America with the Béthouart mission, and was thus anathema to the gaullists, who described him as a 'German agent', and branded Tabouis, Pobers and de Kérillis as traitors for doing business with him. De Kérillis responded with an open letter to de Gaulle (1 May 1943), denying the claims: no money had been spent on the fusion, and in any case, external contributions to the paper did not amount to more than 15 per cent of its operating budget. 'Our paper is poor, but it is pure,' he stated haughtily.

Not as pure as he thought – or as he wanted others to think. The facts were much more complicated. Lemaigre-Dubreuil was the biggest synthetic oil producer in France (Lesueur), and his mission in the United States was designed to set up a business network for post-war trade between France and America. Despite his Cagoule background, his motivations were not ideological in any political sense. He was a capitalist. He had done favours for the Americans, and he was calling in some of his chips. He worked out secret agreements with the Board of Economic Warfare and the War Department that were to his advantage, and he purchased *Pour la Victoire* with the idea of creating a companion paper in North Africa. It is not certain that de Kérillis knew about this deal. Tabouis must have, and it was Pobers who reported it to the Americans, together with the information that the arrangement had been made secretly and that there would be no public announcement of it.[28]

In the light of these events, the takeover of Demilly's *La Voix de France* must be interpreted as a much more deliberate attempt to outmanoeuvre the gaullists, probably masterminded by Lemaigre-Dubreuil, but with the active complicity of Tabouis and Pobers,

28. RG 208, OWI 222, Box 1075, 16 June 1943.

who shared his fears about de Gaulle's strengthening links with the French Communist Party and the Soviet Union. For *La Voix de France*, amalgamation in fact meant disappearing almost altogether. For a few months, on a monthly basis, Demilly edited a small section for schools – a reminder of the paper's origins – but the section gradually became more widely spaced, and Demilly himself was reduced to an occasional by-line column. He did not have the stature for the battle which had begun.

One reason why the gaullist rage against *Pour la Victoire* was so intense was that Tabouis, in January 1943, had broken her contract with *La Marseillaise* on the grounds that the material Quilici was sending from London was too embarrassingly anti-American for it to be printed in the United States. (The British obviously agreed with Tabouis' assessment, for they shut the paper down in the summer of 1943.) More generally, with Béthouart being fêted by Americans and French alike, the intractable gaullists were in the frustrating position of being seen as the main obstacles to the very unity of which they considered themselves to be the designated guardians.

All of this spurred Tixier's efforts to acquire a newspaper that could be used as a weapon to bring *Pour la Victoire* to its knees, and against Aglion's advice,[29] he used Free French money to buy *L'Amérique* from the Lacostes. Just what pressure he brought to bear is unknown, but given Lacoste's attitude towards de Gaulle, it is hard to see that the $3000 paid him – although a tidy sum at the time – would in itself have been enough to make him simply abandon the fruits of ten years' effort, especially since the terms of the arrangement barred him from publishing anything for five years.[30]

In any case the deal was done, and under the cover of the very respectable Eugène Gentil, engineer, and vice-president (with Laugier) of France Forever, Tixier put Buré and Torrès in charge of the paper, renamed *France-Amérique*, and handsomely subsidised. The first number appeared on 23 May 1943, with all gaullist guns ablaze. Philippe Barrès had left *Pour la Victoire* to join the new team, which modelled itself on Tabouis' earlier one, and included a wide range of writers, many of whom had been contributors to *Pour la Victoire* at one time or another.

While *Pour la Victoire* would continue to maintain a high level of journalism – much more sophisticated and dignified than

29. OSS, *loc. cit.*, Box 37, FR 531, 20 April 1943.
30. Ibid., FR 570, 15 April 1943.

France-Amérique – it had begun to play what was to be a long and painful losing hand. Its efforts to lend support to the Giraud camp led it into a complicated path, as it had to smooth over problems posed by Giraud's political ineptitude and his diffidence towards democracy. And then, the paper continued to publish de Gaulle's speeches and to make conciliatory remarks about him. In retrospect, such liberalism, although not without generous spirit, appears as weakness in the face of *France-Amérique*'s single-track polemical approach, which did not hesitate, for example, to bury Giraud's official US visit in a few lines in the social pages.

The effects of the external pressure on the Tabouis–Pobers team were soon intensified by internal conflict, which was perhaps provoked by Pobers, and from which he certainly benefited, as he stood by to pick up the pieces left after a fierce clash between de Kérillis, who was falling prey to a persecution complex, and Tabouis, who panicked. In his *De Gaulle dictateur*, de Kérillis describes in detail his personal evolution away from gaullism, which reached its climax with the gaullist hostility to the US invasion of North Africa and the *Richelieu* affair.[31] Publicly, however, he maintained an even-handed stance, and although he had declared himself for Giraud in *Pour la Victoire* on 24 July 1943, his sense of patriotism made him bow to de Gaulle's October victory: 'For a Frenchman in exile, General de Gaulle and the London Committee have created a *de facto* situation, and in spite of all the reservations one might have, they do represent France.'[32] But henceforth he was in opposition, and he dragged the paper with him, well beyond the point to which Pobers and Tabouis were willing to go. A split became inevitable, and as we shall see, when it came, it destroyed the paper. Tixier had achieved his goal.

Another Tixier obsession was to centralise gaullist power in Washington. After the formation of the FCNL, the symbolic value of a single embassy-type operation became all the more important, since the closer the liberation of France came, the more critical was the question of the Americans' recognition of de Gaulle's authority. When Tixier left Washington, there had been two missions, his own, where he was replaced by Philippe Baudet, and Giraud's, where the civilian counterpart to Béthouart was Henri Hoppenot. With the creation of the FCNL, the two missions were fused, and one of the results was the suppression of Aglion's post in New York.

31. Henri de Kérillis, *De Gaulle dictateur* (Montreal, 1945), pp. 150–223.
32. *Pour la Victoire*, 16 October 1943.

Aglion was convinced that this was Tixier's work – the fruit of their prolonged disputes and of the stubborn independence with which Aglion had managed the New York office. And he was probably right. In Tixier's blunt assessment of the unity needed to ensure both massive American aid and US recognition of France's sovereignty under de Gaulle, there was to be no room for reminders – as Aglion was – of the delegation's humble and scattered beginnings.

Baudet and Hoppenot, both career diplomats, worked together to re-establish the framework and fabric of proper Franco-American dealings. To Béthouart's distress, they kept him subordinate,[33] calmly reasserting the primacy of civilian rule over the military. They were, in the context of Foreign Affairs, excellent examples of what Robert Murphy later called 'the indestructibility of the French civil service'.[34] They were not gaullists in the militant mould; they were not working for a man or a symbol, but for the good of their reborn nation.

To the extent that de Gaulle was still perceived as anti-democratic, they worked to counteract the image and to change its cause. Hoppenot was a close friend of Alexis Léger, and he knew that Léger, in his contacts with Sumner Welles and the OSS, was accusing de Gaulle of every form of totalitarian evil – from having built a fascist organisation, to being irretrievably linked with Russia.[35] His job, and Baudet's, was a difficult one, and it was undoubtedly not to their advantage to have as much criticism of their work as emanated from the New York office. Aglion's removal none the less seems to have been a gratuitous and rather nasty act, a punishment especially unfair in that his service to the gaullist cause had just been crowned by his publication of his *L'Epopée de la France combattante* (New York, 1943). His enforced transfer to Washington in October 1943, to a purely consultative post, left an understandably sour taste.

In June 1943, in a report on the French colony in New York, Aglion had remarked upon the wide-spread relief felt by the various groups at the formation of the FCNL:

> The general feeling of optimism among the most representative personalities of the French colony seems to be based on the satisfaction of national pride, the very natural pride of having recovered, these past few

33. Béthouart, *Cinq Années*, p. 210.
34. Murphy, *Diplomat among Warriors*, p. 57.
35. OSS, *loc. cit.*, Box 37, FR 557; Box 38, FR 624.

days, a lost identity. It is a feeling which, obscurely still, but effectively and surely, is tending to reduce the gap between the two French groups.[36]

Inklings of such a spontaneous, popular desire for unity had been surfacing from time to time since America had joined the war. One especially notable occasion was the funeral of Henri Focillon in early March 1943. It was held at New Haven, at Yale University, where Focillon had held a chair for over a decade. It was attended by a large crowd that contained representatives of all groups: the Ecole Libre was there in force, naturally, to salute their president's passing, and so were Henri Bonnet and Eugène Gentil, representing France Forever, where Focillon had held a directorship. More surprisingly, Aglion, for the gaullist delegation, was balanced by a group from Giraud's military mission, and the arch-rivals Henri Torrès and Michel Pobers were also present.

It would be naive to ignore the political advantage that the different factions sought to derive from their attendance, but it would be cynical not to recognise that there was another dimension to the event. Focillon was a grand and distinguished Frenchman, whose sweeping breadth of vision had made him one of the greatest historians of art of his generation. His thought and work offered a scope that transcended the traumas of France's war experience, and it ennobled his own long illness and death at the relatively young age of 61.

Certainly, from the beginning, he had been an unqualified admirer of de Gaulle, to whom he paid repeated homage as his country's leader and saviour. But he was also a great liberal, a strong supporter of Blum's Popular Front; and above all, he was enormously optimistic about France's long-term vitality and creativity.[37] At his funeral, beyond the political tensions, it was in that image of France that the mourners sought to find themselves and assert their own future.

But such privileged moments were uncommon. Nerves were still sensitive and easily exposed. As a Swiss, Denis de Rougemont could treat the matter more lightly than the French, although he made it clear which side he was on. On 14 July 1943, in his diary, he noted of his work at the OWI:

---

36. 'Note sur l'état d'opinion de la colonie française au 9 juin 1943'. Document kindly provided by R. Aglion.
37. See Henri Focillon, *Témoignage pour la France* (New York, 1945), passim.

Washington, which is anti-gaullist, but careful about being objective, has given me the following directive: Quote ten lines from de Gaulle's speech, and ten from Giraud's. All I have to do is pick ten fine turns of phrase from the first, and ten platitudes from the other – it's easy, and the public will be the judge.[38]

A month earlier, a 'unity' dinner, sponsored by the French-American Club at the Waldorf Astoria, to mark the third anniversary of de Gaulle's 18 June appeal, drew 500 guests. They included the Delegation, the Béthouart mission, all the French societies, and a wide range of American francophiles. But the Chamber of Commerce stayed away, and so did the *Pour la Victoire* group, understandably unwilling to share a meal with people like Emile Buré, whose savage personal attacks in *France-Amérique* were proceeding unabated.[39]

The 14 July celebrations were much worse. A bemused Eleanor Clark followed the events for the OSS. The morning reception given by Giraud at the Waldorf Astoria was largely a military affair, but a civilian representation was invited, including the France Forever group. They were furious that in Giraud's stirring call to national regeneration, there was not a single mention of de Gaulle, or of the Free French Army's triumph at Bir Hakeim. At the Ecole Libre in the afternoon, Geneviève Tabouis, who had been invited, but not asked to speak, had to listen to American radio commentator Johannes Steel deliver a scathing indictment of the State Department's French policy, followed by a bald description of a France divided into two camps: de Gaulle's and Hitler's.[40] Immediately following, there was a mass meeting at Hunter College, held by France Forever. It was attended by 3000 people. After balanced speeches by Maritain – who insisted on the indissoluble links between France's freedom and republican values – and Houdry, who praised Giraud as well as de Gaulle, emphasising how much France's liberation depended on America, the 'unconditionals' – Bernstein and Torrès – took over, with speeches centred exclusively on de Gaulle, and on back-patting of the nations that had already recognised his authority.

Torrès was active too, at the *France-Amérique* banquet. In a midnight speech, he violently attacked the United States for its interference in French affairs. This in turn led to a savage altercation

---

38. Denis de Rougemont, *Journal d'une époque* (Paris, 1968), pp. 535–6.
39. OSS, *loc. cit.*, Box 37, FR 602.
40. Ibid., FR 609–15.

between him and Senator André Maroselli, who recognised that de
Gaulle had saved France's honour, but stressed that the FCNL had
no mandate as any kind of government. It was merely an interim
manager of French affairs. (Maroselli had been senator for the
Haute-Saône. Like Camille Fernand-Laurent, the Paris *député*, he
had taken refuge in the United States after the total German
occupation of France. Both men were staunch republicans.)

The level of agitation maintained by Torrès and his ilk was
directly attributable to Tixier's policies. It was not appreciated by
Baudet, and even less so by Aglion. The latter, in a moment of
exasperation with the divisiveness of partisan politics, expressed the
wish that Torrès could be sent to North Africa, Paul Weill drafted,
France Forever disbanded and *France-Amérique* shut down![41]
Like many others, unquestionably patriotic and loyal supporters of
the spirit of Free French, he was sickened by the cultism and hatred
nurtured by people like Torrès, Weill and Buré, and he agonised
over the rift that such behaviour maintained between France and
America. He knew that if gaullism was ever to be recognised by the
US authorities as a legitimate and representative political force, it
would have to be given a more human and more democratic face.

As de Gaulle moved inexorably towards the consolidation of his
power in Algiers, the major question for debate in exile circles was
whether or not the provisions of the Tréveneuc Law would be
applied. This law dated from 1872, and had been formulated for
precisely the kind of situation in which France found itself: that is, a
return to independence after a national catastrophe had deprived the
nation of effective government. (The founders of the Third Republic were drawing on the Prussian victory of 1870, and the
disorders of the Paris Commune in 1871.) The procedure involved
calling on local governments to send delegates to a special provisional assembly, which would have the responsibility, as soon as
circumstances permitted, of calling a general election.

The text of the first declaration of the FCNL had strongly
intimated that it would respect this law, and in discussions about its
application, it quickly became a symbolic guarantee of France's
democratic future. For Alexis Léger, it was paramount, and even
for less legalistic minds, like Cot and Maritain, there was an
expectation that the law would be applied. Among the émigrés,
only a few of the fanatical gaullists, such as Torrès and Weill,
actually spoke out against its application.[42] Roosevelt, prejudiced

41. Ibid., FR 595.
42. *loc. cit.*, Box 38, FR 646, 648.

against de Gaulle, and perhaps influenced by Léger, would use the non-application as an excuse for not recognising the FCNL's legitimacy as a provisional government, even after the Committee was widely accepted as such in France itself.

In order to create a more democratic image of de Gaulle, a number of his supporters founded, in April 1943, the Comité Républicain Français, which was supposed to be a group with diverse political views, and given to ideas, rather than committed to a particular leader. The OSS wondered, with justifiable scepticism, whether this was another of Tixier's public relations exercises. A perusal of the list of office-bearers and members reveals very much the same people who were heading other gaullist organisations: the editors of *France-Amérique*, Barrès and Buré; the leaders of France Forever, Laugier and Weill; the gaullist scientists, Rapkine, Auger, Hadamard and Perrin; and so on. One unexpected presence, André Géraud (Pertinax) is most plausibly explained by his employment in the OSS. Tabouis was excluded from the group, despite passionate pleas to Aglion to intercede for her. In any case, the group seems not to have accomplished anything. Its meetings were predictably enthusiastic in condemning Giraud as naive and ignorant, and in portraying de Gaulle as the embodiment of the new France.[43]

In September, the former secretary of the French-American Club, Robert Lange, led a breakaway movement called 'United for Liberation', which had the support of Louis Bromfield and the two French parliamentarians Maroselli and Fernand-Laurent. Both of the last had been writing in *Pour la Victoire*, pressing the idea of unity within a republican framework. Maroselli had close links with Jules Jeanneney and Herriot, and reproached de Gaulle for putting his political ambition before the military needs of the liberation. Fernand-Laurent, for his part, was especially concerned with questions of constitutional legitimacy. However, their movement, what there was of it, was even more ephemeral than the French Republican Committee.

De Gaulle had his own idea about democratic representation, which was to constitute it from above. He brought into the FCNL key Third Republic figures, like Mendès-France and Le Troquer. And he had protagonists of the internal resistance, like Henri Frenay and François de Menthon. As the *Echo d'Alger* put it:

> It would have been difficult to assemble a body of people who could better represent every shade of opinion, or speak more authoritatively

43. Ibid., Box 37, FR 586, 594. Also Ent 142, Boxes 1–2, Aglion file.

for the people of France. . . . From now on, we have a central authority which is truly representative of the political traditions of France and the new realities arising from the needs of public welfare.[44]

The broadening process was an ongoing one, and by April 1944, the FCNL had been further enlarged to include the communists Fernand Grenier and François Billoux. In addition, in October 1943, a call went out for the formation of a provisional consultative assembly, where representation was of diverse origins, but included many former parliamentarians of all political groups. The end result – if not the means by which it was achieved – could hardly, in the circumstances, have been more representative.

Of the former parliamentarians in America, Pierre Cot was the only one to go. De Kérillis wrote a five-page letter to Félix Gouin to explain his refusal, which was based on what he saw as the essential illegality of the whole exercise. His ire was especially raised by the so-called election of Henri Torrès to represent the French in exile in America. Torrès was in fact chosen by the executive committee of France Forever, with none of the other French organisations even being informed that an election was to be held. Some ironic justice occurred when Torrès was prevented from leaving the United States because of a libel suit brought against his *La Machine infernale*. He was eventually replaced by Francis Perrin.[45]

On the central committee itself – which had all the power – representation of those who had experienced the American exile was strong. In addition to Tixier, there were Henri Bonnet and Jean Monnet. Bonnet, although a member of the executive committee of France Forever, was never one of its dogmatic members, and his vision had never been limited to sectarian gaullism. As for Monnet, we have already seen that for a long time he was quite negatively disposed towards de Gaulle. His eventual decision to work under him, which was based on pragmatic good sense, could only bring reassurance to the Americans with whom he worked so closely, and whose respect he enjoyed to such a high degree.

By the spring of 1944 it was obvious enough that de Gaulle had won for the circumspect *New York Times* to say so:

Whether de Gaulle would have been the better military leader of French forces, whether de Gaulle is pompous and disagreeable, and therefore a

44. 10 November 1943. Quoted in *Free France*, Nov.–Dec. 1943.
45. *Pour la Victoire*, 30 October, 6, 13, 20, 27 November 1943.

bad leader, forms no part of a useful debate at this time. The race was run in Algiers, and de Gaulle has come out on top.[46]

All that Roosevelt could do henceforth was to withhold formal recognition, and in an atypically ungenerous fashion, he did that until October 1944, well after the extraordinary performance of the French Army's sweep through France, and well after de Gaulle's triumphant reception in liberated Paris.

The deliberate exclusion of French units from the first waves of troops in the June landings in Normandy could only be felt by de Gaulle as a calculated insult. It was the same with the reception he was given by Roosevelt in July, when his twice postponed official visit finally took place. He got a seventeen-gun salute to demonstrate that he was being welcomed as a military leader, and not as a head of government, and any high-ranking civilians were conspicuously absent from the party at the airport. Polite speeches could not hide the deep personal unease that separated the two men. But more important still, Roosevelt's determination not to discuss any serious political matters with de Gaulle – and especially not any global issues – was an indication of his underlying assumption that France, by its collapse in 1940, had forfeited any claim to playing a serious role in the post-war world. De Gaulle, of course, had just such a role in mind.

The July visit was in all other ways a success. The American press was enthusiastic, and the French émigrés flocked to the parades and receptions. There was a lot of back-biting gossip about the keenness of those who had previously been known to be Pétain and Giraud supporters, or to have had reservations about de Gaulle. But the General had only a relatively short list of people he did not want associated with his victory. He refused to see Tabouis, Léger, de Kérillis, Chautemps and Pertinax – to whom he attributed much of the difficulty he had had with the US authorities. He also rejected contact with André Labarthe, who with Raymond Aron, had run a pro-resistance, anti-de Gaulle paper in London, and had recently arrived in the United States to start afresh. In April 1944, he had launched an English-language magazine, *The Tricolor*, which had a liberal programme, and pointedly played de Gaulle down – to the point that in the first two editorials, he was not even mentioned. In August, after de Gaulle's visit, Labarthe described the cheers of the crowd as expressing 'above all American friendship for France'.

46. 16 April 1944.

For Henri de Kérillis it was a time of final decision: to back down and look for an accommodation with de Gaulle, or to make the irrevocable break. He chose the latter path, and his front-page article in *Pour la Victoire* on 9 July, while de Gaulle was engaged in his talks with Roosevelt, was damagingly subversive:

> The only French general who, refusing the orders of the politicians, did not wish to surrender to the Germans in 1940, has become, under the influence of the politicians, the French general who in June 1944 is not fighting, and who is even maintaining a painful clamour of dissent amidst the awesome and grandiose roar of the guns of liberation.

Obviously, such open aggression made things awkward for Geneviève Tabouis and the management of *Pour la Victoire*, though it is unlikely, at that point, that anyone was aware that the end-game for the paper had begun.

Later,[47] Tabouis claimed that it was because of de Kérillis' instability that she decided, in mid-1944, to change the clause in her testament specifying that, in the case of her not being able to continue, he would succeed her as director of *Pour la Victoire*. (The original 1942 contract gave de Kérillis trusteeship of stock in the case of Tabouis' death, and the right to publish an article on page 1 of every issue of the paper for fifteen years.) She paints a picture of de Kérillis wandering the New York streets in a pathological state, drawing the attention of police by his strange behaviour, a man broken by the news of the death of his only son, who was a parachutist during the Normandy landings, and who had been betrayed to the Gestapo.[48]

There is other evidence that de Kérillis was indeed dramatically affected by his son's death, and that in an emotional outburst, he actually accused de Gaulle's secret service of being responsible for the betrayal.[49] In view of his earlier obsessions with the Cagoule and the Fifth Column, this reaction is not out of character.

Nevertheless, OSS documents suggest a quite different situation. Eleanor Clark's July 1944 interview with de Kérillis shows him as pessimistic, but clear-headed and far from unbalanced.[50] As for

---

47. Olivier Gaudry, unpublished *mémoire*, *Henri de Kérillis*, Institut d'études politiques de l'Université de Paris, March 1966, pp. 193ff.
48. Ibid., pp. 198–9.
49. Cf. Fritsch-Estrangin, *New York*, pp. 129–30; also Aglion, *Roosevelt*, pp. 96–7.
50. OSS, *loc. cit.*, Box 39, FR 864.

Tabouis, at the end of the previous summer she had freely expressed her fear that gaullism was leading to communism and would provoke a revolution in post-war France,[51] and was in full support of de Kérillis. Her decision in May 1944 to 'disinherit' him coincided with Tixier's granting her plea for a passport to return to France.[52] Was this Tixier's way of finally getting rid of de Kérillis – or was Pobers, the beneficiary of the change, the one behind the move? Neither possibility is unlikely . In any case, de Kérillis, who had the news leaked to him by the lawyer, still had enough power to insist on a new contract: shares could be transferred, but only with his permission, and the paper would pay him an indemnity of $50,000 if ever one of his articles was refused. Such an agreement could hardly last.

After de Gaulle's visit to the United States, Tabouis was reported to be anxious to break her partnership with de Kérillis, and perhaps arrive at a compromise peace with the gaullists – although privately, she continued to assail the Algiers regime, and advocated a return to the pre-1940 political system. She wanted to take *Pour la Victoire* to liberated territory and express her dissenting views directly to the French people. The paper's conciliatory statements about de Gaulle were also partly motivated by concern about advertising revenue. The dispute between her and de Kérillis continued through to November, when it finally broke into the paper itself: in response to a particularly virulent de Kérillis article predicting that de Gaulle's provisional government, *ad hoc* and authoritarian, could only produce a bastardised form of republic (25 November 1944), Tabouis inserted a note disengaging the paper's responsibility from his views. And the following week, she refused his article altogether.

Her own story was that he submitted two violently anti-gaullist articles entitled 'De Gaulle assassin', and 'Pétain was better'. According to the OSS report, which sounds more plausible, the rejected article was called 'Necessary explanations', and as well as spelling out the terms of his collaboration with *Pour la Victoire*, it quoted extensively from Tabouis' previous writing to show that his article of the previous week was in accord with her views. Negotiation failed to produce any compromise. The stubborn Tabouis broke her contract, and the equally stubborn de Kérillis took her to court.

51. Ibid., Box 38, FR 644, 30 August 1943.
52. Ibid., Box 40, FR 881, 13 September 1944. The information was provided by Robert Valeur, director of the gaullist information centre in New York. Also

He lost. The $50,000 suit was in fact dismissed, thanks to Tabouis' highly placed friends.[53] And so ended the turbulent career of Henri de Kérillis, who retired to his Long Island farm to concentrate on his potatoes and dairy cows, reserving his political views for social occasions, correspondence and private conversations – with old friends visiting America, or during his own rare trips to France. He died of throat cancer in New York in 1958.

To replace him at *Pour la Victoire*, Pobers brought in the staunch gaullist Jules Romains, who was now back from Mexico. But thereafter the paper appeared as only a shadow of what it had been in its heyday. In a sense, the liberation of France had made it redundant. It talked conscientiously about the effects of the Occupation on life in France, about reconstruction and the *épuration*, but the fire was gone. And after Tabouis left, in June 1945, the paper, now under the sole control of Pobers, began to look more and more like *France-Amérique*. Nobody was surprised, in May 1946, when the two papers merged, under the title *France-Amérique*. Tixier had finally had his way. Only one paper remained, integrated into the official French Cultural Mission.

At the Ecole Libre, thanks to the efforts of some of the more idealistically-minded academic staff, the attempt at formal politicisation failed. But the victory for academic freedom was a Pyrrhic one. The battle began in the Spring of 1944, when the FCNL Cultural Attaché in New York, Henri Seyrig, following directives from Algiers, moved to transform the school into an official organisation of the Algiers committee, under its direct control. Within the school, this move was supported by Koyré, Benoît-Lévy, Lévi-Strauss, and Rapkine. An immediate problem arose with the Department of Justice, which required special registration of institutions under the control of foreign governments and agencies. For the school's president, Jacques Maritain, as well as Mirkine-Guetzévitch and the whole of the Belgian group of professors, the takeover move was a blatant attack on the principle of academic freedom.

The Justice Department was willing to compromise: registration could be averted even if the school received some FCNL funding, provided that those who were officially connected with the FCNL – Aglion, Bonnet, Valeur and Benoît-Lévy – were dropped from the staff. The 'politicals' were not satisfied with this solution, and

---

FR 938, 14 December 1944, and Box 39, FR 863, 15 August 1944.
53. Aglion, in a private letter of 19 August 1987 wrote: 'it has been said that the White House had given instructions in her favour.'

the academic year ended in chaos.[54] *Pour la Victoire* lamented the passing of a grand ideal:

> It is no longer in doubt that the attempt by 3 or 4 people to transform the school into a propaganda agency could only lead to the dissolution of an institution of which all French people recognised the importance and high standing. (24 June 1944)

The Ecole staggered into its third year, its courses depleted, and without any effective leadership. At its thinly attended third anniversary celebration, the French were massively outnumbered by the Belgians.[55] Although it would never completely disappear, it was already no longer capable of fulfilling Alvin Johnson's dream of a permanent French higher education institution within the framework of the New School. Claude Lévi-Strauss, during his time as Cultural Attaché, worked in harmony with Ambassador Henri Bonnet to try to breathe some life back into the institution, but it survived only in an extremely diminished form.[56]

This was in part, obviously, because there was no longer any need for a university-in-exile: the war was almost over, and the émigré professors had returned or were in the process of doing so. However, it needs to be said that the turmoil and bitterness with which the Ecole's collapse occurred were the direct result of a monolithic attitude that was simply prepared to destroy what it could not control.

The degree to which such an attitude was necessary is an issue that can never be resolved. Injustices and cruelties were perpetrated on individuals in ways that are difficult to justify, even taking reasons of state into account, and seem too often ascribable to settling of personal accounts. Léger, Labarthe and de Kérillis were all men of good will, but were squeezed out of the debate and subjected to painful ostracism. So was Camille Chautemps, despite his break with Vichy and his persistent attempts to serve his country. And even many who did serve the Free French and resistance cause with unremitting loyalty found themselves treated shabbily.

The case of Geneviève Tabouis is striking. Despite her poor health and great personal anxiety about her family in France, she

---

54. OSS, *loc. cit.*, Box 39, FR 820, 824, 830, 834.
55. Ibid., Box 40, FR 975.
56. P. M. Scott and W. B. Rutcoff, *New School* (New York, 1986), pp. 170–1.

had criss-crossed the United States on morale-raising journeys, she had lobbied the American press and politicians on behalf of Free France, she had raised money, and she had created an extraordinarily fine newspaper in the best traditions of journalism. How could she not resent being named as a person with whom all FCNL officials were expressly forbidden from having any contact? Especially when the letter of interdiction was signed by Henri Hoppenot, who had, after all, continued to serve the Pétain government in Uruguay until the eve of the invasion of North Africa, and who had come to the United States as Giraud's civilian representative[57] – hardly an irreproachable gaullist pedigree.

On the other hand, the argument for discipline and the suppression of dissenting views was based on weighty considerations. Gaining American recognition of the authority of the FCNL was only one of these. More generally, what was at stake was the whole position of France in the post-war world. The nation that was gradually rising out of the shame of defeat and occupation was regaining pride through its strengthening participation in the allied military battle, but its internal fragility was great, and its international position was desperately perilous. How could liberated France be administered in such a way as to avoid internal conflict or the American imposition of the Allied Military Government of Occupied Territories (AMGOT)? How could France negotiate the massive American aid needed to begin the massive tasks of reconstruction without losing sovereign control of its own political and economic processes? How could such a powerless France make its voice heard in an international forum totally in the hands of the British, Americans and Russians?

These questions were the ones that most preoccupied Hervé Alphand and Jean Monnet when they returned from the first World Conference of the United Nations Relief and Rehabilitation Administration (UNRRA) in Atlantic City in early December 1943. Even more than the condescending treatment that they received from their British, American and Russian colleagues, the exclusion of French as an official language was a measure of what Alphand called 'this long calvary of French rebirth'. There was none of the inhumanity of the hard-line gaullists about these men, as they grappled with their seemingly impossible task. Alphand noted in his diary:

---

57. OSS, *loc. cit.*, Box 39, FR 863.

It is ten o'clock at night. In a room in the most modern hotel in the world, where there is a radio, cool or warm air, unlimited iced water, '*servidor*'. . . . I am atrociously anxious. My gaze in the mirror reveals desperate eyes, hair too long, a thin, dark face. A feeling of abandonment, solitude. A feeling, too, of the incredible effort to be accomplished, and of the mediocrity of our means, of too heavy a heritage. De Gaulle just has to be that great Frenchman who can help us to sustain the blaze which is going to die down, and which will have to be reignited . . . Doubt, I have to admit, is constant.[58]

It cannot have been easy to keep a balanced view. One man who succeeded in doing so was Jacques Maritain, whose position evolved from his early rejection of de Gaulle as a politician to a carefully reasoned acceptance of him as France's legitimate leader. Maritain's evolution corresponded firstly to visible and undeniable changes in de Gaulle's own organisation. Maritain had written to de Gaulle as early as May 1942 to warn him about apparent napoleonic political ambitions,[59] and in all his writings, speeches and messages, he constantly returned to the theme that only the people of liberated France could choose a legitimate government.

The 'democratisation' of de Gaulle was of course a slow and complex process. Christian Pineau, the communist founder of *Libération*, who went to London in 1942, emphasises just how hard he and Tixier had to struggle with de Gaulle to get him to understand what was happening in the internal resistance. He portrays de Gaulle as being preoccupied with his rejection of the Third Republic, and inadequately prepared for post-war social planning.[60] Jean Monnet pushed in the same direction, though with different concerns, and indeed, originally along the Giraud path. Maritain, a man of principle, and a theologian as much as a social philosopher, was never tempted to deify de Gaulle, and never inclined to bend to pressures to accept that the end justified the means. He defended Aglion against Tixier, and the Ecole Libre against political takeover. His friend C. G. Paulding, the editor of *Commonweal*, believed that any dictatorial tendencies on de Gaulle's part would necessarily be balked by the likes of Maritain, 'who have enough independence to stay on the outside and howl'.[61]

Another element in Maritain's 'conversion' to gaullism was his

58. Alphand, *L'Etonnement d'être*, pp. 169, 171.
59. OSS, *loc. cit.*, Box 35, FR 209–210.
60. Christian Pineau, *La Simple Vérité 1940–1945* (Paris, 1960), pp. 174ff.
61. OSS, *loc. cit.*, Box 38, FR 636.

concern with the Jewish question. His wife Raïssa was a converted Jew, and many of their friends among the émigrés were Jewish. But Maritain's preoccupations were not merely personal. To a remarkable degree, and from the very earliest stages that information about persecution and the extermination camps began to trickle through to America, he showed forthright hostility to Hitlerian and Vichy policies. He denounced anti-Semitism as an attack against democracy, Christianity, law and ethics, and ultimately, civilisation itself.[62] He espoused the gaullist attacks on Giraud's abrogation of the Crémieux decree, and came to see de Gaulle himself not as an ideal leader, but as the *only* one who was strong enough to reorient France towards a tradition of humane and republican values. More practically, he judged that de Gaulle was politician enough to be adaptable.

At the end of 1944, he travelled to France, where he had an interview with de Gaulle, and stressed the need for the General to understand America. In turn, he gained greater insight into what had happened in France, and understood that the massive tasks of reconstruction entailed the need for much closer collaboration with the Left than he, as a moderate Catholic, had ever imagined. It was after this meeting that he accepted what he had refused six months earlier: to be France's Ambassador to the Vatican.

It was an unconventional appointment. Maritain was an outstanding representative of his faith, but he was not a diplomat. From de Gaulle's viewpoint, the ambassadorship was less a reward for services rendered than a clever one-stone-for-two-birds strategy. On the one hand, it offered the Americans another demonstration (following the appointment of Henri Bonnet as Ambassador to Washington) of his sensitivity to people they liked. On the other, it would help win the support and sympathy of the Christian Democrats in France, in order to be able to tap into the emerging electoral strength of the MRP. For Maritain, it was a way of continuing on the path that Paulding praised at his farewell luncheon at the Waldorf Astoria in May 1945: 'You told the truth always, the truth as it was known to you, and in doing so, you served France, but you served America also, you served the world.'[63]

Close upon the heels of the US recognition of the French Provisional Government in October 1944, Colonel Passy visited America. His visit was arranged by General Donovan, and he worked in close collaboration with the OSS. Eleanor Clark registered the

62. *Pour la Justice* (New York, 1945), pp. 165ff., by 217ff.
63. OSS, *loc. cit.*, Box 40, FR 988.

surprise and dismay of many of the French community, who found it hard to accept that the United States would cooperate with a man who had the reputation of being the leader of the French Gestapo. Passy set up office in New Orleans, where French undercover work was easier, and began to send out his antennae towards South America and the Far East. In the world of espionage, too, the French were back.[64]

64. Ibid., FR 919, 924–925.

– 8 –

Going Home

Everything has changed from the inside. What is misleading is that the set is the same. The set is the same,
but it's a different play that's going on.

Julien Green[1]

Julien Green, who was more committed to France, and more in
exile in his American homeland than most Frenchmen, was at Bear
Trap Farm in Virginia when he heard on the radio the news of the
liberation of Paris. It made him 'mad with joy', and the thirteen
months that passed before he could actually return to the Paris he
loved were full of frustrating paradox. The fragments of news that
began to filter through about the experience of Nazi occupation and
atrocities, were cause for depression and bewilderment: 'Between
France and us, these four years of absence have dug a kind of
chasm. There are too many things I didn't know'.[2]

When he arrived back in Paris at the end of September 1945, the
sense of change was overwhelming. Like many others, he groped
for some sort of understanding of everything from Hiroshima to
his own feeling of being a Rip Van Winkle. Patiently, but with the
growing awareness of an insurmountable gap, he gathered the
reminiscences and impressions of those who had lived through it
all on the *inside*. He talked endlessly with his writer friends: with
Mauriac, who believed that a revolution was taking place; or
with Stanislas Fumet, who told him about the pro-Vichy mood
of the population, the timidity of the Church, the horrors of
Auschwitz.

Whatever relief or pleasure came from finding that his furniture
and books had been saved by friends, was diminished by the rapid
discovery that it was impossible to find an apartment to rent: he
had to search for almost eight months before he could sign a lease.
And after America, the city-scape was simply bizarre, with its

1. Julien Green, *Journal*, in *Oeuvres complètes*, IV (Paris, 1975), p. 855.
2. *Ibid.*, pp. 799ff.

clerics in their habits, its horse-drawn carriages, and its children clacking over the streets in their wooden-soled clogs.[3]

Green's experience was not unusual: there was the romantic yet sad rediscovery of once-familiar places, now condemned to shortages of food and accommodation and to deprivations of all kinds; and yet, at the same time, a gladness at being reunited with the homeland, at the ending of the exile. On his way back to Switzerland in April 1946, Denis de Rougemont found a Paris that had stepped back a century, 'in the direction of a forgotten beauty', but where the inhabitants were part of a broken, anxious nightmare.[4]

Getting back was quite a different affair from the exodus. Papers and travel were not always easy to arrange, but the general climate was one of rediscovered freedom, and there was no longer the threat of dominance or persecution by a hostile power. There was, however, a sense of uncertainty about what was happening in France, and despite the rush for visas that Suzanne Blum had to cope with in the newly re-established New York Consulate,[5] the majority of the émigrés took their time to go home. Geneviève Tabouis was on her way on a 'liberty ship' in the late spring of 1945, after the opening of the United Nations assembly in San Francisco, and after the capitulation of Germany. She was one of the early ones. Most, whether through caution or perhaps some sense of solidarity with America's continued engagement in the war in the Pacific, did not seek to return immediately. They went back only in 1946 or 1947, and sometimes even later.

The more thoughtful ones were aware, in varying degrees, that such radical changes had occurred that their old ways of thinking and seeing were no longer adequate. Maurice Dekobra, whose amused, ironical analysis of the frivolity of the upper-class émigrés made him the Feydeau of the exile, worried about the US–Soviet conflict and the development of atomic science. In his diary, published just after his return in 1946, he looks forward with prophetic hope to the establishment of a United States of Europe, with its own parliament, a common economy, the abolition of national boundaries, and with linguistic problems being solved by an army of instantaneous translators. Such a situation would mean some loss of sovereignty for the old nation-states, but Dekobra saw that as the price of their survival.[6]

3. *Ibid.*, pp. 862ff.
4. Denis de Rougemont, *Journal d'une époque* (Paris, 1968). p. 558.
5. Suzanne Blum, *Vivre sans la patrie* (Paris, 1975), pp. 207ff.
6. Maurice Dekobra, *Sept Ans chez les hommes libres: Journal d'un Français aux Etats-unis 1939–1946* (Paris, 1946), pp. 360–76.

The formulation of this vision picks up on ideas that had been widely discussed among the European émigrés during the war. Count Richard Coudenhove-Kalergi, the founder of the pan-European movement, had promoted the concept of a united Europe since the end of the First World War, and had been active in organising conferences and discussions in America throughout the 1940–5 period. His dream was an idealistic one, based on a desire for harmony and peace, and it reached its fullest expression in the 1948 Congress at The Hague, when the Council of Europe was formed.

On a more practical level, Jean Monnet had been mulling over the creation of unity through amalgamations in Europe's heavy industry and the abolition of customs barriers. As early as October 1943, he had discussed the idea with de Gaulle, who had dismissed it as fanciful.[7] De Gaulle, at that stage, was still primarily concerned with re-establishing France's prestige and power, and did not find appealing ideas of international authorities that would supersede national sovereignty.

What Dekobra the novelist saw – as did the Transylvanian dreamer Coudenhove-Kalergi, and the little economic genius from Cognac, Jean Monnet – was that European unity was no mere ideal projection, but an absolute condition of France's survival. In a strange way, this realisation, for Dekobra, was a release from the caricatural romance and adventure novels with which he had made such a successful career. They too were largely concerned with survival – but of the privileged classes that had somehow managed to weave their way down through the century and a half of social and political upheaval since the Revolution. But in his American novels, such as *La Madone à Hollywood*, a new seriousness and edge of urgency begins to cut through the formulaic slickness and familiar satire, with the awareness, both ominous and exciting, that a world revolution has begun, brought about not by ideology, but by science and technology.

Louis Rapkine had never been in doubt about that. The approaching liberation of France brought to him a renewed desire to ensure that French science could have access to the enormous advances that had taken place in the United States and Britain during the time that France had been completely cut off. He had failed to integrate, as a distinct Free French group, into the American war effort, the scientists he had managed to save; but his disappointment was largely outweighed by his success in creating the

---

7. Hervé Alphand, *L'Etonnement d'être* (Paris, 1977), p. 168.

Free French Scientific Mission in Great Britain. By September 1944, he had regrouped the dispersed scientists, and arranged their passage to England.

Through contacts and friendships developed in Britain before the war, he was able to set up a network of laboratories and factories willing to open their doors to the French visitors – the members of the Mission at first, and then scientists from liberated France. The members of the Mission, through their own work in America, were the bearers of significant new knowledge. They had also laid the groundwork for new exchange contacts between French and US scientists. At the same time, Rapkine's continuing links with the Rockefeller Foundation gave him an opportunity for regular briefings of the US authorities on the upgrading and updating needs of French laboratory systems. His contribution to the rebirth of French science was thus multiple and considerable. The long list of scientific dignitaries who continued to pay tribute to his work, long after his early death (he died of lung cancer in 1948, at the age of 44), bears lasting witness to its importance.[8]

Almost all of the émigrés returned to take up their lives again in France. Of the few that did not, some, like Yves Tanguy or Jacques Schiffrin, chose to stay on because it suited their personal lives and work. Tanguy's marriage to Kay Sage was the choice of a whole way of life: spacious living in the gentle woods and hills around Woodbury, Connecticut, and at the same time, ready access to New York, which had become the most dynamic art centre in the world. It was much the same for Schiffrin, who discovered in the New York publishing world a field in which his imagination and creativity could once again develop freely.

For some others, the decision to stay was forced upon them. De Gaulle's major political opponents – Alexis Léger, Henri de Kérillis, and Camille Chautemps, were all on the blacklist of French to be refused re-entry visas. An actual list existed, and although it was never formally used,[9] the sentiments it expressed were genuine enough in their hostility to make those listed aware that they would not be welcomed back in France.

On a broad symbolic level, this was a rejection of the Third Republic, or at least of significant aspects of it. (Tabouis too was originally blacklisted.) Chautemps, part of a whole political

---

8. See B. and V. Karp (eds), *Louis Rapkine 1904–1948* (North Bennington, Vt, 1988).
9. OSS, RG 226, Ent 100, Box 39, FR863, 15 August 1944. Also a private letter from R. Aglion, 28 August 1987.

dynasty, was emblematic for the gaullists of the instabilities, secret deals, and social conflict that characterised the former regime. He had also worked with Vichy and defended the Armistice. From that point of view it was easy to condemn him. Léger and de Kérillis were more difficult targets, since they had to be attacked simply on the grounds that they did not accept the legitimacy of de Gaulle's political strategies, and that they had advised the US government accordingly. At the same time, de Kérillis' trumpeting nationalism – which had made of him a brave and rare voice at the time of Munich and the Armistice – had suddenly begun to appear old-fashioned in the context of the new geopolitical realities. As for Léger, he had after all been the lynch-pin of French foreign policy in the 1930s, and however distinguished and dignified his conduct, the policy itself could hardly be declared a success, and was certainly no model for the development of future directions.

The decision to put Chautemps on trial was one of the excesses of the *épuration*, and derived from the new-born Fourth Republic's zealous desire to legitimise its origins by separating itself from both Vichy and the Third Republic. Even Emile Buré, who had been one of Chautemps' most violent critics, was shocked by what he saw as deliberate persecution: 'his conduct could not be judged severely from a national viewpoint, except by the gaullist fanatics – of which I was one.'[10] Sumner Welles sent a statement of support to Chautemps' defence lawyer, Maurice Ribot: 'I consider that he demonstrated convictions totally opposed to any form of collaboration with Germany, and totally in favour of French resistance to Hitler's regime.'[11]

The trial on 25 March 1947 took place in Chautemps' absence.[12] Interestingly, the French government did not even seek to extradite him, and in view of the flimsy nature of its case, one can understand that it was better, from the prosecution viewpoint, that he not be there to defend himself. The proceedings were farcical. The charge – that Chautemps had contributed to the Armistice – was, in terms of the facts, undeniable. But the only way that this could be portrayed as a crime against the nation was in terms of the myth that the true France, the *real* nation, was not made up of the forty million who applauded Pétain, but of the few hundred who had joined de Gaulle in London.

---

10. In *L'Ordre*, 8 January 1948.
11. Quoted in Camille Chautemps, *Les Cahiers secrets de l'Armistice* (Paris, 1963), p. 326.
12. Transcript of trial kindly provided by Mrs H. Samuels.

The two major witnesses were André Maurois and Jules Romains. The former, understandably anxious not to have attention drawn to his own support of Pétain, now that he had rejoined the Académie Française and the ranks of the respectable, was stricken with complete amnesia about his life in America. (At the same time, he was in the process of rewriting the memoirs he had published in New York in 1942, in order to present a less embarrassing picture of himself.) He was of no help to Chautemps. Romains, on the other hand, was very supportive of the former prime minister. He defended his old friend's patriotism and his positive influence on France's behalf with the Americans. None the less, Chautemps was condemned to five years' imprisonment – a term which he waited out in America until the general amnesty of 1953.

Any one of them could, had he so wished, have returned to France eventually, but for all of them, France had ceased to be home. Léger was in a way more fortunate than the others, in that he had a whole other life to turn to, as the poet Saint-John Perse. His physical exile could be, and was, transposed into the metaphysical dimension of the poet's condition in the world.

Another poet, Saint-Exupéry, was also haunted by the idea of exile, but his experience and destiny were very different from those of Léger. His last winter, spent in Algiers, was full of anguish and despondency. Denied the possibility of flying, because of his age, and in severe pain from a back injury, he passed the cold nights huddled in the converted laundry of a friend's apartment. The gaullists had banned the sale of his books in North Africa, and missed no opportunity to humiliate him publicly. In particular, Henri Laugier, the former France Forever president who had been named as rector of Algiers University, persisted maliciously in keeping alive the myth of Saint-Exupéry's membership in Pétain's infamous National Council. Saint-Exupéry was hurt – and more by the attacks on his honour and his patriotism than by the vague threats of post-liberation imprisonment. It was in a state of despair, verging on suicidal paranoia, that he struggled with his unfinished masterwork, *Citadelle*, sick with pessimism about France's future, and his own.

During the following spring, he talked his way back into being accepted as a pilot and rejoined the 'fighting' war, regaining some measure of peace with himself. To use one of his obsessive images, he felt 'pure'. Disentangled from the political complexities that knotted his stomach and his thinking, he could lose himself in a destiny that transcended the belittlement of enforced civilian status.

His final disappearance at the end of July 1944, while returning from a reconnaissance mission over France, is a neat symbol, and from his own viewpoint, a good resolution of his dilemma, for he could see no place for himself in a post-war France represented by the Laugiers and Le Troquers.

While it can be argued that Saint-Exupéry's image of France was too romanticised to be realistic, the treatment he received from the gaullists was vindictive and in no way merited. Henri de Kérillis went as far as to insinuate that Saint-Exupéry was killed by a gaullist – cagoulard plot[13] – which is highly unlikely. However, it is not an admirable episode in gaullism's development that when he died, the creator of *The Little Prince* had given up hope. The push to exclude him, and everything he stood for, from the post-war ethos, is a telling example of how imperfect, at that time, were de Gaulle's assumptions about the overall mood of the mainland French. Later, he was more conciliating, but his November 1944 gesture in granting Saint-Exupéry a French airforce citation for distinguished service, remains, in view of everything that preceded, an insulting irony.[14]

Many of the exiled journalists made a successful transition to the post-war era. Philippe Barrès, adaptable and strengthened by his gaullist connections, founded *Paris-Presse* with Eve Curie. Pierre Lazareff, while directing the enormous '*Air du Temps*' collection for Gallimard, would also become the czar of the *France-Soir* empire, while his wife Hélène would direct *Elle*. But perhaps the most striking itinerary is that of Geneviève Tabouis, the prewar Cassandra who made so many apparently wrong choices towards the end of her direction of *Pour la Victoire*, but whose unerring instinct for survival allowed her not only to live through all the eruptions of the post-war period, but, with her regular radio broadcasts, to become familiar to a whole new generation. This feisty woman, who outlived her contemporary Charles de Gaulle by more than a decade, was surely inhabited by the spirit of Marianne. Among the representatives of French journalism in the United States during the war, she stands out as the most luminous symbol of French republican continuity.

Once dispersed, the exile community passed almost immediately into oblivion. It was as if it had never existed. And yet, without it, the fate of France and the shape of the post-war world might have been very different. The enormous impact of some individual

13. In *De Gaulle dictateur* (Montreal, 1945), p. 66.
14. See Antoine de Saint-Exupéry, *Ecrits de guerre* (Paris, 1982), pp. 370–500.

refugees is immediately apparent. Jean Monnet's extraordinary clarity of vision and his wizardry in negotiation provided France with the entire economic base of its recovery, while at the same time guaranteeing maximum independence and sovereignty. His friend and co-worker. Hervé Alphand, summed him up thus:

> Jean Monnet astonishes me. It is he who draws up the memoranda that are submitted to the President of the United States; it is he who incites Eisenhower to send the telegrams that will finally tip the scales in our favour. All that with extreme modesty and complete selflessness. I shall be the only Frenchman to know how much we owe him in this phase of the war. When it is all over, people will think it happened naturally – or others will take the credit. . . . But he doesn't care.[15]

Louis Rapkine, through his efforts in rescuing so many important French scientists, in finding them places to continue their work, in building structures to allow new scientific skills and discoveries to flow back into France, made an utterly essential contribution to the nation's technological renewal. Claude Lévi-Strauss, from his encounter with Roman Jakobson, conceived a new philosophical paradigm that became one of the essential markers in the post-war French intellectual landscape.

Of the three, Monnet was probably the least obviously dependent on the émigré community in carrying out his work, since he was principally involved with the British and the Americans, especially in the early years of the war. Later, however, as Monnet began to turn his mind to specifically French questions, he did in fact draw on projects and ideas that had been taking shape within the community for some time.

As we have seen, the community itself did not form immediately. Initially, America was simply a refuge for a relatively small number of individuals who were fleeing the advance of Nazi Germany. There was no organising principle. It is not an accident, however, that so many of the refugees were people whose very lives were driven by the value of free thought and expression: artists, film-makers, musicians, novelists, poets, intellectuals, journalists and so on. Many of them had known each other in pre-war France. Some, like the surrealists, the academics, and the journalists, were already part of a community. In America, they were drawn together by the need to go on working, for their own

---

15. Alphand, *L'Etonnement d'être*, p. 73.

cultural survival. Perhaps even more powerfully, there was a sense too, with France under the shadow of totalitarian repression, that they had become guardians and voice of a heritage that, without them, might simply waste away. That such a view was distorted is evident, since it takes no account of the clandestine cultural networks that flourished in France itself under the Nazis and Vichy. On the other hand, precisely *because* cultural freedom had been driven underground in France, the United States became something of a privileged cultural space, that allowed continuity of free artistic and intellectual development no longer possible at home.

The dynamic produced its own institutions. The French book publishing industry, the newspapers, the art galleries and the schools all did well because they had sprung from an organic need, and not from any artificially imposed construct. The level of activity attained is proof of extraordinary vitality. And at a time when France, under Pétain and the Germans, was projecting an image of shamed defeat and social decay, the presence on American soil of such a vigorous and independent image of French culture was of critical importance. It was something far more real, to the American people, than the distant rhetoric of Charles de Gaulle.

The émigré community was not insular. Its journalists wrote for American newspapers and periodicals as well as their own; its filmmakers made American films; its intellectuals taught in American universities and colleges; its artists engaged with the spectacular revolution that was occurring in American art. French cultural maintenance was firmly based on the practice of free and open cultural exchange.

The other major pillar of the French community in exile was its determination to continue the war, its refusal to accept the finality of the 1940 defeat. This general stance was a natural corollary of the desire for freedom that had brought them to America in the first place, and it preceded any development of explicitly political strategies or programmes. The realisation was widely shared that Europe's freedom depended on America's abandonment of isolationism and acceptance of an active role in the fight. That was the priority, and the birth of organisations like France Forever resulted from the need to persuade and seduce the United States into believing that Europe in general, and France in particular, were worth fighting for.

De Gaulle's 18 June call from London was, in this respect, inspirational, but it was not instrumental. Free France, as perceived in America, was a spirit – of resistance, of a refusal to bow to defeat and oppression – and it was more evident in the cultural integrity and pride of the exile community than in the particular movement begun by de Gaulle and his London committee. Those charged with the formulation and expression of US policy about US–French relations – Roosevelt himself, but also Secretary of State Cordell Hull and Undersecretary Sumner Welles – had access to an exceptional range of informed opinion from immensely experienced and gifted people: political figures such as Cot, Chautemps, de Kérillis, Léger; and also intellectuals like Maritain, or military men like General Odic and Saint-Exupéry. These were people vouched for by Americans; they were close at hand, available; their behaviour could be scrutinised, their views sifted, assessed, reassessed. They were heard more often, and more sympathetically, than de Gaulle's representatives.

Many among the longer-settled expatriates – particularly those in business, those in official organisations (Alliance Française, Lycée, Institut), or the more conservative sections of the Catholic Church – tended to remain respectful of the Vichy government, especially early in the war. Sometimes this was because of atavistic admiration for Pétain, going back to his hero's role in the First World War; sometimes – though rarely – it was because of pro-German sentiment. Most often, it was simply the practical thing to do. As long as the United States maintained relations with Vichy – and it had good political reasons for doing so – ordinary daily business required using the established structures. Once the United States entered the war, and even more so after the allied invasion of North Africa, Vichy ceased to be an issue, and the long-term expatriates joined the recent émigrés in the push for resistance and national resurgence.

It would be hard to imagine a better example of the gallic stereotype of fractiousness and internal fighting than the wartime exile community in New York. Arguments, violent and often personally vicious, raged between individuals, between all sorts of groups, and within groups. Those who thought the Armistice was necessary were vilified by those convinced it was treason; those who thought that relief should be provided to France snarled at those who believed it would serve Germany; those who gave unquestioning support to US policy were attacked by those who were equally unquestioning about de Gaulle. And some of the worst squabbles were among the most committed gaullists. None the less, although the Americans were irritated by this behaviour, they were remarkably tolerant of it.

The reason for that was twofold. First, personal relations between many of the major French figures and the Americans were excellent. And secondly, whatever side they belonged to, the

French émigrés – once Vichy had been eliminated – all agreed that the most important thing was to help America win the war. The concern about who would run France, and how, after the war, was a matter of serious conflict, but not many of the refugees shared de Gaulle's overwhelming preoccupation with it. The degree to which they were willing to set aside their own battles to work for the allied cause is illustrated in the French section of the Office of War Information, where Lazareff had the cream of France's cultural diversity – gaullists and anti-gaullists, surrealists and Catholics – serving together in a situation outside of which they would have been angrily fighting.

De Gaulle had a real rival in Roosevelt, and he was right in seeing that France's post-war sovereignty would be hard to achieve. America had established itself as a superpower, and France was in every way vulnerable. He was wrong, however, to believe that to reach his goal required some kind of uniformity and orthodoxy of views, and a repression of dissenting voices. His attempts, and those of his agents, to bring the exiles under strict control were counterproductive, and lost him more support than he gained.

Ironically, the cultural and political pluralism of the exile – where many talented people were able to use the heightened sense of freedom and space that America offered to great creative purpose – served France, and de Gaulle, to a far greater degree than the General realised. Through their writing, their teaching, their artistic creation, their press, they helped maintain, in American public opinion as well as in the minds of the major policy-makers, the view that no post-war world could be complete without an independent France among its significant powers. Conversely, they projected to the gaullist camp a strong sense of democracy, which through the likes of Pleven, Tixier and Aglion, played its part in gradually nudging de Gaulle towards a more democratic vision. This, in turn, helped the eventual realisation in America – whose arbitration in the matter had become paramount - that de Gaulle might, after all, be an acceptable democratic leader, and that France was once again ready to take up a prominent role in world affairs.

Bibliography

SOURCES

In addition to the published sources listed below, material has been used from the French National Archives, the Institut de l'Histoire du Temps Présent, the Institut Charles de Gaulle, the US National Archives (Washington and Suitland), the Library of Congress, the New York Public Library, the archives of the New School for Social Research, and the Alliance Française in New York. This material is acknowledged in notes as appropriate.

Access to private papers was granted as follows: to Camille Chautemps' papers, by his daughter Mrs Howard Samuels; to some Louis Rapkine documents, by Mrs Sarah Rapkine; to numerous documents from the gaullist delegation in New York, by Mr Raoul Aglion.

Personal interviews and correspondence were conducted with: Raoul Aglion, Michel Bloit, Alain Bosquet, Alfred Jodry, Georges May, Isaac Molho, Henri Peyre, Antoinette Samuels.

Aglion, Raoul, *L'Epopée de la France combattante*, New York, 1944
—— *De Gaulle et Roosevelt: La France libre aux Etats-unis*, Paris, 1984
—— *Roosevelt and de Gaulle: Allies in Conflict – a Personal Memoir*, New York, 1988
Alphand, Hervé, *L'Etonnement d'être: Journal 1939–1973*, Paris, 1977
Aumont, Jean-Pierre, *Souvenirs provisoires*, Paris, 1957
—— *Le Soleil et les ombres*, Paris, 1976
Balakian, Anna, *André Breton: Magus of Surrealism*, New York, 1971
Barrès, Philippe, *Charles de Gaulle*, New York, 1941
—— *Sauvons nos prisonniers*, New York, 1941
Bellanger, Claude et al. (eds), *Histoire générale de la presse française*, Paris, vol. III, 1972
Bernadac, Christian (ed.), *Dagore: les carnets secrets de la Cagoule*, Paris, 1977
Bernstein, Henry, Nine anti-Pétain articles in the *New York Herald Tribune*, 9, 11, 13, 16,, 18, 20, 23, 25, 27 June 1941
Béthouart, Marie-Emile, *Cinq Années d'espérance: mémoires de guerre: 1940–45*, Paris, 1968

Blum, Suzanne, *Vivre sans la patrie*, Paris, Plon, 1975

Bosquet, Alain, *La Grande Eclipse*, Paris, 1952

—— *Les Trente premières années*, vol. 3, *Les Fêtes cruelles*, Paris, 1984

Bourdrel, Philippe, *La Cagoule: trente ans de complot*, Paris, 1970

Breton André, *Entretiens (1913–1952)*, Paris, 1969

Cate, Curtis, *Antoine de Saint-Exupéry*, New York, 1970

Chautemps, Camille, *Cahiers secrets de l'Armistice*, Paris, 1963

Cohen, Gustave, *Lettres aux Américains*, Montreal, 1942

Cot, Pierre, *Le Procès de la République*, New York, 1944

Coudenhove-Kalergi, Count Richard, *An Idea Conquers the World*, London, 1953

Crawford, W. Rex (ed.), *The Cultural Migration: The European Scholar in America* (The Benjamin Franklin Lectures, Fifth Series), Philadelphia, 1953

Curie, Eve, *Voyage parmi les guerriers*, New York, 1944

Dalio, *Mes Années folles*, Paris, 1976

Danan, Yves, *La Vie politique à Alger de 1940 à 1944*, Paris, 1963

David, André, *75 Années de jeunesse*, Paris, 1974

Dekobra, Maurice, *Les Emigrés de luxe*, New York, 1941

—— *La Madone à Hollywood*, New York 1943

—— *Sept Ans chez les hommes libres: Journal d'un Français aux Etats-Unis 1939–1946*, Paris, 1946

Désert, Joseph, *Toute la Vérité sur la Cagoule*, Paris, 1946

Doering, Bernard, *Jacques Maritain and French Catholic Intellectuals*, Notre Dame, 1983

Ducattillon, Joseph (O.P.), *La Guerre, cette révolution: le sort de la civilisation chrétienne*, New York, 1941

Duroselle, J.-B., *L'Abîme*, Paris, 2nd edition, 1986

Fermi, Laura, *Illustrious Immigrants: the Intellectual Migration from Europe 1930–1941*, Chicago, 1968

Fernand-Laurent, Camille, *Un Peuple ressuscite*, New York, 1943

—— *Gallic Charter: Foundations of Tomorrow's France*, Boston, 1944

Focillon, Henri, *Témoignage pour la France*, New York, 1945

Fritsch-Estrangin, Guy, *New York entre de Gaulle et Pétain: les Français aux Etats-unis de 40 à 46*, Paris, 1969

Fry, Varian, *Surrender on Demand*, New York, Random House, 1945

Gaudry, Olivier, *Henri de Kérillis*, Mémoire présenté à l'Institut d'Etudes politiques de l'Université de Paris, March 1966 (unpublished)

Gaulle, Charles de, *Lettres, notes et carnets*, 12 vols, Paris, 1980–8

Géraud, André (Pertinax), *Les Fossoyeurs*, 2 vols, New York, 1942

Gillois, André, *Histoire secrète des Français à Londres de 1940 à 1944*, Paris, 1973

Giraud, General Henri, *Un Seul But, la victoire*, Paris, 1944

Gold, Mary Jane, *Crossroads Marseilles*, New York, 1980

Bibliography

Goldschmidt, Bertrand, *Les Rivalités atomiques: 1939–1966*, Paris, 1967

—— *Pionniers de l'atôme*, Paris 1987

Goll, Claire, *La Poursuite du vent*, Paris, 1976

Green, Julien, *Journal*, in *Oeuvres complètes*, Paris, Editions de la Pléïade, 1975

—— and Maritain, Jacques, *Une Grande Amitié: Correspondance 1926–1972*, Paris, 1979

Guerdan, Léon, *Je les ai tous connus*, New York, 1942

—— *Des Minarets aux gratte-ciel*, New York, 1943

Guggenheim, Peggy, *Out of This Century: Confessions of an Art Addict*, New York, 1987

Harris, Mary Emma, *The Arts at Black Mountain College*, Cambridge, 1987

Hélion, Jean, *They Shall Not Have Me*, New York, 1943

Henry-Haye, Gaston, *La Grande Éclipse franco-américaine*, Paris, 1972

Hull, Cordell, *Memoirs*, 2 vols, New York, 1948

Jackman, Jarrell C. and Borden, Carla M. (eds), *The Muses Flee Hitler: Cultural Transfer and Adaptation 1930–1945*, Washington, Smithsonian, 1983

Johnson, Alvin S., *Pioneer's Progress: an Autobiography*, New York, 1952

Jules-Romains, Lise, *Les Vies inimitables: souvenirs*, Paris, 1985

Karp, B. and V. (eds), *Louis Rapkine*, North Bennington, Vt, 1988

Kérillis, Henri de, *Français, voici la vérité*, New York, 1942

—— *De Gaulle dictateur*, Montrèal, 1945

Laugier, Henri, *Service de France au Canada*, Montreal, 1942

Lazareff, Pierre, *Dernière Edition: souvenirs d'un journaliste français*, New York, 1941

Lévi-Strauss, Claude, *Tristes Tropiques*, Paris, 1955

—— *Le Regard éloigné*, Paris, 1983

—— with Didier Eribon, *De Près et de loin*, Paris, 1988

Levy, Julien, *Memoirs of an Art Gallery*, New York, 1977

Lourié, Arthur, *Profanation et sanctification du temps*, Paris, 1966

Manévy Raymond, *La Presse de la IIIè République*, Paris, 1955

Mann, Klaus, *The Turning Point*, London, 1944

Marchal, Léon, *De Pétain à Laval*, Montréal, 1943

Maritain, Jacques, *A Travers le désastre*, Paris, 1942

—— *Pour la Justice*, New York, 1945

—— *Messages (1941–1944)*, New York, 1945

Marlio, Louis, *La Révolution d'hier, d'aujourd'hui et de demain*, New York, 1943

—— *Problèmes d'aujourd'hui*, Montreal, 1944

Massu, Suzanne, *Quand j'étais Rochambelle*, Paris, Grasset, 1969

Maurois, André, *Tragédie en France*, New York, 1940

—— *Mémoires*, New York, 1942

—— *La France change de visage*, Paris, 1956

Bibliography

Milhaud, Darius, *Ma Vie heureuse*, Paris, 1974

Monnet, Jean *Mémoires*, Paris, 1976

Murphy, Robert, *Diplomat among Warriors*, New York, 1964

Ornano, Henry d', *L'Action gaulliste aux Etats-Unis 1940–45*, Paris, 1948

Ozenfant, Amédée, *Mémoires 1886–1962*, Paris, 1968

Palmier, Jean-Michel, *Weimar en Exil*, Paris, 2 vols, 1988

Philip, André, *Par lui-même ou les voies de la liberté*, Paris, 1971

Pierre-Gosset, Renée, *Expédients provisoires: le coup d'Alger*, Paris, 1945

Renoir, Jean, *My Life and my Films*, New York, 1974

—— *Lettres d'Amérique* Paris, 1984

Romains, Jules, *Salsette découvre l'Amérique*, New York, 1942

Rougemont, Denis de, *Journal d'une époque*, Paris, 1968

Roussy de Sales, Raoul de, *L'Amérique entre en guerre*, Paris, 1948

Rutcoff, P. M. and Scott, W. B., *New School: a History of the New School for Social Research*, New York, 1986

Saint-Exupéry, Antoine de, *Ecrits de guerre*, Paris, 1982

Saint-Jean, Robert de, *Démocratie, beurre et canons*, New York, 1941

—— *Passé pas mort*, Paris, 1983

Saint-John Perse (Alexis Léger), *Lettres à l'Etrangère*, Paris, 1987

Tabouis, Geneviève, *Ils l'ont appelée ʿassandre*, New York, 1942

—— *Grandeurs et servitudes américaines: souvenirs des USA 1940–1945*, Paris, 1945

—— *Les Princes de la paix*, Paris, 1980

Taylor, John Russell, *Strangers in Paradise: The Hollywood Emigrés 1933–1950*, London, 1983

Torrès, Henri, *La Machine infernale*, New York, 1942

—— *Accusés hors série*, Paris, 1957

—— *De Clémenceau à de Gaulle. Ce que je n'ai jamais dit: chronique du temps retrouvé*, Paris, 1958

—— *Souvenir, souvenir, que me veux-tu?*, Paris, 1964

Welles, Sumner, *The Time for Decision*, Cleveland and New York, 1945

Index

Index

Index

Index

Of Related Interest

Voices from the North African Immigrant Community in France

Immigration and Identity in Beur Fiction

Alec G. Hargreaves

Well over a dozen members of the so-called Beur generation, a popular name in France for the sons and daughters of first-generation North African immigrants, have so far published narrative works. This study combines careful analysis of the formal structures of Beur fiction with a wealth of insights derived from interviews with the authors and extensive access to unpublished writings.

Alec G. Hargreaves is Senior Lecturer in French at Loughborough University.

Published in 1991
ISBN 0 85496 649 8

Forthcoming

Victor Serge

The Uses of Dissent

Bill Marshall

This study introduces the reader to Victor Serge's life and extraordinary novels, locating them amidst crucial debates about revolution, communism and anarchism, literature and representation, and in comparison with his contemporaries. From the prisons of France and Siberia, through the Russian Civil War and the purges of Stalin to the Second World War and the last exile in Mexico, the voice of Serge speaks out with authority and compassion. Bill Marshall demonstrates that the voice of Serge, in all its contexts, is unified by a notion of dissent – an active dissent far removed from the quietism and conservatism of other dissidents.

Bill Marshall is a Lecturer in French at the University of Southampton.

January 1992
ca. 240pp
bibliography, index
ISBN 0 85496 766 4

Collaboration and Resistance Reviewed

Writers and the *Mode Rétro* in Post-Gaullist France

Alan Morris

This volume examines the renewal of interest in, and extensive re-evaluation of, the wartime occupation of France by the Nazis. The author places the phenomenon in its literary and historical context, revealing how, until 1970, a collective and predominantly Gaullist 'myth' of the resistance was able to establish itself in France. The subsequent undermining of this 'myth' is discussed through a survey of the works of prominent writers and through more detailed studies of some of the younger of these writers, showing how, in the effort to escape a problematic heritage, new myths are created.

Alan Morris is from the Department of Modern Languages at the University of Strathclyde.

January 1992
ca. 208pp
bibliography, index
ISBN 0 85496 634 X